THE NORMA

History

THE NORMAN CONQUEST

H. R. Loyn

Professor of History, Westfield College, London

HUTCHINSON

London Melbourne Sydney Auckland Johannesburg

Hutchinson & Co. (Publishers) Ltd

An imprint of the Hutchinson Publishing Group

17–21 Conway Street, London W1P 6JD

Hutchinson Group (Australia) Pty Ltd
30–32 Cremorne Street, Richmond South, Victoria 3121
PO Box 151, Broadway, New South Wales 2007

Hutchinson Group (NZ) Ltd
32–34 View Road, PO Box 40–086, Glenfield, Auckland 10

Hutchinson Group (SA) (Pty) Ltd
PO Box 337, Bergvlei 2012, South Africa

First published 1965
Second edition 1967
Reprinted 1971
Third edition 1982

Set in Times Roman

Printed in Great Britain by The Anchor Press Ltd
and bound by Wm Brendon & Son Ltd
both of Tiptree, Essex

British Library Cataloguing in Publication Data
Loyn, H. R.
   The Norman Conquest. – 3rd ed.
   1. Great Britain – History – Norman period, 1066–1154
   I. Title
   942.02'1   DA195

   ISBN 0 09 149530 x cased
        0 09 149531 8 paper

CONTENTS

Preface to first edition   vii
Preface to third edition   viii

List of abbreviations   ix

1   NORMANDY AND EUROPE   11
   (a) The European background: general constitutional
      problems of the age   11
   (b) The Norman duchy   20
   (c) The Normans in eleventh-century Europe   27

2   NORMANDY AND ENGLAND   32
   (a) William II, duke of Normandy, 1035–47   32
   (b) William II, duke of Normandy, 1047–66   38
   (c) The church in Normandy   44
   (d) The Normans and the English before 1042   49
   (e) The Normans in England during the reign of the
      Confessor   53

3   THE ENGLISH BACKGROUND   61
   (a) The House of Godwin   61
   (b) The nature of the earldoms   67
   (c) The Old English monarchy   70
   (d) The Old English church   79

4   THE CONQUEST   85

5 THE NORMAN SETTLEMENT   101

   (a) The political settlement   101

   (b) The feudal and military settlement   111

   (c) Feudalism and the church: some general
       conclusions   131

6 NORMAN GOVERNMENT   137

   (a) The government of the realm   137

   (b) The government of the church   153

   (c) The government of the duchy   168

7 THE EFFECTS OF THE CONQUEST   173

   (a) Some general effects   173

   (b) The towns   175

   (c) The countryside   185

   (d) Conclusion   194

   Bibliographical note   198

   Index   207

TABLES

1 *The Norman ducal dynasty*   22
2 *The House of Godwin*   62
3 *The making of Domesday Book*   145

MAPS

1 *Normandy during the reign of William the Conqueror*   41
2 *England during the reign of William the Conqueror*   122

PREFACE TO FIRST EDITION

This book sets out to provide an interpretation of the Norman Conquest in a relatively small space. It is intended for the general reader and for the undergraduate. Emphasis has been placed on continuity with the Anglo-Saxon past, but full credit has been given to the Normans for their innovations, and especially for their skill in the arts of secular government and of war. The heritage was sound. It was well employed.

For help in the preparation of this book I am under a great debt to the late Sir Maurice Powicke who first suggested the project, and to Professors S. B. Chrimes and R. F. Treharne for their encouragement in the early stages. My special thanks go to Dr C. H. Knowles who read through the typescript and made many helpful suggestions, to Mr M. C. Ede who read through the typescript at a slightly later stage and who also made many emendations in style and content, and to Professor S. B. Chrimes and Mr I. A. Roots who read the page-proofs and saved me from several errors and infelicities. Lastly my thanks go to my wife for her constant support and for preparing the index.

I acknowledge the help of Mr A. Frearson who prepared the diagram of 'The making of Domesday Book' (based on the work of Professor V. H. Galbraith), and the courtesy of Messrs Eyre and Spottiswoode for permission to use the material contained in the genealogical tables (based on the tables in *English Historical Documents*, vol. ii, ed. D. C. Douglas and G. W. Greenaway). I also wish to acknowledge here in the preface to a volume which has few footnotes the help given by the published work of many scholars to which it has not been possible to give precise reference in the text. Without the hard thought which has been put into the problems of the Norman Conquest during the last generation by a succession of distinguished scholars the task of attempting a general synthesis would be impossible. My sincere thanks go to the staff of Hutchinsons, particularly to Miss Ann Douglas, for seeing the book safely through the press, and also to many librarians, especially to Mr F. G. Cowley of the library of my own college, for their care and patience.

H.L.

University College, Cardiff
1964

PREFACE TO THIRD EDITION

The text of this edition is substantially unchanged though detailed alterations have been made from time to time to incorporate new material, or to alter emphasis in the light of recent investigation. A full bibliographical note has been added to bring the attention of readers to the most important contributions of the last decade or so. I wish to thank my pupils, colleagues and fellow-scholars for their help in preparing this revised edition. I owe special thanks to Dr. David Bates of University College, Cardiff for his very helpful, constructive comments and for allowing me to read a typescript of his valuable forthcoming book *Normandy before 1066* before publication.

H.L.

Westfield College, London
1982

LIST OF ABBREVIATIONS

A.H.R. : *American Historical Review*

Battle Conference 1978 (etc.) : *Proceedings of the Battle Conference 1978* (etc.), ed. R. Allen Brown, Woodbridge, 1979 (etc.)

B.I.H.R. : *Bulletin of the Institute of Historical Research*

D.B. i, ii : *Domesday Book*, ed. Abraham Farley, London, 1783 (republished Record Commission, ed. H. Ellis, 1811 and 1816)

Dudo of St. Quentin : *De moribus et actis primorum Normanniae Ducum*, ed. Jules Lair, Caen, 1865

E.H.D. ii : *English Historical Documents*, vol. ii, ed. D. C. Douglas and G. W. Greenaway, London, 1953 (2nd edn, 1981)

E.H.R. : *English Historical Review*

Econ. H.R. : *Economic History Review*

Florence of Worcester : *Chronicon ex Chronicis*, ed. B. Thorpe, London, 1848–9

Freeman, *Norman Conquest* : E. A. Freeman, *The History of the Norman Conquest of England*, Oxford, 1867–79 (five vols.)

Guy of Amiens : *Carmen de Hastingae Proelio*, ed. Catherine Morton and Hope Muntz, Oxford, 1972

Liebermann : *Die Gesetze der Angelsachsen*, ed. F. Liebermann, vol. i, Halle, 1903

Ordericus Vitalis : *The Ecclesiastical History of Orderic Vitalis*, ed. Marjorie Chibnall, Oxford, 1969–80 (six vols.)

T.R.H.S. : *Transactions of the Royal Historical Society*

V.C.H. : *Victoria County History*

Vita Ædwardi : *Vita Ædwardi Regis*, ed. F. Barlow, London, 1962

Wace, *Roman de Rou* : *Maistre Wace's Roman de Rou et des Ducs de Normandie*, ed. Hugo Andresen, Heilbronn, 1877–9 (two vols.)

Wilkins, *Concilia* : D. Wilkins, *Concilia Magnae Britanniae et Hiberniae*, vol. i, London, 1737

William of Jumièges : *Gesta Normannorum ducum*, ed. J. Marx, Rouen and Paris, 1914

William of Malmesbury, *Gesta Regum* : *Willelmi Malmesbiriensis, Gesta Regum Anglorum*, ed. W. Stubbs, London, 1887–9 (two vols.)

William of Poitiers : *Guillaume de Poitiers, Histoire de Guillaume le Conquérant*, ed. Raymonde Foreville, Paris, 1952

1

Normandy and Europe

(a) *The European background: general constitutional problems of the age*

To ATTEMPT to read the Norman Conquest in isolation is easy, but misleading. This great crisis in English affairs has so direct a bearing on problems which are specifically English that the European context can be relegated in dangerously casual a fashion to a subordinate position. In fact, concentration on the purely English problems, such as the constitutional significance of the Conquest, its effects on the monarchy, the baronage, and the peasantry, and the element of social revolution involved, can lead to serious distortion. The Norman Conquest of England was a phenomenon of European importance, as significant in the development of French as of English history, as much a feature of the vitality of the eleventh century as German pressure to the east, Norman adventures in the Mediterranean, or even the First Crusade.

A decisive change came over the state of Western European society in the middle of the eleventh century. Any division of history into periods is arbitrary, and tends to be unsatisfactory, but all students of history know that changes can occur in a surprisingly short space of time. The difference between the Western Europe of 1000 and 1100 is unmistakable, and critical events towards the middle of the century at Rome, in connection with the papacy, and in the Mediterranean dramatize the period of change. Western Europe began to grow more prosperous, a prosperity of continuous development which produced in the course of the twelfth century the wealth and luxury of the central Middle Ages: cathedrals, universities, literature, the whole complicated cultural achievement that is sometimes known as 'the twelfth-century renaissance'. Methods of thought altered; among scholars greater emphasis on logic and human reason took the place of a cruder acceptance of past authority. A movement from epic to romance can be traced in fields less obvious than the merely literary. The changes are so great that many, notably the French-speaking historians, have attempted a formal division of European history at about 1050, between the early Middle Ages and the central Middle Ages, or between a first Feudal Age and a second Feudal Age. If the concept of 'the Dark Ages' were still tenable the mid-eleventh century would be a serious contender for the honour of being the date at which Western Europe entered the true 'Middle Ages'.

The reasons for the revival of prosperity are controversial, and are bound up with the complicated arguments that surround the economic developments of Western European society in the early Middle Ages. At a simple level the main reason for revival is clear: the containing and absorption of the barbarian invasions. From the fifth century A.D. Western Europe had been subject to invasions by the unsettled peoples from without the Roman Empire: Germans, Slavs, Moslems, Magyars, and Scandinavians. After the turn of the eleventh century Western Europe was free from the dislocation which attended such raids, with their inevitable consequence of disastrous break in continuity to agrarian communities and to settled territorial government. The sometimes rough-and-ready feudal and pre-feudal institutions gave protection; the reviving monarchies and churches of the West offered hope of peace. Freedom from successful barbarian invasion is continuous from 1100, an immunity that Western Europe was alone in enjoying—except for Japan—in the second millennium A.D.

Yet the simple answer is not completely satisfying in spite of all its logical force. It is true that freedom from barbarian attack gave opportunity for the peasant to cultivate his land in peace, and so to supply the surplus upon which could be built the structure of successful church and monarchy. But effective resistance to the barbarian invader is certainly no mere abstraction, and there are many economic historians who would look deep into the structure of society to explain how it was that the Scandinavians and the Magyars in particular were successfully halted or absorbed. Fruitful work on technical developments in agrarian practice and organization has suggested that an achievement of mastery over arable farming may be the chief factor both in the reviving prosperity of Western Europe and in its capacity to resist the invader. Parallel to the more conspicuous symptoms of late eleventh-century prosperity—reviving trade, notably in the Mediterranean, intensification of urban life, the extension and consolidation in permanent form of urban institutions—there exists also evidence of agrarian expansion, colonization, and the taking in of more land from the waste. The more obvious advantages of prosperity applied only to fairly closely defined trade-routes, and to fairly closely defined urban classes. None the less important to the Western European economy was the prosperity of the arable farmer, especially in the countryside which lent itself to the growth of large and efficient manors: France north of the Loire, England south of the Humber, Lorraine, and Franconia. In this context the Norman Conquest, with its achievement of unified political control over such a large area of fertile, surplus-producing country, Normandy and prosperous England, is a fact of first importance to economic and political historian alike.

The Norman Conquest also needs to be considered against the background of other general European political developments, which are themselves products in some sense of the vitality of the eleventh century. Outside Western Europe there were three principal movements which helped in their various ways to provide the Westerners with a greater sense of security. To the north and east there had been an extension of the Christian faith to Scandinavians, Slavs, and Magyars, with a resulting increase in stability among the Western Christian communities, notably among the Germans. To the south-west a similar extension of Christian power at the expense of the decaying Caliphate of Cordova resulted in the capture of Toledo in the heart of the Iberian peninsula in 1085. In the central Mediterranean the Normans established themselves in South Italy, and their leader, Robert Guiscard, was recognized as duke of Apulia by the Pope in 1059. Their conquest of Sicily from the Moslems (1071–92) coincided with the effective conquest and settlement of England by their cousins at home. Meanwhile the rise of the Turks in the east at the expense of the old Moslem powers of Baghdad and Cairo forced the Eastern Empire to the defensive, particularly after the Battle of Manzikert in 1071. The establishment of crusading states in the Holy Land at the end of the eleventh century, in which Normans played a prominent part, was the final stage in Christian reaction to this intensified threat, and was a symptom both of the efforts to make the Mediterranean once again a Christian lake and of Western vitality.

Within the principal political units of the Western world—Germany, France, and England—grave constitutional problems came to the forefront concerning the nature of the monarchy and the special powers of the king in relation to the church, the baronage, and the community in general. It is possible to trace, with reasonable historical logic, later divergences in constitutional practice back to this formative period of the later eleventh century. The German monarchs failed to increase either their control of wealth or the number of permanent royal institutions. The quarrel with the papacy and the resulting civil wars, known as the Investiture Contest, are rightly held to bear a large part of the responsibility for this failure. In France the peace-giving monarchs cut poor figures, but the work of creating peace-giving institutions was done for them in the provinces by formidable rulers, such as the dukes of Normandy and the counts of Anjou. The Anglo-Norman monarchy in England gave the lead that was needed, and transformed a wealthy but conservative community into the most advanced feudal monarchy in the Western world.

Yet while it is useful to reflect on these divergences, it is also true to say that socially the Western world was settling into similar moulds.

The direction of social development can conveniently be defined as a movement towards the creation of a feudal order. This is as true of communities such as England, which in strict terms can scarcely be called feudal before the mid-eleventh century, as it is of communities where feudal institutions early received recognizable form. An essential social characteristic of the new order was the financial and judicial authority exercised by the landlords over dependent peasants. Such authority stemmed from a king. The king was an integral part of the feudal order. Landlord power and royal authority did not grow in opposition to each other: they developed unevenly side by side from the ninth century onwards. Historically there were two principal sources of such development: Carolingian kingship, and the growth of landlord power under the stress of barbarian invasions. The Carolingian Empire, though short-lived and politically inglorious in decline, left a heritage of ordered government to Western Europe which was strong even in areas such as England which had not enjoyed direct rule by Charlemagne. This heritage was both Roman and ecclesiastical in inspiration. Theocracy is the word which sums up most conveniently the essential nature of the Empire in its prime. The church co-operated actively with the monarch because, even with Christian reservations as to the sin-imposed limitations of earthly government, the state offered some fulfilment of God's purpose in establishing an ordered framework of society within which the church could be protected, iniquities against moral and positive law be suppressed, and individual rights be respected. The majestic ceremonial of coronation, elaborated in the course of the tenth century, symbolized this acceptance of a monarch who was the immediate source of authority under God—and some would add under the church. Splendid though these ideas were in theory, political reality in the persons of marauding Magyars and destructive Danes was forcing in practice a different form of political authority upon the West. Recognition in law of royal authority persisted to a varying degree, most concisely in Western Frankish lands where by apparent paradox the direct political and military power of the king shrank into the small but potentially powerful fief centred on Paris. In practice fragmentation of political authority was the consequence of barbarian raiding. There were sound military reasons for such fragmentation. The barbarians travelled swiftly in Viking ships or on Hungarian horses. Their attacks were widespread, unexpected, and devastating. Mobility gave them the element of surprise. No area was completely safe. The cumbersome formal armies of Carolingian days, an excellent offensive weapon for an aggressive settled people against unorganized barbarians, were helpless in face of swift-moving and well-organized thrusts. Defence was effective only in smaller units, bristling with fortified townships and controlled by resolute warriors in a state of constant preparedness. The great fief presided over by a lord who would bind himself by Christian oaths to the king was the necessary answer to the turbulence and unrest of the time. In origin the fief owed much to the March policy of Charles the Great. Royal methods of coping with difficult border situations had in time to be applied to the peaceful, settled hinterland. The Flemish monk who wrote the Life of King Edward (the Confessor) portrayed the earls Harold and Tostig as such military lords of the border. King Edward lived secure because 'the one [Earl Harold] drove back the foe from the south and the other [Earl Tostig] scared them off from the north'.[1] In the continental communities fragmentation of royal authority went further than in England. Two chief heirs emerged to the supreme power of the Carolingian theocracy: the kings of Germany who, after 962, also took to themselves mastery of much of Italy and the imperial title, and the kings of France, after 987 members of the Robertian House, better known as the Capetians. Effective defence and effective authority passed into the hands of the great vassals in the more settled 'French' and Lotharingian lands.

[1] Superior figures refer to notes at end of chapters.

These vassals, dukes, margraves, or counts, were themselves
Frankish counts, descendants of Frankish counts, or successful
military commanders who had usurped or succeeded to the
royal-derived authority of Frankish counts. In the duchies of
Normandy, or Aquitaine, or the counties of Flanders, Anjou, or
Blois, they in small compass exercised and developed the royal
authority. The king in France was left indeed with only his name
and his crown, both powerful instruments for the future. In the
eleventh century present responsibility for the growth of peace-
giving institutions rested in the hands of the great vassals. William
of Normandy by his conquest of England brought the most
advanced of these feudal fiefs into direct contact with an ancient
monarchy, and the chronicler William of Poitiers tells how there
was great rejoicing in Normandy after William had gained the
English throne: 'never dawn more serene had arisen there than
that on which they learned the certain news that their prince,
author of their peace, had become a king. Towns, castles, villages,
monasteries rejoiced in the victory, more so in the crown (*multum
pro victore, maxime pro regnante*)'.[2] His acceptance of the title of
king brought an elevation in rank that was more than a mere
style of words. The man who had proved himself competent to
rule a province was now faced with the task of governing a
kingdom. On his own death-bed King William is reported as
saying that he alone acquired a royal diadem, which none of his
predecessors had possessed.[3]

In this acknowledged difference between a king and a provincial governor is a clue to the basic constitutional ideas of the
period, and, incidentally, a clue to the constitutional divergences between England, France, and Germany in the eleventh
century. At the practical level the degree of control which the
king was able to achieve over the provincial governors who were
also his great vassals was the vital element in determining
the strength of an eleventh-century monarchy. On this score
England under the strong Norman hand, and, to a lesser extent,
Germany, stand well, while the Capetians in France are conspicuous only by their weakness. The constitutional historian,

seduced by his abstractions and also by his knowledge of later events, is tempted, however, to plumb greater depths and to say, with considerable justice, that the key to strength or weakness in a feudal community consisted in the degree of integration that was achieved between the community, the feudal vassals, and the king. This seeming jargon becomes intelligible when translated into terms of who held legal courts and by what right, who exacted fines and penalties and by what right, and who collected dues and tolls and by what right. In these respects England and, in potential, France emerge as the strong constitutional units. Germany, by contrast, shows up in its weakness. Ottonian theocracy had come late with only partial success. The German nobility was independent, claiming powers of jurisdiction that were of the soil and blood, not delegated by the king. In some areas independent holdings, technically known as alods, predominated over fiefs. Excessive reliance on the church brought great dangers in its train at the time of the Investiture Contest. Over an area as vast as Germany and its imperial extensions it was difficult to insist that authority over freemen was a delegated right from the king. The greater compactness of the economic centres of the Western monarchies gave greater opportunity to the constructive feudal monarchies.

The constitutional historian, following this line of thought, can too easily reach the over-simplified conclusion that England gained the best of both worlds. He may be right, but it is wise to remember how grasping and inefficient Norman government could be at its worst, before we mask the inadequacies under a set of bland abstractions. In Germany the splintering of sovereign power can be foreseen: folk-elements were assimilated by local magnates in their own right during the time of invasion; the monarchy was too ambitious. In France the great vassals did their work only too well; the result was the formulation of the strongest of feudal monarchies, and the way was prepared for royal despotism. In England folk-elements remained strong in public courts and in ideas of public justice. William and his Norman successors were also able to strengthen an already powerful monarchy. The resulting feudal monarchy provided a more even blend of folk-power and royal power than elsewhere in Europe. On such high abstract levels the contribution of William seems two-fold and limited: to foster the continuity of an existing wealthy monarchy, and to bring knowledge of full-formed feudal society with its potentially unifying force to a society in the pre-feudal stage.

This last phrase demands a little elaboration. It is true that England had suffered from barbarian attack, that she had survived, and that she had done so by acceptance of a compromise between central power and local responsibility similar to that which was common on the Continent. Yet in two respects she differed. The kings themselves had taken the lead against the Danes, and the triumph of the tenth century was the triumph of the ancient royal house of Wessex, not the triumph of the house of Rollo, of the Angevin counts, nor indeed of the descendants of the house of the counts of Paris, nor of the dukes of Saxony. England had also in the eleventh century suffered political conquest, not from barbarians but from settled communities. The dynasty of Canute in some respects became more English than the English. With full co-operation from the church it carried forward the task of unification and deepening of royal government so characteristic of the West Saxon house in the tenth century. Yet it had one dramatic effect on society which has not fully received proper attention. The change of dynasty delayed the growth of secular fiefs on continental lines. The personnel at the royal court changed; in the localities new men took charge. Continuity and time firmly to establish hereditary succession were not given to the English provincial dynasties. Even so, as will be suggested later, the great earls in less than half a century built up their control of delegated power to the point where, in their magnificence and wealth, they could treat on equal terms with the magnates of the Continent. But their military and political strength was not sufficient, even at the end of their Anglo-Saxon period, to hide the fact that their offices were appointments held of the king, and that they were in the last resort officers, who might be removed by action from above or pressure from below.

(b) *The Norman duchy*

It is generally held that the English monarchy in the eleventh century was strong, but that nevertheless the Normans had much to contribute to English developments, particularly their skill in the arts of feudal government. How was such skill acquired and is there anything in the early history of the duchy that will enable the historian to point to a special Norman virtue?

The duchy owed its foundation to a grant made by Charles the Simple, Carolingian king of the Franks, at St. Clair-sur-Epte in 911 to Rollo, one of the most powerful of the Viking leaders. The chronicler Dudo of St. Quentin, writing it is true nearly a century after the event, told how Charles arranged a marriage between his daughter and Rollo, giving to the latter: 'A defined tract of country as an alod and in proprietorship (*in alodo et in fundo*), from the river Epte to the sea, and all of Brittany, from which he could draw sustenance (*de qua posset vivere*)'.[4]

There were further embroideries to the tale. Dudo wrote that the Vikings had been offered Flanders, which they refused because it was too marshy. Charles demanded homage, but the Viking to whom the task was delegated, instead of abasing himself on the ground to kiss the foot of his lord, bent down, grasped the royal foot, and drew it smartly upwards towards his mouth to the discomfiture of the king and the amusement of some of the onlookers. Unfortunately Dudo cannot be relied on in detail. Later authorities state that the Normans received further territorial grants in 924 and 933, and it is now generally accepted that in 911 Rollo became lord of Upper Normandy only, essentially count of Rouen. The nature of the grant has been matter for dispute. If the terms '*in alodo et in fundo*' mean what they say, the feudal nature of the bond between Viking leader and Frankish king should not be exaggerated. The events of 911 could be interpreted as little more than a grant of a wife and lands to a troublesome warrior, bound to his new lord by a bond of commendation that might or might not prove effective, though it is hard not to recognize some element which can be expressed in Carolingian terminology as the grant of a county, or even the grant of a 'march'.[5] The most significant clause in Dudo's account of the settlement was, perhaps, that which gave Rollo a free hand against the Bretons. 'Normandy', or, more accurately at this stage in its history, the ancient region of 'Deuxième Lyonnaise', the ecclesiastical province of Rouen, had suffered greatly from the devastating attacks of Vikings and of Bretons who were in full political control of the Cotentin during the last quarter of the ninth century. The establishment of a prominent Viking in a devastated and perilous frontier district showed sound sense on the part of the Carolingian Charles. It is also possible, as recent scholars have suggested, that the arrangement meant very different things to the two principals: to Rollo no more than a vague friendship for the king whose daughter he had married, to Charles a commendation that might later be turned to good account.

The grant of Normandy to Rollo certainly proved to be more than a personal arrangement between a Frankish king and a warrior lord who, with a small personal retinue, a hearth-troop, would be capable of holding the Breton frontier. It marked an important stage in the settlement of the surplus Scandinavian population which had burst into Christian Europe in the course of the late ninth century. Rollo himself was a Norwegian, presumably the Hrolfr, son of Rognvald, earl of Möre, of the saga record. His followers who settled the land and who passed on their names to many villages were, as recent careful and authoritative work has suggested, predominantly Danish. Indeed, of the eighty-two Scandinavian names attested in pre-1066 Normandy only two are accepted as exclusively Norwegian in contrast to twenty-six exclusively Danish; the majority, of course, could be either one or the other. These names indicate colonization, and are particularly strong in the area around Rouen, le Pays de Caux, le Roumois, the north and north-west of the Pays d'Auge, and the north and the north-west of the Cotentin. The situation is

TABLE I—THE NORMAN DUCAL DYNASTY

Rollo (First duke of Normandy, 911–930?)

William Longsword (duke of Normandy, 927–42)

Emma, d. of Hugh the Great = Richard I (duke of Normandy, 942–996) = Gunnor

Richard II, duke of Normandy, 996–1026

Emma, died 1052, m. (1) Ethelred, k. of England, 979–1016 m. (2) Cnut, k. of England, 1016–35 [mother of Edward the Confessor, k. of England, 1042–66, by (1), and of Harthacnut, k. of England, 1040–2, by (2)]

Robert, held lands of county of Evreux, archbishop of Rouen, 989–1037

Richard, c. of Evreux, died 1067

William, c. of Evreux, died 1118

Godfrey

Gilbert of Brionne, the count, died c. 1040

Richard fitz Gilbert (dead by 1090) → Family of Clare, earls of Hertford, Gloucester, and Pembroke

Baldwin of Meules, sheriff of Exeter

William, c. of Eu, died c. 1054

Robert, c. of Eu, died 1090

William II, c. of Eu, died 1096

Henry I, c. of Eu, died 1139–40

Hugh, bishop of Lisieux

William Busac

Richard III, duke of Normandy 1026–7

Robert I duke of Normandy, 1027–35 = Herleva = Herluin, vicomte of Conteville

Odo, bishop of Bayeux, 1049–97, e. of Kent

Robert, c. of Mortain, large land-owner in England esp. in Cornwall and Sussex, died 1091

William, a monk at Fécamp

Alice = Renaud, a count of Burgundy

Guy 'of Burgundy,' pretender to Normandy in 1047

Eleanor = Baldwin IV, c. of Flanders = (1) Ogiva

Baldwin V, c. of Flanders

Matilda [Married William the Conqueror]

Mauger, archbishop of Rouen, 1037–55

William, c. of Arques, dispossessed, 1054

Adelaide = Lambert, c. of Lens

William I, duke of Normandy 1035–87 k. of England, 1066–87 = Matilda, d. of Baldwin V, c. of Flanders

Judith = Earl Waltheof

analogous to that in the Danelaw in England; and there is some evidence for movement from the Danelaw to Normandy, particularly to the Cotentin and the Pays d'Auge.[6] Both Normandy and the Danelaw received new settlers and suffered profound modification to their social structure at much the same period of time. The Scandinavians settled in both communities in numbers sufficient to leave permanent trace on agrarian institutions, vocabulary, and place-names. They also brought with them an ability to govern and to organize which expressed itself strongly in the Norman duchy. The Carolingian Empire was falling into disruption. Under new vigorous ducal direction the Norman duchy escaped the worst consequences of such disruption. Professor de Bouard is able to give his considered opinion that by the middle of the eleventh century Normandy was a 'century or so in advance of the rest of the kingdom'.[7]

Rollo, the first 'duke', is a shadowy figure in spite of efforts by later chroniclers to bring out heroic attributes relating to his immense size, strength, and capacity to rule. Chroniclers and later poets were also at pains to stress the equality and independence of the northern warriors. French envoys are said to have asked Rollo's followers the name of their lord, only to have received the proud reply: 'He has no name for we are all equal in power'. Benedict of St. More, in his chronicle of the Norman dukes, elaborated this element of staunch independence:

> Over us there is no prince nor baron
> We are all of one lordship alone
> And all live equal and alike
> Each one is there lord (*sire*) of himself
> And each is faithful to the other.[8]

A certain respect for things past or strange must be accounted for before these stories can be fully accepted, but independence was stressed consistently—in relation, for example, to a serious peasants' revolt in the early eleventh century—as an outstanding Norman characteristic. Rollo died about 930 and was succeeded by his son William Longsword (927–42). William Longsword had been designated duke by Rollo, and associated in the dukedom before his father's death. Rollo had asked the chief men of Normandy, the *comites principesque*, to elect William, which they did in pious form with the request that he should be their 'hereditary duke'. The need for consent on the part of the chief men was strong in the tenth century, but the right of the ruling kin was also established practice. The Normans were clearly fortunate in the strength of their dynasty. In the hundred and sixty years from the accession of William Longsword to the death of William the Conqueror none of the dukes was negligible, and two at least, Richard II (996–1026) and William the Conqueror, were men of outstanding ability. The difficulties which they had to face were partly the difficulties confronting all rulers of the tenth and eleventh centuries, partly difficulties peculiar to Normandy. In common with all other 'state builders' in the West they had to construct permanent institutions of government in troubled times with slender economic margins. They succeeded conspicuously in this task by placing themselves firmly in control of the military forces of the duchy, and in acting as the sole intermediary between the nominal royal source of government and the exercise of comital power in the duchy. Peculiar to the rulers of Normandy were the problems facing a new dynasty in an old but devastated community. Three special difficulties stand out: the turbulence of the Norman warriors, an inadequate tradition of legislation (in marked contrast to the English situation), and a native weakness in institutions. Not until the time of the Conqueror was a reasonable solution to these special difficulties brought in sight.

Yet at the ducal level there were indeed elements of strength. The hereditary principle was applied firmly in practice to the duchy. The chief men had some say in the succession, which nevertheless was transmitted within the ducal line. There were even two minorities, that of Richard I and that of William the Conqueror himself, whose own succession was further complicated by the fact of his notoriously illegitimate birth. When William Longsword considered retiring to a monastery in 942 the barons acclaimed his son Richard I duke, with a common accord, and after William's assassination the young Richard was made duke, ruling the Normans for more than half a century until his death in 996. Memorable for his numerous progeny, the first Richard, known as Richard the Fearless, also has the odd distinction of being the only Norman duke to receive mention in a *Chanson de Geste*. His son and heir Richard II was a most powerful political figure. He ruled Normandy until his death in 1026, and left three sons by Judith, his wife: Richard III (died 1027), Robert the Magnificent (died 1035), and William, a monk at Fécamp. A daughter, Alice, married a Burgundian count, Renaud I. Her sons played a prominent part in the early stages of the rule of Robert's illegitimate son William (1035–87). Another daughter, Eleanor, married Baldwin IV of Flanders.

Robert died in 1035 at Nicea on his way back from a pilgrimage to the Holy Land. The career of his illegitimate son and legal heir, William II, duke of Normandy, William I, king of England, provides the subject-matter for most of the rest of this volume. Two special aspects of ducal Normandy need to be examined before the achievements of William can be seen in the proper context: the relationship of the duke to the king of France, and the relationship of the duke to his own nobility and people. In 1066 the Norman duke became the English king with obvious advantages in relation to his constitutional position. In England he was king, the administrator of law as well as the head of his military feudal hierarchy. In France he confirmed the close political association of the Normans with the Capetian house of Paris, and experimented with new titles such as 'marquis' to describe his own dignity. The contrast is real, and in later centuries of great practical importance. The curious limitations even of the vigorous Henry II in his French fiefs, and the sequestration of the French possessions of John by Philip Augustus, are historical facts that illustrate the difficulties of the Norman and Angevin position. The potential strength of the Capetian king was unquestioned. Yet this strength grew slowly, and twelfth-century conditions must not be read back to the tenth. The apparent inevitability of the growth of royal authority in France can be misleading. The splendid geographical position of Paris, the gradual achievement of law and order in the Capetian fief, the consequent spectacular economic growth of the city, and the realization of the popular and of the mystical elements in the monarchy were factors that led to the development of strong, unitary rule. But they did not fully apply until the late twelfth century, and in some respects not until the full potential value of Paris was realized towards the end of the century. Only then did the special elevation of the Capetian in the feudal hierarchy find true expression. He alone, the Capet, stood above the feudatories; he alone received the mystical royal unction. But for 'ducal Normandy', in the period 911–1066, these ties with the ruler of Paris, Carolingian or Capetian, significant as they might be for later development, were tenuous. Allies rather than vassals is the term which most accurately describes their relationship. The Norman dukes accepted the suzerainty of the Capetian 'dukes of France', but their political support was so necessary to the new dynasty that no effective service could be demanded of them. Norman historians stressed as a matter of moment that the duke held, as if he were a king, the sceptre of the monarchy of the Norman land. When King Henry I, chased from his central fief by his mother Constance, took refuge at Fécamp, his protector, Duke Robert the Magnificent, is said to have claimed to hold his duchy from God alone.[9] The Angevin count feared that Normandy had almost achieved the status of a kingdom. In the south of France similar independence led to similar manifestation of pride. The eleventh-century rulers of Aquitaine were referred to as dukes 'of all the monarchy of Aquitaine'. The constitutional historian, looking backwards, writes accurately of the principles of concentric centralization at work. The king's work was done for him in the localities. The Capetian sat, obese and slow-moving, in his Paris fastness and all was brought to him. Proud Norman, cruel Angevin, rich lords of Aquitaine, all worked to his advantage. Such is a simplification, element of truth though there may be in it. To the eleventh-century world the independence of the princely fiefs and the regionalization of the Western Carolingian Empire were the conspicuous features.

Yet the potentialities of the French monarchy must not be ignored. In two respects it was especially important. The feudal princes themselves had no united purpose. Their rivalries, particularly the rivalries of Anjou and Normandy, could leave the Capet in the pleasant position of recognized arbiter. Royal rights, too, became more than mere theory during a minority, and, as we shall see, the Capetian Henry I played what may well have been a decisive part in protecting the young Duke William, 1035–47, though this was an extraordinary intrusion.

The key to much of the history of Western Europe in the late eleventh century has been found recently in the simple phrase the 'search for law', that is to say in the need of more settled communities to achieve a final settlement to legal disputes at a permanent tribunal. The papal court at Rome, and royal courts in England and Germany (and more slowly in France), came to provide such tribunals. For the earlier period, 911–1066, the 'search for peace' in a technical sense might provide a better clue. In England the king, English or Danish, was able to provide such peace-giving institutions. In France similar success was achieved by the intermediate units, the powerful principalities. The strength and virtual independence in the arts of government of Normandy can best be understood in this context. Their neighbours and rivals, the counts of Anjou to the south and the counts of Flanders to the east, performed similar tasks. In all these principalities, fiefs as they were when seen from Paris, the hereditary principle was firmly established.

One of the big problems of Norman history is to decide how much its strength owed to William the Conqueror himself. Soured as his early years were by the troubles of the minority, William enjoyed a heritage far from negligible. Nor was it only in the duchy itself that Norman energy found expression.

(c) *The Normans in eleventh-century Europe*

The eleventh century was in many respects the Norman century.

At critical moments and in critical places Normans were to be found. Conspicuously in 1066 the Norman duke himself brought about one of the formative conquests in Western European history. But in the early eleventh century the skill and talents of the Normans had already been fully exercised, not only in the political consolidation of the duchy, but south to Spain and, more significantly, in southern Italy. About 1018 or 1020 a strong contingent of Normans took part in what was virtually a Catalan crusade, the beginnings of a new stirring among the Christian peoples of North Spain which reached a climax in 1085 with the capture of Toledo and the Christian domination of more than half of the Iberian peninsula. William in his death-bed speech is said to have freed Baudri FitzNicholas whom he had imprisoned for foolishly going to Spain 'without my permission (*sine mea licentia*)'. He admitted the knight's bravery, but objected to his wanderlust (*sed prodigus et levis est, ac per diversa vagatur*).[10] After the initial impetus the Normans did not, however, find much outlet for their energies in Spain. Their greatest contribution to recovery of Christian unity in the Mediterranean was made further east, in Italy.

Norman adventures in Italy started even before 1016, but in that year a party of pilgrims, returning from the Holy Land, landed in Apulia, and found a political situation ready for exploitation. They travelled back to Normandy, gathered reinforcements, and intervened, ultimately decisively, in a complicated, tortuous struggle between Byzantine, Moslem, Lombard, and papal interests. For nearly two generations before the Norman Conquest of England—and intensively from the first arrival of the Hauteville family in Apulia in 1035—active Norman military leadership transformed the political shape of Italy. A decisive moment was reached in 1059 when their leader, Robert Guiscard the 'Wizard', was recognized by the pope as duke of Apulia and Calabria, holding lands and rights from Pope Nicholas in return for a payment estimated at the annual rate of twelve pence of the mint of Pavia for each yoke of oxen. The pope invested Robert in his ducal office, and promised further support in Sicily; the duke offered in return general support, especially at the critical time of papal elections, and promised that all churches in his lands would come under papal authority.[11]

This arrangement was to have important repercussions on the conquest of England, and it was not the end of Norman endeavour in the south. From their already secure base in South Italy the Normans conducted, side by side with their conquest and settlement of England, a conquest and settlement of Sicily, 1071–92, under the leadership of Robert's young brother Roger. Robert Guiscard himself, fifth son of Tancred de Hauteville, played a very stormy role in the dramatic politics of the seventies and eighties of the eleventh century. His domination of the south, his designs on the Eastern Empire, and his virtual sack of Rome as an ally of Pope Gregory VII in 1084, stamped his reputation on European history. An English monk of the following generation, William of Malmesbury, told how Norman monks from St. Évroul sang chants over his tomb at Venosa, on which tomb was inscribed the following record of the scope of his ambitions:

Here lies Guiscard, the terror of the World.
He expelled from the city of Rome the lord of Italy.
No Parthian, Arab, or band of Greeks could protect Alexis;
Only flight could save him. For Venice there was no safety in
    flight nor the sea.[12]

The prominent part played by Normans, from their homeland as well as from England and South Italy, in the First Crusade was a culminating, dramatic expression of their military and political activity throughout the century. The Normans were at one and the same time the political masters and the irritants of the age.

Why did the Normans come to the forefront in such fashion during the eleventh century? Agrarian wealth and the success of the peace-giving early dukes provide possible answers. There is some evidence for successful commercial revival in Norman ports towards the end of the tenth and the beginning of the eleventh centuries. Evidence drawn from the quantity and distribution of coinage suggests a positive detachment of Normandy from the Scandinavian world and a strengthening of ties with the Romanic World during the first two decades of the eleventh century. Technical mastery should also not be disregarded; the Normans were the best cavalrymen of their age. They were also the best trainers of cavalry, and it is likely that an unrecorded skill in the stable as well as a recorded skill in the saddle may have contributed much to their success. The war-horse, the destrier, capable of carrying a mounted armed warrior, and capable too of the manœuvring and flexibility demanded in that type of warfare, was the final product of generations of skilled breeding and experience in stable management. Norman capacity to use this instrument of war in very unlikely conditions, such as those of Palestine, is not the least of the qualities of a remarkable people.

There is one special quality which seems to distinguish the eleventh-century Norman—a capacity for organization. This is no empty generalization. The fruits of such a gift are to be found wherever the Normans settled. They were not creative thinkers. There is no institution, not the fief, nor the developed castle, nor the jury, nor the fine Romanesque architecture, to which a specifically Norman creation can be ascribed. They were supremely the men who made things work, the assimilators who took over existing institutions and gave them a new efficiency unattainable by their originators. On the Welsh border a Robert Fitzhamon or a Bernard of Neufmarché was an efficient Welsh lord to his Welshry as he was an efficient feudal lord to his vassals who gave him his military authority; in Apulia and Sicily a succession of Hautevilles ruled and preserved their mixed communities of Normans, Greeks, Moslems, and Lombards. Welsh food-rents helped to feed the Norman lords in one instance; a tax levied on estates surveyed and recorded in Arabic in the other. In the Norman province of Antioch the local customs and social structure of the Syrian population remained intact under the hand of Bohemund and Tancred. Within the erratic limits of the eleventh-century world the Normans, like their Viking ancestors before them, exercised an incisive, pragmatic gift for government. They gave their peoples good peace, even when they plundered them.

1 *Vita Ædwardi*, pp. 32–3
2 William of Poitiers, p. 226
3 *Ordericus Vitalis*, iv, p. 90; *E.H.D.* ii, p. 285
4 Dudo of St. Quentin, p. 169
5 There is a useful discussion of the settlement of 911 by L. Musset in *Annales de Normandie*, vii, Caen, 1957, pp. 345 ff.
6 J. Adigard des Gautries, *Les Noms de Personnes Scandinaves en Normandie de 911 à 1066*, Lund, 1954, p. 264
7 M. de Bouard, *Annales de Normandie*, i, Caen, 1951, p. 160; also *Guillaume le Conquérant*, Paris, 1958, p. 61
8 Dudo of St. Quentin, p. 154; Benedict of St-More, *Chronique des Ducs de Normandie*, vs. 3299–3303, ed. F. Michel, 1836–44 (Docs. Inéd. de l'Hist. de France)
9 Dr. Bates has kindly pointed out to me how explicit William of Jumièges is against this claim (*Normandy before 1066*, London, forthcoming, p. 105), and that William of Poitiers also considered that all Norman rulers before William the Conqueror himself were royal vassals. William of Jumièges makes specific reference to Robert: '*apud Fiscannum Normannorum ducem adiit, Robertum per debitum fidei petens sibi ab eo subveniri*'. See also H. E. J. Cowdrey, 'Anglo-Norman *Laudes Regiae*', Viator (1981), pp. 37–78.
10 *Ordericus Vitalis*, iv, p. 100; *E.H.D.* ii, p. 289
11 Baronius, *Annales ecclesiasticii*, xi, Antwerp, 1608, p. 272
12 William of Malmesbury, *Gesta Regum*, p. 322

2

Normandy and England

(a) *William II, duke of Normandy, 1035–47*

THERE is undoubted good sense in looking to a broader context for the phenomenon of the Norman Conquest of England. Without some sketch of the scope of Norman endeavour, no proper account is possible of the vitality that made the enterprise successful. Yet we must not obscure the fact that we are also dealing with the personal exploits of an extraordinary man. William would be powerless without his Normans. But it is hard to envisage Norman success in such a venture without William. An older generation of historians celebrated this statesman king as one who brought order out of anarchy, and who first used France to conquer Normandy, then Normandy to conquer France, then Normandy to conquer England. Such simplification is perhaps unnecessary, though there is some truth in it. Although the present generation is rightly sceptical of ascribing long apprenticeships to men who afterwards 'fulfil their historic tasks', there is a curious rhythm about William's career that makes his later success intelligible. Consistency in ultimate objective, tenacity, courage, the ability to make the right decision at the right time—these are qualities which attract the historian as they attracted contemporaries. As an object-lesson in hardening by adversity William's early career is difficult to equal; it resembles an extract from a moralist's case-book. Only fight against physical weakness is lacking. Physical strength never seems to have deserted William, except for a few perilous weeks

between his victory at Hastings and his coronation at Westminster on Christmas Day, 1066.

William was born at Falaise in 1027 or 1028. His father,
Robert the Magnificent, to whom later generations attributed
the characteristics of a seducer of heroic proportions under the
nickname of Robert the Devil, was the son of Duke Richard II.
Robert was born about 1008 or 1009 and succeeded to the
County of Hiémois in the south-west of the duchy with its *caput*
at Falaise in 1026. During the short reign of his elder brother
Richard III, 1026–7, Robert was not a loyal vassal, and was
accused in popular legend, almost certainly falsely, of fratricide
when his brother died on 6 August 1027. While still count of
Hiémois, Robert took as his mistress Herleva (Arlette was her
pet-name), daughter of Fulbert, a tanner of Falaise. By her he
had two children: Adelaide, who married Lambert, count of
Lens, and William. His union with her was not casual, though
not recognized by the church. In twelfth-century Scandinavian
law (which probably resembled the customs by which the
Norman aristocracy governed their social affairs) three types of
marriage were acknowledged: Christian marriage, which carried
with it full rights to compensation and to property; union with
a freewoman, a *frilla*, which also involved rights, though subject
to some legal disabilities; and union with a concubine. Robert
and Herleva probably came into the second category; a tanner's
daughter could be free. Yet the predatory seizing of an attractive
female, which is how later chroniclers read the liaison, did not
provide the best hope of security for the offspring. William was
known as 'the Bastard' throughout all Europe until the more
honourable title of 'the Conqueror' came to be given.

The young William was brought up at Falaise, probably at his
mother's house. There is an odd story, told by a later chronicler,
of William Talvas, the evil head of the house of Bellême, cursing
the infant William to whom he had been taken 'in a cottage in
Falaise'.[1] The tanner's family prospered as a result of the liaison.
Fulbert himself became chamberlain at the ducal court and was
succeeded by his son in that office. Herleva herself, to whom her

son remained devoted, was married successfully to Herluin, viscount of Conteville. Her sons by this marriage, Odo of Bayeux and Robert of Mortain, were among the most prominent and influential of the Normans who made their fortune in England with Duke William. There are mysteries about Herleva herself which open the field to conjecture. She had a distinguished Germanic dithematic name; she appeared to retain the affection of Duke Robert, but even when he was setting out on a dangerous pilgrimage with the full support and blessing of the church he did not receive her into Christian marriage. This failure is a sign of one of two things: either Christian marriage was unimportant at the ducal court—where Christian oaths were not; or there was some ban to marriage which created too many difficulties even for the complaisant Norman episcopate. The evidence is not conclusive, and to some extent is contradictory on the critical question of the date of Herluin's marriage to Herleva. Ordericus Vitalis states that this took place after Robert's departure for Jerusalem. Many believe, however, that the eldest son of this marriage, Odo of Bayeux, must have been of reasonably mature age before succeeding to the bishopric in 1049 or 1050. If indeed Herleva was married to Herluin, and producing her three known children by him in the early thirties, a formidable barrier to Christian marriage to Duke Robert would have been apparent to all, more formidable than any scandal concerning possible earlier marital entanglements of the duke. Duke Robert took such pains to ensure the succession of his illegitimate son that it is hard to imagine him failing to take the obvious step of Christian marriage to Herleva (and so legitimizing their children *ex post facto*, an act for which there was precedent in the ducal family), had such marriage been possible.

Duke Robert set out on his pilgrimage, probably an act of penance for his high-handed sequestration of church lands, late in 1034. He commended young William to his barons:

Il est petit, mais il creistra
Se Deu plaist, si amendera.[2]

(He is little, but he will grow
if God so wills, and grow better)

Robert died in early July 1035, at Nicea in Asia Minor. There succeeded a very troubled period for his duchy and for his young successor.

The chronology of the following years is still uncertain, but their nature is not. Normandy suffered from a straightforward minority crisis which was not resolved until the decisive battle of Val-ès-Dunes in 1047, and the effects of which lingered on until William defeated his overlord, the French king, in the campaign which culminated at Varaville in 1057. Recent work has emphasized the personal nature of the troubles. In the strict sense of the term the period was not anarchic, that is to say there was not a concerted move against ducal power as such. But the results are difficult to distinguish from anarchy, and the minority may well be held up as a typical example of the dangers which beset any feudal regime. Powerful nobles took their opportunity to settle old scores with their neighbours. They fortified their homesteads, and used them as centres from which to conduct private war. Some ducal officers were faithless enough to fortify ducal castles which had been entrusted to them, and to indulge in the search for private gains—though only, it is true, towards the end of the troubles. Emphasis is properly placed on the private nature of the gains. Even Roger of Tosny, one of the most notorious of the nobles, a veteran of the Spanish wars, who is credited with the taunt that no bastard should rule over the Normans, limited his direct objectives to private encroachments against his neighbours. Assassination was used freely as a means of policy. Feuds sprang up and intensified. The temporary absence of a ducal authority led to widespread distress. Gilbert, count of Brionne, a grandson of Duke Richard I, had become guardian to the young prince in 1039 or 40. He was assassinated at the instigation of a kinsman, Ralph de Gacé, son of Archbishop Robert of Rouen. Turold, the young duke's tutor, and Osbern, his seneschal, were also killed violently, the latter by William of Montgomery at night in the duke's own room.

Yet Normandy suffered less from these battles and feuds than might have been expected. A prosperity in the duchy, a precocious awaking of urban life, a special prosperity in the ducal house itself, helped to soften the blow. Ducal administration remained relatively intact. By a strange twist of fortune Ralph de Gacé, assassin of the former guardian, was received as Duke William's guardian, and proved himself capable of keeping the ducal feudal army formidable and effective. The savagest fighting and feuding were confined to the province of Lower Normandy, and associated especially with the House of Bellême. Unauthorized castle-building was the greatest menace, a public act which could be met with public reaction once the ducal authority was again securely implanted.

William survived this tumultuous period, partly because of the support of Ralph de Gacé, of the episcopate, and of administrators loyal to ducal traditions, and partly because it was not in the interest of any one of the powerful predators to assassinate him. There was no effective Norman rival, and not even the most stupid of the Norman barons wished to provoke outside interference from Angevin or Capetian. Duke William received a very thorough tuition in the exercise of arms, and the contemporary historian, William of Poitiers, transmits probably sound tradition when he calls the reception of arms by the duke a moment when all France feared. This formal coming of age probably took place in 1044, and we are told that Gaul possessed no such armed knight as he: 'It was a splendid sight, delightful yet terrible, to see him, holding the reins, girded about with his sword, gleaming under his buckler, menacing with his helmet and lance'.[3]

The troubles of the 'anarchy' may well have been, as M. de Bouard has suggested, symptoms not so much of decadence as of 'a crisis of growth'.[4] This magnificent young warrior was a man well equipped to settle such a crisis. Rebellion and unrest flared up into a specifically anti-ducal move in 1046. William's cousin, and to this point his friend, Guy of Brionne, a Burgundian noble on his father's side, but of the Norman ducal house by maternal descent, provided the leadership. The result went far beyond the sporadic outbreaks of violence of the minority. Some modern investigators hold it to be the last reactionary effort of the more Scandinavianized section of the duchy against the ducal house at Rouen and the peaceful Gallicized valley of the lower Seine. Certainly the men of the Cotentin and le Bessin made up the backbone of the army of revolt. William showed at this early stage in his career the great political skill that was to distinguish him later in life. He was surprised by the rebellion, and very nearly captured ingloriously. But his instinctive reaction was sound. He escaped to safety, first to Falaise, then to Poissy, and made an appeal for help to his overlord, Henry I of France. It was to Henry's interest as well as William's to subdue a revolt that threatened to place a Burgundian noble in authority in the Norman duchy, and so, in 1047, the French king and the young Norman duke crushed the insurgent army at Val-ès-Dunes. All records agree on William's personal bravery and leadership. There is some disagreement on the relative part played by the French and the Normans in the victory. It seems that the credit should be evenly balanced; the duke was certainly not re-established as a mere creature of his Capetian overlord.

William's actions after his victory also exhibited his political sense. He treated the surviving rebels with marked clemency. Only Grimold of Plessis forfeited his lands, to die a miserable death in prison, and he seems to have been guilty of treachery excessive even in that age. As a step towards a re-establishment of permanent peace, William held at Caen soon after his victory a great assembly of dignitaries, lay and ecclesiastical, at which he had proclaimed a Truce of God for his duchy. By its terms all private war was forbidden from Wednesday evenings to Monday mornings, from the beginning of Advent to the octave of Epiphany, from the beginning of Lent to the octave of Easter, and from Rogationtide to the octave of Whitsun. Penal clauses, invoking penance and exile, indicate that the peace was intended to be effective.[5] Only the duke and the king were excluded from its provisions. In the development of the ducal constitution this promulgation of formal peace marks an important stage. For long the church had been trying ineffectively to establish such a close season for fighting. Now ducal authority was thrown decisively in its support. William at the very beginning of his personal rule had quelled a serious revolt, and had demonstrated in the most dramatic fashion his intent to impose, with the active help of the church, peace on his ducal lands.

(b) *William II, duke of Normandy, 1047–66*

The following years, from 1047 to 1066, witnessed the consolidation of the duchy. Principal interest switches from the internal state of the duchy to its position in the delicately balanced political situation in north France. Yet within the duchy events were taking place that presaged later mastery of feudal statesmanship. Many of the rebels of 1046–7 came to terms and were afterwards to be found among the most loyal of the duke's followers. Guy himself fled to the great fortress of the castle of Brionne, stone-built, well defended by nature as well as by art, on an islet situated between two arms of the river. William cautiously invested this fortress, built rough 'castles' around it to provide protection for the besiegers, and let shortage of supplies and boredom do their work for him. It says much for the duke that he did not rush headlong to an attack on this strong place, but merely waited—in all probability three whole years—for the prize to fall into his grasp. Guy was treated generously, and was offered the chance of living on at Brionne with his family. He chose instead to depart for his Burgundian lands. William's experience in investing the fortress served him well in the later campaigns in north France. His methods illustrate both the good sense and the command of resources enjoyed by the young duke. To keep an army of besiegers in the field successfully for such a long period implies wealth as well as strength of character.

It is probable, though unfortunately the details are only

scantily recorded, that this period, in particular the early part of the period, saw the elaboration of a systematic imposition of feudal service which provided the Norman duke with the strongest feudal army in France. Guy of Brionne's preference for Burgundy may well be associated with new stringent demands made by the vigorous, confident duke from his vassals. A quiet revolution took place in the obligations and duties of land-holding within Normandy. The 'Old Guard,' many of them descendants of Richard I or Richard II, were replaced by men on whom Duke William could place more trust. His two half-brothers, Odo and Robert, both received substantial promotion. Odo received the powerful bishopric of Bayeux in 1049 or 1050. Robert, on the exile of William Werlenc, a descendant of Duke Richard I, received the county of Mortain, possibly later in the 1050s rather than early. William in this respect completed a process initiated by his forbears Richard I and Richard II, both of whom had tended to reserve or to create 'counties' such as Arques, Eu, Hiémois, Évreux, Brionne, and Mortain itself for relatives, conditional on the satisfactory performance of military service to the duke, and on loyal care of ducal fortresses.

A general tightening up of ducal administration occurred, notably in connection with the imposition of military service. Castles, though still often quite rudimentary structures of the type we know as mottes with their baileys, were tending to become more elaborate, and to play an increasingly important part in the warfare and also in the machinery of government of the age. William was able to intrude his own garrisons into the castles held by even the strongest of his barons, a right that was unquestionably his in feudal law but which was not enforced over much of feudal France. The French king himself would have received a frosty answer had he attempted to place Capetian knights in any of the castles belonging to his Norman vassal. Military control of the duchy passed securely into ducal hands. Economic resources in the way of revenues, tolls, dues, and feudal rights were at his disposal, and he saw that they were well employed. Some of the methods are reminiscent of methods later to be used extensively in England. Ducal castles were built and garrisoned at strategic points. Great fiefs were carved out of royal demesne, but the terms upon which they were granted were clearly defined and heavy. To all appearance—a point, of course, that could not apply to England—some effort was made in Normandy to avoid granting fiefs to a military vassal in an area where he already held a patrimony of importance. Viscounts remained ducal officers well charged with the duty of looking after ducal interests in the local communities (and well prepared, incidentally, to undertake in later years the more complicated function of an English sheriff). Central institutions, a chancery, financial offices, a law-declaring court, were slow in development, although this apparent slowness may be attributed among the Normans to an element of Scandinavian emphasis on oral communication. Town life flourished. William deliberately fostered the growth of Caen, so that it became the second city of Normandy. He fortified it extensively as the strategic centre of ducal power in Lower Normandy, and founded two great abbeys there in 1059 as part penance for the uncanonical nature of his marriage. A highly successful series of archaeological excavations has succeeded in revealing the shape and nature of the substantial stone fortress erected at Caen by the Conqueror. Bustling prosperity was a feature of the duchy at this period, a prosperity which may well have been a carrying forward of the enterprise and activity in the North Sea and the Baltic areas during the preceding century. French historians agree that William found much in the Anglo-Saxon heritage which he could use to perfect Norman institutions. They also rightly remind us that Normandy was among the best-founded feudal states in Europe.

To contemporary historians the solid unobtrusive building up of a powerful feudal principality was incidental to the outside political developments of the period. These may be summarized shortly as prevention of Angevin expansion on the southern Norman border, effective resistance to Capetian military intervention, and finally, in the years 1062–4, the conquest of Maine, which may be read as the prelude to the Norman Conquest of

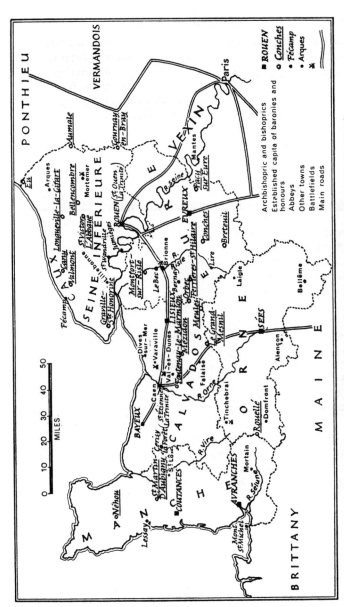

NORMANDY DURING THE REIGN OF WILLIAM THE CONQUEROR

England. An extraordinary feature of the campaigning was the loyalty of the Normans to their duke even when, as happened in 1054 and again in 1057, he was attacked by his overlord, the French king, at the head of formidable feudal armies. William at this time was under sentence of excommunication from the pope, a sentence which seemed to have no effect on the loyalty of his baronage. With the details of the campaigns we have no concern, but the methods used have considerable interest. An eye for the strategic castle, an ability to use surprise, and a prudent hesitation over pitched battles are characteristics of his military enterprises. Chroniclers and poets found little to admire—except the successful results—in the campaigns of William of Normandy during this stage in his career. At Le Mans, at the castle of Mayenne, at Alençon, as at the two best known engagements of the 'French' campaigns, at Mortemer in 1054 and at Varaville in 1057, it was guile as well as strategic sense that led him to victory. He could be cruel, as when, in revenge for the taunts of 'tanner's child' which were hurled at him, he hacked off the hands and feet of thirty-two captives taken at the siege of Alençon. During his victorious campaign in Maine he used a scorched-earth policy similar to his later activities north of the Humber. Natural accidents favoured him. His two principal opponents, Henry I of France and Geoffrey of Anjou, died in 1060, leaving him with a free hand to accomplish his immediate designs. There followed a slow, cautious, effective campaign against Maine, which resulted by 1064 in full Norman control of the south-east frontier of the duchy. Settlement of Breton unrest in 1064 in a feudal campaign (in which Harold, earl of Wessex, played an honourable part) completed the process by which William established himself as undisputed master of north-west Gaul. The fortunate death of Duke Conan of Brittany in December 1066 removed a potential danger from the Norman political scene. In this long series of successful feudal wars William built up and tested the feudal armies that were to lead him to great victories across the Channel.

The main emphasis in this period should be placed on military organization and on military activity. Yet an account would be defective if it did not contain reference to William's diplomatic skill, notably in relation to the county of Flanders. The Flemings had been ancient rivals and sporadic open enemies of the Normans. Both groups had English interests which were more likely to bring them into conflict than alliance. Conditions were, however, changing. The counts of Flanders were turning their attention more from their imperial lands and to the possibility of strengthening 'French' interests. After the battle of Val-ès-Dunes William turned wisely to the thought of a Flemish alliance, and made plans for a marriage alliance which was to bring great benefit to him, politically and personally. Envoys were sent to the powerful Baldwin V, count of Flanders, before 1049, and William proposed marriage to Matilda, the count's daughter, who brought with her the prestige of a descendant of Charlemagne and also of a descendant of King Alfred. For some reason, the details of which are not known, the Reformed Papacy forbade the marriage. At Rheims in 1049 Pope Leo IX held a great Council, and a formal decree was set forth against the union. Political interests may have played their part. Leo's cousin, the Emperor Henry III, and the Capetian King Henry I, were likely to be opposed. The reason for papal opposition was consanguinity, but how this came about is uncertain; the known ties of blood do not appear to be sufficiently close. Not apparently until 1050 or 1051, perhaps not until 1053, did William marry Matilda, and then only at the cost of alienating temporarily the stiffest and in the end the most loyal of his ecclesiastical supporters, the great Lanfranc. Lanfranc eventually sided with William and by his efforts the Papacy in 1059 recognized the marriage. The stormy beginning anticipated a calm continuation. The marriage was very successful, and the loyal affection given by William to his wife stands out as one of his most attractive characteristics. *Fortunata viro mulier, vir coniuge felix.*

Politically the marriage brought him what he desired, additional security in north French politics. Baldwin V proved a loyal friend who worked well with his son-in-law. Up to 1060 his

contribution to William's welfare was important but negative; he
did not help his own overlord, Henry I of France, in the Capetian
campaigns against the Norman duchy. After 1060 Baldwin's
support was even greater and positive. When Henry I died in 1060,
leaving an eight-year-old heir, Philip I, with his Byzantine name
and Russian mother, Baldwin, a mature and able feudal statesman in his own right, became chief guardian of the young Capetian heir. From 1060 to 1067, that is to say during the period of
preparation for the succession to England and over the crisis of
the Conquest, William's father-in-law occupied a position of the
first importance in the counsels of the French monarchy. He
handled the regency in a fair and tolerant fashion, but his presence at the key post helped William greatly, first in the conquest
of Maine and then in the more ambitious English expedition,
Baldwin's effective control of his own county of Flanders and of
the regency of France ensured in fact that all the harbours of
north France were in friendly hands on the eve of the Conquest
of England.

(c) *The church in Normandy*

There remains one very important element in ducal Normandy
to discuss before we turn to examine the relationship of the
Normans and of their duke to England. The Norman church has
to this point received only passing attention. Yet in some respects
ecclesiastical history in the eleventh-century duchy presents the
historian with one of his most challenging and rewarding
problems. Recent work, parallel in this respect to recent work on
the Old English church, has given a more favourable account of
the Norman church than used to be considered plausible. There
was much in the Norman church that appeared wrong to the
most advanced ecclesiastical thinkers of the day. The duke kept a
rigid control of all higher ecclesiastical preferment. He invested
his bishops and demanded feudal military service from them in
respect of their fiefs. He endowed abbeys, but again expected
military service in return for the endowment. Favour was shown
to men of high rank, particularly to members of the ducal house,

in the matter of preferment. Even those not of noble birth who attained a bishopric tended to be noted for their loyal service to the duke rather than for any special piety of life. The organization of the church favoured ducal control. There was one archbishopric—at Rouen—and six bishoprics at Coutances, Bayeux, Avranches, Sées, Évreux, and Lisieux. Within his duchy William expected good order to be maintained through ecclesiastic synods presided over by the metropolitan at Rouen. Only very reluctantly did he acquiesce in the interference of the outside world in matters of ecclesiastical polity. Some of the episcopal appointments were bad by any standard. Archbishop Mauger of Rouen (1037–55), son of Duke Richard II, was probably under twenty years of age when he was appointed. He made some effort to play his part, was generous to churches, confirmed many charters, and presided at the important Council of Rouen, which partly anticipated the papal reforming Council at Rheims (1049). But he never received the pallium, nor the apostolic benediction. In 1055 William deposed him in a public synod at Lisieux with the full consent of a papal legate and of the other bishops of the province, apparently as part of the complicated negotiations concerning the recognition of William's own marriage to Matilda of Flanders. William of Poitiers stressed Mauger's extravagance, and his disobedience to Rome. William of Malmesbury clearly placed opposition to Duke William's marriage as the root cause of the deposition. There were also accusations of intrigue, and of excessive indulgence in the chase and cockfights. Legends grew fast around the deposed archbishop, who retired with his wife and child to Jersey. William of Jumièges declared that Mauger went mad; Wace was certain that he had a private devil who answered to the name of Toret.[6] Such scandals echoed earlier scandals relating to Norman bishops from the ducal house; it was held as a special virtue in William that he had not allowed kinship to interfere with his sense of justice. Avranches and Bayeux, as well as Rouen itself, were something of a ducal preserve. Lisieux also had bishops from the ducal house, though Sées was strongly under the influence of the marcher lords of Bellême. Some of William's own appointments must have appeared unsatisfactory to church reformers. He made his half-brother, Odo, bishop of Bayeux in 1049 or 1050, when Odo cannot have been much older than twenty and may have been a mere boy of thirteen or fourteen. William also appointed to the new see of Coutances in 1048 Geoffrey of Mowbray, later to be one of his right-hand men in England, for political rather than for religious reasons. Yet there are positive redeeming features which suggest something more than just an even balance of good and ill. The Norman church in the twenty years before the Conquest became especially rich in three respects: in men, in learning, and in monasteries.

Outstanding among the men were Archbishop Maurilius, archbishop of Rouen, 1055–67, who was appointed to the archiepiscopal see as an earnest of good intentions towards the reformed papacy, and Lanfranc, who was later to become archbishop of Canterbury, 1070–89, and a most prominent figure in the settlement of England. Archbishop Maurilius was essentially a papal man, in marked contrast to Mauger, his predecessor. Maurilius was experienced in a harsh monastic observance at Florence, and later at Fécamp, before he became archbishop. He was remembered as much as a saintly person, as a representative of advanced ecclesiastical thought, as for any decisive reforming actions. Yet the Council which he summoned to Lisieux in 1064 took important steps towards bringing Normandy into line with papal views on moral reform. It affirmed the orthodoxy of the province of Rouen, ordered priests and deacons of the countryside not to marry, nor to keep concubines, and in relation to secular canons laid down the principle that those who were in major orders, yet lived maritally, were to break such 'marriages'. Secular canons in minor orders were to be dissuaded from marriage by 'means of persuasion', a somewhat weak reaction to a very difficult problem. The other great personality in ducal Normandy before 1066 was Lanfranc. In contrast to the English stage in his career, when his administrative gifts were dominant in Normandy his chief contribution came as a teacher, as an

active organizer of monastic life, and as an active diplomatic
agent on behalf of the duke. He was born about 1010 in Pavia,
and was distinguished as an early student of civil law. About
1046, when already a scholar of great reputation, he settled down
in the humble post of prior in the new Norman foundation at
Bec. He became one of William's closest advisers, was present at
Pope Leo's reforming Councils at Rome and at Vercelli, and
eventually came to act as William's chief representative in the
dispute over the validity of his marriage to Matilda. His relationship with the duke was stormy in the early stages of the dispute.
Lanfranc was disturbed at the question of consanguinity
between William and Matilda, and was at one point sentenced to
exile. The story is told how on his slow progress out of the duchy
on a lame horse (the best that the poor house of Bec could
provide) Lanfranc met the duke, professed his obedience to the
ducal sentence, and said that he was making his way out of the
duchy as fast as he was able. He then asked for a present of a
better horse so that he could obey yet more quickly. William—it
is one of his few recorded jokes—is said to have laughed, and to
have exclaimed that never before had he heard of a criminal
asking a present of a judge. The scene ended properly with
reconciliation—a pleasing reconstruction of a relationship
between two blunt and formidable men. William is said, in later
years, to have venerated Lanfranc like a father, respected him
like a master, and cherished him like a brother or a son.[7]

In his early days as prior of Bec, Lanfranc added to his already
powerful international reputation as a scholar by emerging as a
spokesman for conservative theological belief concerning the
Eucharist in a controversy with the acute but unorthodox
Berengar of Tours. This controversy was distinguished not only
by subject-matter but by the method of disputation. Lanfranc
clearly established himself as the foremost exponent of new
logical methods of argument. It was this grasp of principles of
logical argument which no doubt contributed to his skill as a
teacher. Under his guidance Bec became a force in the scholarly
world of the day, and when he left the house—with the greatest

reluctance—in 1063 he could count among his pupils the reigning pope, Alexander II, a future archbishop of Canterbury, Anselm of Aosta, and a number of other men, such as William of Bona Anima, later archbishop of Rouen, and Ernost and Gundulf, both later bishops of Rochester, who rose to prominence in church and state. In June 1063 Lanfranc was made abbot of William's new foundation of St. Stephen's (the *Abbaye aux Hommes*) at Caen. Later, in 1067, he was offered the archbishopric of Rouen, but refused it, a refusal which at first sight seems strange but which is in perfect harmony with the Norman career of this extraordinary man who attracted scholars to Bec and who made the reputation of Norman monasteries illustrious throughout Europe.

The past history of Norman monasticism itself presented an interesting reflection of general European development. In the tenth century the great Burgundian house of Cluny was in the forefront of monastic reform. Its influence on Normandy was effective, particularly through the work of William of Dijon (961–1031), who had received his early training in Cluny and in Italy, and who built up a fine reputation as a scholar in medicine, mathematics, architecture, and art. It has been estimated that twenty-one out of the twenty-eight or so monastic houses in the duchy on Duke William's accession derived directly from William of Dijon's work. Fécamp in particular was famous for its intellectual achievements. Duke William fully supported these monasteries. He found in them useful allies in the government of his duchy. They were not withdrawn from the world in any strict sense, but were part of the social and feudal organization of the duchy.

Independent of this solid basis of reformed Benedictine order there grew up in the early 1040s the monastic house which came to be most influential in Anglo-Norman affairs during the succeeding century: the abbey of Bec. Its founder was a feudal warrior, a knight named Herluin, who sought spiritual relief in harsh asceticism and in withdrawal to the desert places. He established a small community organized in the most rigorous discipline, and at this stage in its existence the abbey of Bec was very close to other similar ascetic movements which proliferated in the later eleventh century, many of which were eventually absorbed in the new Cistercian order. The arrival of Lanfranc was probably responsible for a transformation which took place, and Bec, in spite of some strain between Herluin and Lanfranc (the peaceful settlement of which is regarded by his contemporary biographer as symptomatic of saintliness and humility on the part of Lanfranc), came to conform more closely to the other Norman houses, and developed into a centre of learning and typical Benedictine observance, a training-house for intellect and administration. The English church was far from decadent in 1066, but it stood to gain greatly from the more intense contact with continental reform, particularly that associated with the conservative house of Bec. Three of the outstanding medieval archbishops of Canterbury, Lanfranc, Anselm, and Theobald, received a substantial part of their training and spent a substantial part of their careers in this Norman house.

(d) *The Normans and the English before 1042*

It would have been surprising if the Normans, whose outstanding characteristics were vitality and energy, had not found some outlet for their energies overseas. The wealthy kingdom of England lay half-a-day's sail to the north, and in the tangled political state of the tenth century there was great interchange between Scandinavia, England, and Normandy. Recent analysis of personal name elements embodied in place-names in Normandy suggests some flow of peasantry from the English Danelaw to Norman lands. During the time of Duke Richard I (942–96) there was friction between the Normans and the English over the harbouring of Viking pirates in Norman ports. The pope himself brought about a concord between Duke Richard and King Ethelred, but, in spite of this, the Normans welcomed a Viking fleet in the year 1000. The English sent an expeditionary force to France to take reprisals against the population of the Cotentin. The reprisals were unsuccessful; the men of the Cotentin proved more than a match for the English, and the sole survivor of the harrying party reported back to the English fleet that if they did not fly at once they would be killed 'come mutuns'.[8]

It was probably as a settlement, and presumably a final settlement, of such dispute that a very important marriage settlement was achieved in 1002. There may have been a commercial reason behind the arrangement. From the document known as IV Ethelred, that is to say a statement of law (in Latin) made probably during the reign of Ethelred, we learn that important trading contracts existed between England and Normandy. Among the specially privileged traders at London were the men of Rouen who came trading with their fish and their wine.[9] King Ethelred, a widower in his mid-thirties, married as his second wife Emma, a sister of Duke Richard II (996–1026). Emma was probably only in her teens at the time of her marriage. She was long remembered in England for her piety:

> Emma, richardes daughter, duc of normandie
> Þet holi womman was, and god withoute ech folie

Emma was certainly a remarkable woman. She left a reputation in later days as a patron of Normans in England; Ordericus Vitalis describes the company that went with Henry I's daughter Matilda to Germany, on the occasion of her marriage to the emperor, Henry V, hoping for preferment such as their ancestors had achieved in England through Queen Emma.[10] There is some positive evidence of the existence of such place-men: a reeve Hugh at Exeter in 1003, appointed to look after the queen's interests in the city; a lady-in-waiting Matilda who married Aelfgeard, a powerful man, at Worcester; Herluin and his son Baldwin who received valuable estates, notably in Warwickshire. Queen Emma, during her long stay in England, provided a focus for Norman interest and Norman friendship. She accustomed the royal court to contact with Normandy. Her wealth was so great that her son Edward the Confessor had to move against her at Winchester in 1043, early in his reign. He sequestered for his own use much of her great wealth (possibly control of the royal treasure), and gave her firm advice that the time had come for a life of dignified retirement at Winchester. The Old English Chronicle recorded in 1052 the death of Emma (Aelfgifu, 'the lady, widow of King Ethelred and Cnut', ms D, 'mother of King Edward and of King Harthacnut', ms E).

The Chronicle, by the correct references to Emma's dynastic position, gives us the proper clue to her importance. We can assume, an analogy with other such alliances, that Norman chaplains, Norman serving-maids, and Norman retainers were common enough in Emma's household. Contact between the Norman ports and Hampshire was easy, and though, to pass her years of exile during the reign of Harold I (1037–9), Emma sought refuge in Flanders rather than in Normandy, there were good reasons of an immediate political nature why this should be so. Her niece's step-son, Baldwin V, was in powerful control of his county at the time; her other great-nephew, William of Normandy, was still a young boy at a perilous moment in his career. With the exception of these years, Emma spent a complete half-century in England. She returned on the accession of her son Harthacnut, and so provided the one strong personal link in high place between the England of Ethelred, the England of Canute, and the England of Harthacnut and Edward. Dynastically she had a special importance in providing the Norman court with a possible right of blood which they could use in favour of William. The chronicler William of Poitiers, admittedly after stressing rights of election and consecration, stated openly: 'And if a claim by blood is demanded it is to be noted that the son of Duke Robert touches King Edward in near kinship, for Robert's aunt, Emma, sister to Richard II and daughter to Richard I, was Edward's mother.'[11]

The element of continuity provided by Emma requires emphasis. The English were accustomed to the presence of a strong-minded, energetic, Norman queen. She was no mere cipher in the days of Ethelred, and Canute found it expedient and helpful to marry her himself (keeping, it is true, his other wife *more Danico*, Aelfgifu, the English lady of Northampton, mother of Harold I, in a position of authority and responsibility in the Danelaw). William of Malmesbury considered that Canute's reasons were purely political: the English were accustomed to the rule of their lady; through her they would become accustomed to Danish rule. Her three children by Ethelred—Godgifu, who later married Dreux, count of Mantes, Edward, and Alfred— went into honourable exile in Normandy, but it is likely that their mother kept in touch with them. Her influence on Canute was truly considerable in ecclesiastical matters; a land-grant near Winchelsea was made to the thriving abbey of Fécamp, probably at her instigation. Some of the principal missionaries to Scandinavia seem to have been of her entourage, and probably Norman in origin: Rudolf, her own kinsman, Bernard, her chaplain, and William, a chaplain in Canute's household. Her continued presence helped to keep alive the idea of the legitimate West Saxon dynasty in high circles in England, and this idea became focused on the Norman exiles, her own sons Alfred and Edward, rather than, for example, on the heirs of Edmund Ironside, far away, first in Scandinavia, then in Hungary, who nevertheless on a strict law of succession were the next in line.

On Canute's death his son Harold I succeeded to effective authority in England, a succession which represented a strengthening of the Scandinavian and Anglo-Scandinavian elements in the country. It was quite natural that the Norman princes should attempt to assert themselves. The young Alfred crossed to England with a small force, was received hospitably but then was betrayed by Earl Godwin of Wessex who handed him over to King Harold and his henchmen. Alfred was savagely blinded, and died as a result of the treatment he received. This political assassination, expedient though it might be on purely technical grounds, shocked opinion in the Christian world. It left a heritage of enduring hate towards Godwin and his house. The Normans justified the slaughter at Hastings as revenge for the death of Alfred. Emma's son by Canute, Harthacnut, seems to have been genuinely moved by the assassination of his half-brother. When he succeeded to the English throne in 1039, on the death of Harold, he sought to redress the wrong. The recall of Prince Edward in 1041, and the recognition of his right to succeed, may have been influenced by remorse for this deed. Emma herself played a mysterious part in all the political troubles of these complicated years. Her attachment to Harthacnut, the strange, doomed young man, who died as he stood at his drink at a wedding feast in 1042, was great and genuine. She had not the same affection for her other son, Edward, and yet it is hard not to believe that she had much to do with his summons from Normandy and recognition as heir. It may have been his realism in recognizing that he had to work with his brother's murderers which caused the rift; it may have been the sheer political and financial influence built up by the great lady who had in 1042 been queen of England for the best part of forty years. As mentioned above, the political influence of Queen Emma came to an end before her son had been on the throne a year. But it would be wrong to neglect the Anglo-Norman ties that were a direct product of this extraordinary woman's career.

(e) *The Normans in England during the reign of the Confessor*

From the Norman point of view it is easy to read the reign of Edward the Confessor (1042–66) as a prelude to an inevitable Norman Conquest. Yet much of the shrewdest modern work has shown the limited nature of the Norman influence, and also a curious tide in the process of Normanization. It was natural that Edward, who had spent nearly all his adult life in the duchy, should look to his Norman friends for help in the new task confronting him. He had been well looked after in the duchy. Canute was not vindictive towards the young princes; indeed, Canute had maintained friendly relationship with the Norman duke, Richard II. Under Robert I friction developed (later associated with the failure of a supposed ducal marriage to Canute's sister). There were strong rumours of projected invasion on Robert's part; but his efforts seem to have been made in favour of the young princes, Edward and Alfred, protected by him in their exile. Edward was not creating any great break with tradition when he looked across the Channel for advisers; Canute himself had been happy to recruit bishops from Lorraine.

Edward did not, however, indulge in a conscious policy of Normanization. For the first ten years of his reign (1042–51) there was little more than a normal infiltration. The composition of his early courts was more Scandinavian than Norman, and the endowments offered to his Norman friends, although significant, were not on a scale sufficient to warrant a radical change in the composition of the aristocracy. Some important appointments were made: Robert Fitz-Wimarc, a relative of the king and also of the Norman duke, was well endowed with estates and responsibility, especially in the eastern counties. At some point after 1050 Ralf the Timid, the king's nephew, was given great estates in the West Country, notably in Herefordshire, where he appears to have borne the title of earl and to have exercised a function akin to that of a Lord Marcher in a later age. Osbern, who was a Norman by birth, was also established in Herefordshire, founding the lordship of Ewias Harold on marcher lines. Ralf the Staller, probably a Breton, was prominent in East Anglian affairs; the Conqueror later made him earl of East Anglia. These four were men of great authority locally and in the royal court; it would be wrong to underestimate their influence. There were also many lesser men, Normans and Bretons, who received substantial secular rewards in England as a result of Edward's accession. But, as the careers of the great English earls alone would be sufficient to suggest, there are no good grounds for postulating the build-up of a royal anti-Godwin party by the lavish endowment of foreign favourites. Many modern historians, bearing Edward's quarter of a century of exile in mind, have been surprised at his moderation.

In the church the effect of his return is more pronounced. He made some personal appointments to his household and his chapel from Normans and Bretons. As royal appointment to the greater ecclesiastical offices was often made from his chapel, these appointments were more influential than their number would suggest. Indeed, the paradox has been pointed out that this king, of saintly reputation, was responsible for the appointment of men more fit for the needs of secular duty than had been the monks, who had predominated in episcopal appointments during the preceding century. But, even so, of the ten vacancies which occurred in the episcopate between 1043 and 1050 six were filled with Englishmen, and a seventh with an Englishman (or, perhaps, a Cornishman) trained in Lorraine.

The most important of the Norman appointments was one which on the surface seemed reasonably sound. In 1044 Robert, a monk of Jumièges, was appointed to the see of London. He turned out to be a churchman of a familiar type, more interested in politics than in religion. His reputation on the Continent remained respectable; the reformed papacy continued to support him. In England, however, he became a focus for anti-Norman feeling and, in particular, a target for the supporters of Godwin, earl of Wessex, and his kin. In 1051 Robert was translated to Canterbury at the royal command and in spite of an earlier election of Aelfric, a relation of Godwin. This appointment, together with its political consequences, helped to provoke the exile of the house of Godwin. During their twelvemonth of absence from England, from autumn 1051 to autumn 1052, there was a more serious attempt to Normanize the hierarchy and the administration. Some good men were introduced, such as William, bishop of London, who remained in occupation of his see through the Conquest to 1075. Others, introduced as royal agents, had no more than a fleeting taste of the prizes of rich English office. In 1052 Godwin returned, and (as part of what bears the mark of an agreed settlement) many Normans fled, and the remainder were reduced to political impotence. Robert himself, as the Anglo-Saxon Chronicle (ms E) tells us, went overseas, 'leaving behind him his pallium and all Christendom here in this land'. He was declared an outlaw solemnly in the Witan, and Stigand succeeded to his archbishopric. It is possible that in English eyes he had forfeited his office, both by his behaviour and by leaving behind him the pallium, the symbol of his archiepiscopal rank. To the reformed papacy it was none the less iniquitous that an archbishop (Stigand) should be appointed in the lifetime of one who had been canonically and properly ordained to the office.

Godwin's return, and the agreed settlement, marked a dramatic end to the short-lived attempt at systematic Normanization, but not a complete victory for an 'anti-Norman' party. Relationships with the duchy continued good, though there were fewer Norman appointments. The king's physician, Baldwin, is the most interesting of later appointments from overseas; he had been a monk at St. Denis, Paris, and was especially famous for his skill in medicine. He numbered both King William and Archbishop Lanfranc among his patients in the succeeding reign. He was made abbot of the wealthy house of Bury St. Edmunds in 1065, and continued to exercise a great part in affairs right through the Conquest to his death in 1097. The king maintained close personal contact with Normandy. As late as 1064 he sent Earl Harold himself on a most important embassy to the Norman court. For, in spite of the partial success of Godwin and the growing power of his son and successor, Harold, in the later years of the Confessor's reign, it seems certain that William, duke of Normandy, was at some stage recognized as probable successor to the English throne. Most would agree that 1051 (or possibly the winter of 1051–2) was the most likely time for such recognition.

Much that is obscure in the immediate pre-Conquest period would become clearer if it could be said with certainty that for fifteen years before 1066 a substantial body of opinion in England and overseas regarded William as the lawful successor to Edward. Some mysteries would naturally remain. For example, the return of Edward, son of Edmund Ironside, from Hungary in 1057, a return that would surely need the royal assent if not the royal initiative, does not make sense if we read Edward as thoroughly consistent in his recognition of William. We are told by the Anglo-Saxon Chronicler (ms D) that the aetheling

Edward died mysteriously before he was allowed to visit his cousin, the king. The aetheling's children, Edgar the Aetheling and Margaret of Scotland, lived on to enjoy lives of some note and adventure. It may be that the Godwin party compelled the recall; it may be that anti-Norman feeling made some insurance essential to Edward. Yet designation of Duke William in 1051 clears up some problems, and recognition of this designation may have been among the hardest of terms imposed upon the Godwins when they made their reconciliation under arms in the autumn of 1052. It would certainly explain why hostages from the Godwin family, Wulfnoth and Hakon, a son and grandson of Godwin, were brought up at the court of Duke William.

Recent work of outstanding interest on this problem has concentrated on two facets in particular: the events of 1051–2 and the embassy of Harold to William sometime before the Conquest, probably in 1064. Most are agreed that Edward offered the succession to William in 1051, and most now accept the idea that the recognition was coupled with the translation of Robert of Jumièges to Canterbury early in 1051. Robert visited Normandy on his way to receive the pallium at Rome before 21 June 1051, and this seems the most likely moment at which a formal announcement of the royal decision would be made to the duke. If such recognition were made known in the summer the revolt of Godwin and his family in the autumn would be much more intelligible. On the other hand it may be argued that the unsuccessful revolt and the absence of Godwin gave Edward his chance to recognize William. One of the copies of the Anglo-Saxon Chronicle (ms D, not the best source, it is true, for events in south-east England) tells that William visited England in the winter 1051–2, accompanied by a large force of Frenchmen, and it is hard to see for what reason, other than the most pressing, he could have been prevailed upon to leave his duchy at that delicate moment. This 'inherent political improbability' coupled with the utter silence of other sources, Norman and English, has led D. C. Douglas to reject the source, and most now agree that the Chronicles were probably confused, very possibly in relation to the visit of

Robert of Jumièges to the ducal court.[12] William is not likely to have stirred from his Norman duchy that winter, but even so Edward was wise in the political circumstances of his time to look to his energetic young kinsman (his first cousin's son) as the man best equipped to ensure peace in England.

The second event that has caused much discussion recently is the visit of Harold to Duke William sometime before King Edward's death. Most agree that this visit took place in 1064 and that its purpose was to confirm the recognition of William as successor. There are difficulties in accepting this view completely. The Bayeux Tapestry shows a rather dejected-looking Harold returning from his embassy. Edward on his death-bed undoubtedly entrusted the kingdom to Harold, at first sight a somewhat odd action on the part of a man who had already named Duke William as his successor. The probable solution to this last puzzle is that put forward by D. C. Douglas and Mlle Foreville independently, though both from an exact study of the text of the Norman chronicler William of Poitiers, according to whom Harold pledged himself by a solemn oath during his meeting with Duke William at Bonneville in the following terms, after swearing fealty to him by the sacred rite of Christian peoples: 'first to be the *vicarius* of the duke at King Edward's court, second to employ all his influence and wealth to confirm the duke in possession of the kingdom after Edward's death, third to place a garrison of the duke's knights in Dover castle at his own expense, and fourth to maintain and supply garrisons in other parts of England at the duke's will and his own expense'.[13]

In return Harold is said (after paying homage to the duke) to have been confirmed in all his lands and dignities. Although this is a Norman party statement it rings true in detail, and Mlle Foreville has suggested that there was ground in this settlement at Bonneville for genuine misunderstanding and genuine conflict of laws. Harold placed himself by his oath in the position of an executor under Roman law, pledging himself in detail to look after William's interests after formally promising to become his man. The reception from Edward as he lay on his death-bed was then a reception in trust preparatory to handing over to the rightful heir. Norman indignation at Harold's assumption of the kingship was directed against him as a perjuror, a breaker of his oath, a false executor. William's challenge of Harold to single combat can be read as correct judicial action, the challenge to a judicial duel. Such an interpretation would help to clarify the tragic nature of the situation in 1066. The Normans undoubtedly pleaded their case with a savage indignation against the perjurer Harold. There is more than mere statement of case in their indignation. They themselves genuinely believed in the justice of their cause.

Finally, before we turn to the events of 1066, one point should be emphasized. King Edward himself retained the strong Norman sympathies of his upbringing. In church and state he conformed to the custom of his rich English kingdom. The construction of Westminster Abbey, one of his chief interests in later years, was as typical of English kings and great lords as it was of Norman dukes. Indeed there are close parallels between the work at Westminster and the work the other side of the Channel at Jumièges. The intrusion of Normans into high office, apart from during the year 1051–2, was not excessive. There was a distinct slackening off in the number of Norman appointments later in his reign. But friendship for his kinsman, the highly successful and powerful William II, duke of Normandy, remained one of the strong elements in his make-up, a friendship that was to facilitate the advent of William I, king of the English, duke of Normandy, self-styled lawful successor of the house of Alfred.

1 Wace, *Roman de Rou*, v. 8059 ff.; *en cest oestel chaenz entrez* (1.8068)
2 ibid., vs. 8107–8
3 William of Poitiers, pp. 12–14
4 M. de Bouard, *Guillaume le Conquérant*, Paris, 1958, p. 20
5 M. de Bouard, 'Sur les origines de la Trève de Dieu en Normandie', *Annales de Normandie*, ix, 1959, especially pp. 171–4
6 William of Poitiers, p. 132, with notes by Mlle Foreville, pp. 130–3; *Ordericus Vitalis*, iii, p. 86; Wace, *Roman de Rou*, vs. 9681–9758, for Toret (Thor?), vs. 9713–22

7   *Lanfranci Opera*, ed. J. A. Giles, Oxford, 1844, p. 287; Freeman, *Norman Conquest*, iii, pp. 102–3; William of Poitiers, p. 126
8   Wace, *Roman de Rou*, v. 6303
9   IV Ethelred, 2.5; Liebermann i, p. 232
10 *Ordericus Vitalis*, vi, p. 168; R. L. G. Ritchie, *The Normans in England before the Norman Conquest* (inaugural lecture), Exeter, 1948, pp. 14–15
11 William of Poitiers, p. 222
12 D. C. Douglas, 'Edward the Confessor, Duke William of Normandy, and the English Succession', *E.H.R.* 1953, pp. 526–45; also Mlle Foreville, 'Aux Origines de la Renaissance Juridique', *Moyen Age*, 1953
13 William of Poitiers, pp. 102–4; *E.H.D.* ii, p. 218

3

The English Background

(a) *The House of Godwin*

To THIS point emphasis has been placed on the preparatory
work done in the Norman duchy, and the firm statement has
been made that William the Norman expected to succeed Edward
as king of England. In fact he did not do so, and in order to
understand this failure it will be necessary briefly to look at the
background of the man who anticipated him, Harold Godwinson,
earl of Wessex. There has been argument about the constitutional significance of the house of Godwin; there can be no
argument concerning the political importance. In 1066 Godwin
and his family had been in the forefront of political life in
England for nearly fifty years, and at various critical moments
had appeared to dominate it. Yet this domination was very much
a personal matter. Godwin and his sons were not Mayors of the
Palace, controlling royal revenues, taxes, the army, and administration. Even as late as 1064 Harold was sent by King Edward on
an embassy (as he had been to Flanders in 1056). His royal lord
and master was no *roi fainéant*. Harold was a powerful earl,
described by a Norman chronicler as *secundus* to King Edward.[1]
The subtlety and truth of the situation is lost completely, if it
is not realized that he was indeed 'second' to the king, a royal
servant for all his military prowess and exalted position.

The family fortunes were founded by Godwin, an Englishman, probably the son of a thegn, Wulfnoth, who had prospered by an act of piracy in the Channel in the early years of the

TABLE 2—THE HOUSE OF GODWIN

Godwin, earl of Wessex
1018–53
=
Gytha (sister of Earl Ulf and aunt of Sweyn
Estrithson, k. of Denmark, 1047–76)

| Sweyn (earl 1043, died 1052) | Edith Swannehals · · · · · · · · illegitimate children | Harold (earl 1045, earl of Wessex 1053, k. of England, 1066, killed at Hastings) = Edith 1066 (d. of Aelfgar, earl of Mercia, and sister of Edwin and Morcar) | Tostig (earl of Northumbria, 1055–65, killed at Stamford Bridge, 1066) = Judith of Flanders | Gyrth (earl of East Anglia, 1057–66, killed at Hastings) | Leofwine (earl of Kent and Essex, 1057–66, killed at Hastings) | Edith (m. 1045, Edward the Confessor, k. of England, 1042–66) |

Note: There was also a son of Godwin, Wulfnoth, and a grandson, Hakon, who were hostages at the court of Duke William from 1052 (see p. 57) eleventh century. Godwin attracted the notice of Canute, was appointed earl of Wessex in 1018, and married the Danish Gytha, sister of Ulf of Denmark, Canute's own brother-in-law. During the troubled reigns of Harold I and Harthacnut he played a discreet but powerful role as an elder statesman who had supported loyally the new Danish dynasty. His part in the death of the aetheling Alfred has already been referred to, but, in spite of it, he seems to have been ready and willing to work for Edward's succession. In the early years of Edward's reign the Godwins flourished mightily, a point to be borne in mind against those who would over-emphasize the Normanizing influence of the Confessor. Godwin's personal authority came from his office as earl of Wessex, and from his possession of landed wealth in that ancient kingdom, most of which came to him as earl rather than in his personal right. 1045 represents a climax in the rise to authority of his house, for in that year King Edward married Edith, daughter of Godwin, who was clearly one of the influential women whose part in affairs has been obscured by the nature of our records. Later hagiographers, searching for an essential justification for sainthood, asserted that the marriage was never consummated, but this is improbable. At that date Godwin, the new father-in-law of the king, was earl of Wessex; his eldest son Sweyn was an earl with authority in the West, probably in control of the Bristol Channel; his second son Harold was exercising the functions of an earl in part, if not all, of East Anglia; his nephew Beorn Estrithsson held an earl's office in the south-east Midlands, including the shire of Hertfordshire in his sphere of office; there were also promising younger sons Tostig, Gyrth, and Leofwine, who appeared to ensure the continuity of the family stock. The other earls, Leofric of Mercia and Siward of Northumbria, powerful men as they were in their own areas, could not compete in dignity and authority with the West Saxon earl. Danger to Godwin's position came from two directions: the first and less important from inside the family, and the second from inadequate personal control of the *sources* of authority. Inside the family, Sweyn, the eldest son, was the weakness. He was a man of uncontrollable passions. In 1046 he seduced the abbess of Leominster; in 1049 he murdered in hot blood his cousin Beorn. For both offences he was exiled, yet soon recalled and reinstated. He was exiled again with the rest of his family in 1051, and met a pious end to a turbulent career on pilgrimage to the Holy Land in 1052. Much more important was the general opposition to the house of Godwin, which reached a critical point in 1051. The king was the centre of discontent, and Edward was no cipher, content that the West Saxon earl should assume royal authority from a subordinate position. Royal administration was strong, and honeycombed the earldoms. Edward himself was responsible for disbanding a powerful, mercenary section of the fleet in 1049–50, an act which was surely connected with his friendship for the Norman duke, and was probably a necessary preparatory step to the recognition of William as his successor. During the exiles of Sweyn, Normans were intruded into the West Country, notably into Herefordshire. Godwin and his sons appear to have maintained their position by their capacity for rule and military ability; they were excellent soldiers. But the other earls looked with no great favour on the power of the family of the earl of Wessex. Rumblings of discontent were also apparent in the church. The appointment of Robert of Jumièges to Canterbury in preference to a candidate from the earl's own family was a grave blow to the Godwin cause. 1051 was a bad year for the Godwins and if, as is likely, William was offered the succession to the throne in early 1051, the desperate nature of the autumn crisis is readily explained. A secular dispute brought matters to a head. The king's brother-in-law (Count Eustace II of Boulogne, second husband of Godgifu, Edward's sister) was involved in a brawl at Dover. King Edward, convinced that the townsmen were at fault, ordered Godwin to ravage the area. Godwin refused, took up arms against the king, and confronted him in open array in Gloucestershire on 1 September, a week before the projected date of the council which had been summoned to hear the dispute. The other earls rallied to the king's side; the king was able to summon a formal council; and Godwin and his family escaped into exile, some to Flanders and some to Dublin. Queen Edith herself was sent to a seemly retreat at the nunnery of Wherwell.

The most interesting feature of the events of 1051 was the unwillingness of both sides to come to open conflict. The Anglo-Saxon Chronicle (ms D) reported that 'some of them thought it would be a great piece of folly if they joined battle because in the two hosts there was most of what was noblest in England, and they considered that they would be opening a way for our enemies to enter the country and to cause great ruin among ourselves'; Chronicle (ms E) reported perhaps more significantly a reluctance on the part of Godwin and his supporters to 'stand against their royal lord'. The strength of the king and of the nation against over-mighty subjects is shown by these happenings. It is also significant that, before granting a safe-conduct to Godwin, the king demanded that all the thegns possessed by the rebellious earls should be handed over to him. Edward knew from his Norman days the danger that the power of the 'feudal' hierarchy would rest in the subordinate ranks. In ensuring that commendation would not be halted at the 'earlish' level, Edward was acting in the full line of continuity from earlier Anglo-Saxon kings, such as Ethelred, who stated in his laws (III Ethelred, 11) that no one should have jurisdiction over a king's thegn except the king himself.

The Godwins, however, had too firm a hold on the wealth and loyalty of much of the kingdom to be thus arbitrarily dismissed. They busied themselves in exile, recruited mercenaries, made exploratory raids, and in the autumn of 1052, supported by a combination of mercenaries (their movable wealth must have been substantial), men of the Cinque Ports, Londoners, and men from their earldoms, they forced a peace on the king. The settlement was moderate, guaranteed by the northern earls and, possibly, as has been earlier suggested, by the Norman duke. Godwin was reconciled to the king, but died in the following year, in the royal presence. On Easter Monday, 1053, Godwin was sitting at a meal with the king at Winchester when he had a seizure which deprived him of his speech and his strength. He died three days later on 15 April. Harold succeeded to his earldom of Wessex.

For the rest of Edward's reign, 1053–66, the rivalry of the great 'earlish' families has been considered a fatal weakening of united English resistance to Norman invasion. There is a danger of over-dramatizing political events, and yet an account of the background to the Norman Conquest would be defective without some sketch of the succession to the various earldoms. The essential facts are as follows. When Harold of Wessex succeeded his father in 1053 he gave up his East Anglian earldom, which passed to Aelfgar, the son of Leofric of Mercia. In 1055 Siward of Northumbria died, and Harold's brother, Tostig, was appointed in his place; for the succeeding ten years Tostig, though personally unpopular, governed the north harshly but effectively. In 1057 Leofric of Mercia died, and was succeeded by his son Aelfgar, who was replaced in East Anglia by Harold's other brother, Gyrth. As Harold himself was very active along the Welsh March in Hereford, and as yet another of Godwin's sons, Leofwine, held prominent office in Kent and Essex, it is easy to see how the house of Leofric must have felt itself constricted and encircled by the military authority of Harold and his brothers. The years 1057–63 were in fact dominated politically by the growing military prowess of Harold against a combination of Welsh and Mercian forces. Harold gained great prestige from his Welsh victories. With the help of Normans as well as Englishmen he stabilized the perilous Hereford border, extended effective English overlordship to the lands between the Wye and the Usk, and ruined the precocious attempts of Gruffydd ap Llywelyn to impose unity upon the Welsh. Aelfgar was forced into exile at one point, and only with great difficulty, possibly because of his strong hold as a landlord in north-west Mercia, did he resume his comital functions. Even so, in 1063, on the death of Aelfgar, the prestige of his house in Mercian affairs was sufficient to ensure the succession to the earldom of his young son Edwin.

The military successes of Harold, the political success of his house, and his general prestige in the country must not blind us to the fact that he was a subordinate, a very powerful military commander, but not an autonomous governor of men. He could be sent on embassy by his royal master, and perhaps in no respect is the subordinate nature of his office better demonstrated than in the last great political crisis of the reign, the Northumbrian crisis of autumn 1065. This crisis was a direct prelude to the Norman Conquest, and it unfolded dramatically into the events of 1066. In October 1065 the Northumbrian thegns, greatly dissatisfied with the harsh rule of Tostig, flared into open rebellion against the earl, massacred his hearth-troop, declared him formally deposed, elected Morcar, the younger brother of Earl Edwin, in his place, marched south in a devastating campaign into Northamptonshire, and forced King Edward to acquiesce in their choice. Harold played a distinctly equivocal part in the revolt, and in the negotiations between the rebels and the king. His failure to give Tostig his full support led to a rift in the family which the author of the *Vita Ædwardi* declared in poetical terms was fatal to the Old English state. King Edward seems to have been genuinely loyal to Tostig, and his humiliation in agreeing to the Northumbrian demands is said to have hastened his death. With the removal of Tostig from his office as earl Harold was left as incontestably the ablest and most experienced man of affairs in the realm. The course of the crisis shows how powerful thegns, if they acted together, could unseat an unpopular earl. Nevertheless, the royal assent was needed to create an earl.

(b) *The nature of the earldoms*

Much recent work of interest has concentrated on the internal workings of the Old English monarchy and church, and these themes, concerned with the strength of the Old English realm, require some consideration before we turn to the events of 1066. The scope of the battle cannot be assessed until the value of the prize is realized.

The first important problem concerns the nature of the earldoms, of which so much mention has been made above. There are analogies with the constitutional position of some of the great continental fiefs; there are also some analogies with the great German duchies of the tenth century. But the likenesses are deceptive. Two factors in particular point the contrast: the age of the Old English monarchy, and the difference in constitutional position between even the great earldom of Northumbria and the duchy of Bavaria or the county of Anjou. Northumbria, Mercia, East Anglia, and Wessex, it is true, represented ancient kingdoms in which there survived some sense of communal cohesion. The earldoms were new. The typical early tenth-century royal officer was the *ealdorman*, who was normally in charge of one shire. In the course of the tenth century, as the range of the West Saxon monarchy extended, it became common for an *ealdorman* to be entrusted with rule over several shires. It was Canute, however, with his imperial background, who finally gave the earldoms both their names (Scandinavian *iarl*, replacing Anglo-Saxon *ealdorman*) and their familiar pre-Conquest forms. The earldom was not a compact constitutional unit similar to the county of Anjou in France. The potential danger to the English monarchy consisted in the risk that the earls would intrude themselves as a permanent class between the king and the thegns, and that their offices would become hereditary possessions. At the time of the Conquest neither of these developments had reached completion. Earls remained great officers subject to the king and his council from above, and to the pressure of communities from below. Tostig's career was illuminating in both respects. Even Harold's success had been essentially military and political. Very significant, too, is the shift in appointments to earldoms which occurred in the Confessor's reign. The house of Godwin and the house of Leofric, partly because of their territorial possessions, had gained what amounted to a prescriptive right to the earldoms of Wessex and Mercia respectively. In Cheshire in 1066 there was not a single acre of royal demesne, but Earl Edwin held no fewer than twenty manors, assessed at more than a hundred hides. Elsewhere the 'earlish' families were not so deep-rooted. King Edward asserted his authority in the north when he appointed Tostig to the earldom of Northumbria. East Anglia provides the best example of the changes that were possible in the person and the kin of the holders of an earldom. Harold had exercised some comital authority as early as 1045–6; in 1051 he was exiled and Aelfgar, son of Leofric, took his place, only to yield it quietly during the winter of 1052–3 on the restoration of the Godwins. In 1053 Harold succeeded to Wessex and Aelfgar came back to East Anglia. In 1057 Aelfgar succeeded to Mercia, and Harold's brother Gyrth now took over the East Anglian office. Men of mature age in the two families were regarded as the most fitting to succeed to earldoms, but the appointments themselves were matter for political choice, exercised to all appearance by the king in his witan.

The functions of the earl were more elaborate than those of his predecessor, the *ealdorman* of the tenth century, in one special field. His military office was much more marked. This is in part a result of the more elaborate military organization of an age that knew the dangers of constant hostile attack. The earl was the man who co-ordinated military defence, and presumably the collection of revenues that made such defence practicable, over a widening area. It is probable that he had to pay special attention to maritime defence; the earls of Northumbria to the Humber, the East Anglian earls to the Wash, the Mercian earls to Chester and the approaches to the north-west, the West Saxon earls to the south coast and to the Bristol Channel. They continued to draw the revenues that had supported the *ealdorman*, a third of the profits of justice from the shire courts and the same proportion of customs rendered by the boroughs. The earl, or his deputy, normally a king's reeve, a shire-man, later a shire-reeve or a sheriff, presided over the shire court, acting as a colleague to the bishop. There are traces of estates permanently assigned to his maintenance; Aldermaston preserves in its name *ealdormannestun* evidence of one such estate. But the earl

remained the king's officer. He was entitled to one-third of
certain revenues, but the remainder went to the king. The
powers of the earl were great, vice-regal in the military sphere,
but somewhat vague. His special importance was in the political
field, as the representative of the king. The existence of the earldoms was not a sign of a deep-rooted disruptive tendency in the
English constitution. Under the Norman kings the title of earl
was retained in an increasingly honorific context, except on the
frontiers where special palatine jurisdictions were set up.

(c) *The Old English monarchy*

England was in some respects the wealthiest monarchy in Western
Europe, and modern scholars have consistently stressed the
advanced nature of its institutional growth. In spite of social
differences in regional custom there was a genuine sense of
community in England centred on the person of the king.
Edward himself could claim the antiquity of his dynasty as a
special source of strength. There was a mystical quality to the
house of Cerdic which Henry I, for example, afterwards exploited
on behalf of his wife Matilda, the daughter of Margaret of
Scotland, grand-daughter of Edward Aetheling, in direct descent to
the main stock of Alfred's line. William I's insistence on the legitimacy of his succession was connected with an appreciation of the
loyalty due to the ancient house. To the northern world, also,
the West Saxon dynasty had a special appeal. Athelstan was a
saga-hero; and, as Christianity spread, Alfred and Edgar were
singled out as heroes of the Christian world. The church
throughout the early Middle Ages supported the monarchy in
Western Europe; the king was the best hope of a more secure and
peaceful order in which the church could flourish. There was a
long tradition of anointing and an elaborate coronation ritual
in England where the king was as much a man set apart as was
the Capet in France. King Edward himself heightened this
Christian sense of office. He was an anointed king, and his
dignity and effectiveness derived in no small part from his
exploitation of this aspect of his office. Edward's contemporary

biographer even claimed therapeutic powers for the king, who is said to have touched for the king's evil—though this special gift of healing was held as a mark of personal sanctity, not as an attribute of royal dignity.[2] Harold had every intention of emphasizing the special sanction which came from coronation; he was crowned by the archbishop of York, not by Canterbury, whose title was doubtful. It was left to William firmly to emphasize the spiritual quality of consecration, and he also took care that his first coronation, at Westminster on 25 December 1066, should be at the hands of Ealdred of York, not at the dubious hands of Stigand of Canterbury.

The strength of the English monarchy did not depend, however, on mystical, partially intangible, elements. Techniques of government were well developed. In financial matters England seems to have been well in advance of other West European monarchies. A system of national taxation existed, a land-tax that worked. Methods of assessment were elaborate, varied from region to region, and were ultimately connected with food-rent levies that had been used to support early Anglo-Saxon kings on their peregrinations. Greater efficiency developed through grim experience in buying off the Danes. Under Ethelred it has been estimated that £167,000 was paid formally in Danegeld, to be followed in 1018 with £72,000 to Canute, a further £10,500 coming from London alone. Although Edward had cut government expenditure by disbanding a mercenary element in the fleet, the geld remained, and it is generally accepted now that the geld was levied annually. The rate of geld in the mid-eleventh century seems often to have been at two shillings to the hide, and each landowner would know that the royal officers in the shire would expect to receive, presumably at a fixed date, possibly half on Lady Day and half at Michaelmas, the amount chargeable to his estate. The term hide itself, originally a measurement of land calculated to support one family, had developed into a unit of assessment, particularly important in the levying of the geld. The shire court was the institution through which decisions concerning geld could be made known to the neighbourhood.

It is now generally agreed that there was a much freer circula-
tion of money in pre-Conquest England than used to be considered likely. The monetary system itself was one to be admired.
The only coin was the silver penny, but this was of high standard
and circulated vigorously. English experts were employed in
Scandinavia by Canute to make dies after the English model,
and to help create a native coinage in the northern kingdoms.
Central control of the currency was a remarkable feature of the
late Old English state. Dies were cut, either in London (or
possibly for a brief period at regional die-cutting centres) under
royal supervision, and then sent to each borough. Royal control
was exercised through the dies, and royal profit also came from
the dies. In Hereford, at the time of Domesday Book, there were
seven moneyers who, when the coinage was changed, paid
eighteen shillings for their dies and a further twenty shillings
within one month of their return. One of these moneyers belonged to the bishop of Hereford—an unusual feature, as the
vast majority of moneyers were directly answerable to the king.
Recent work has shown that the coinage was changed regularly
from 973 onwards, at six-yearly intervals to begin with, at three-
yearly intervals during the reign of the Confessor. The old
coinage was called in, and new coins minted from the silver.
The weight of the coins remained good; harsh legal penalties
ensured the standard of the money. There were close on seventy
mints in the country during Edward's reign. Each borough
possessed the right—in some sense it was a duty—to establish a
mint. The moneyer himself, whose name appeared on the reverse
of the coin, was probably a man of substance; his office may
have been hereditary, and was certainly a source of considerable
profit. The scope of operations was remarkable, and Sir Frank
Stenton has pointed out that our firmest indication of continuity
of administration in Harold's day comes from his voluminous
issue of coinage from forty-four different mints. The distribution of coins which survive, for example, from the mints of
York, Chester, Romney, and Exeter suggests that an active
stimulus was given to local economy by war preparations. In its

financial aspects the Old English State was advanced and un-usually centralized.

The work of the royal secretariat was also efficient and advanced. We cannot now accept the existence of a chancellor, by that name, before 1068, but there were highly skilled clerks and plentiful signs of continuity in administration from the time of Athelstan. A permanent body of clerks was maintained, centred at the royal chapel; bishoprics were the prizes for the most successful or the most highly favoured. In calligraphy, in general format of diplomatic instrument, and in continuity of type of charter and writ, there is sufficient evidence to indicate continuous institutional growth in the royal secretariat. Anglo-Saxon charters were elaborate documents, written records of solemn government acts, controlled by royal clerks, though at times drawn up by beneficiaries according to set forms, and approved by the king and witan. They were solemn, formal, and expensive documents. Much more interesting was the writ, a more effective and simpler instrument of government, which was visibly replacing the charter in popularity and efficiency during the last generation of Anglo-Saxon England. In essentials the writ was a letter under seal. Mention of such letters occurs as early as the reign of Alfred; and throughout the tenth century, certainly from the reign of Ethelred, there is sufficient evidence to indicate continuity in form and substance of a recognizable writ, attested by the royal seal. From the reign of Canute (who was probably responsible for the introduction of the double-faced Great Seal) the writ was used increasingly in place of the solemn charter, the land-book or *privilegium*. All surviving Anglo-Saxon writs are essentially title-deeds, preserved because it was important to the owner that they should be kept, but they are not only title-deeds. They concede rights of jurisdiction and financial rights as well as title to land. The strength of the writ lay in its simplicity. It was a straightforward royal order that a thing should be attended to, a parcel of land made over to its rightful owner, or a right be bestowed. It was sent to the royal officer in the shire court and was intended to be read and made public in that assembly. Jurors at the time of the Domesday Inquest in 1086 took the royal writ as one of the surest proofs of legitimacy of land-holding. Complaints were made to the effect that land was held 'without livery, without writ and without seisin'. The following example indicates the strength and simplicity of the matured writ: it was a government order.

'King Cnut sends friendly greetings to Bishop Eadsige and Abbot Aelfstan and Aethelric and all my thegns in Kent. And I inform you that I have granted to Archbishop Aethelnoth all the landed property which Aelfmar had, and which lawfully pertains to Christ Church, within borough and without, in woodland and in open country, as fully and completely as Archbishop Aelfric owned it or any of his predecessors'.[3]

The writ was also remarkable in that it was issued in the vernacular. The earliest surviving writs of William the Norman were still issued in Anglo-Saxon. It was not until 1070 that Latin began seriously to replace Anglo-Saxon as the language of the writ, and even then the form continued substantially unaltered. Care must be taken not to exaggerate. The invention of the writ was a splendid achievement, but only slowly did it become an ordinary instrument of government. Under Canute it was still essentially confined to transmit favour to individuals on extraordinary occasions. Some would even state that the writ did not come into its own until after the Conquest 'as a means of establishing a title with which to defend rights and properties against the conquerors'.[4] This perhaps goes a little too far. There is enough evidence from the reign of the Confessor to show that the writ was in widespread use as a flexible instrument of government, prepared by clerks in the royal secretariat. In this respect, however, as in so many, we are confronted with yet a further example of Anglo-Saxon skill in invention—and Anglo-Norman in use.

At the time of the Conquest England possessed a royal administration with forms of government further developed than those of the Norman duchy. There was also a long tradition in

England of the king as the guardian of the laws of the community and as the framer of law codes. The legislative activity of the Anglo-Saxon kings was great. There were also peculiarities in the royal relationship to land-holding and the ancient renders from land which helped to give the English king a special position.

Part of Godwin's authority, and of Harold's after him, stemmed from his earldom of Wessex. King Edward lacked a consolidated territorial block of unmediatized political authority; indeed with a sufficiently efficient royal administration he did not need it. He did not lack wealth. Land was the prime essential of material possession, and, although there was some slight shrinking of royal wealth in land during the reign of the Confessor, royal demesne—the ancient demesne of the Crown—remained very extensive. It is difficult to assess the exact general position in 1066 (the holdings of the earls provide a complicating factor), but Edward was clearly the most substantial landowner in the country. William, by virtue of conquest and of gradual abolition of 'earlish' office, clarified and intensified the position. By 1086 nearly a quarter of the landed wealth of England was in the hands of the royal house, an estimated £17,650 out of a total of £73,000 in annual value. This figure represents an extension in breadth as well as in depth. William possessed a substantial share in every county, except Sussex and the three 'earlish' counties of the Welsh Marches, that is to say Hereford, Shropshire, and Cheshire. Edward had held little in Norfolk, Suffolk, and Yorkshire, and (in 1066) not a single manor in Hertfordshire, Middlesex, Essex, Lincolnshire, Rutland, Cheshire, and Cornwall, though in several of these counties land ascribed to the great earls bore a relationship to royal demesne. And the main point stands. King Edward, last of the Anglo-Saxon kings, held great royal possessions; in Wiltshire alone his annual return from land exceeded £500. King William, by exacting an increased render in place of the 'farm of one night', and by sequestrating the property of Harold and his family, drew well over twice this sum from the exceptionally fertile shire.

There was inevitable variety in the nature of this landed wealth, but great estates tended to predominate, some of them royal land as far back as written record could carry the story, some possibly a primitive allotment made to the petty king in tribal days. The assessment of the royal estates to geld was light, particularly in Wessex, though the obligations laid on them were heavy in other respects. In parts of Wessex royal manors were grouped into farm-paying units that contributed £80 or even more as composition for the royal right to be entertained on his progress, for the farm of one night (the *firma unius noctis*). Recent work has established that there was much leasing of estates in late Anglo-Saxon England, and royal lands were as subject to this process as were the lands of the great tenants. The valuation recorded in Domesday Book, often in round numbers, suggests considerable trafficking in the proceeds of land; the annual rent was established, and would presumably be the basis on which the owner made his bargain with the 'farmer'. The agrarian economy was well developed; the use of money widespread; financial organization was advanced and efficient.

The problem of landowning is one of the most complicated facing the Anglo-Saxon historian, but certain essential points are now agreed. It is generally accepted that land was not all held of the king, as in later feudal theory, and that all land, unless specially exempt by official act of the king and the witan, was subject to folk-burdens, especially to an obligation to contribute to the maintenance of the king himself, his court, and his officers. The object of special exemption, which came in the form of a solemn charter or specific writ, was to free estates from such folk-burdens, and also to give the new owner by charter (of bookland) the right of testamentary bequest out of kindred—in the first instance so that it could be granted to religious houses, but later so that it could be bequeathed to lay beneficiaries. Three communal burdens remained on bookland as well as on folkland, obligations to provide service in the fyrd, at bridges, and at fortifications. Full feudal military service was not known, nor the fief, though dependent tenures evolved in the course of the tenth and eleventh centuries. At Worcester, in particular, Bishop

Oswald, during the reign of King Edgar, reorganized his estates so that he obtained service, sometimes of a military kind, in return for dependent tenure, normally granted for a period of three lives. The lack of definition in service, which could range from hunting to escort duty and bridge-building, coupled with the fact that military service in the 'Oswaldslaw' remained a matter of status, not tenure, precludes the use of the word feudal in a strict modern sense, though clearly feudal tendencies existed in these great ecclesiastical estates.

The English king was the greatest landowner in the realm. He was also the head of the army and of the navy. There were two principal elements in the royal army: there was the body of personal retainers, and there was the much more complicated organization of the national army, the fyrd. No prominent men could afford to be without his personal hearth-troop, the king no less than any other great lord. In pitched battles they bore the brunt of the fighting, or, perhaps it is more accurate to say, their exploits were the best recorded. Earl Byrhtnoth's hearth-troop at the Battle of Maldon, Canute's housecarls, Godwin's retainers during the threatened rising of 1051, Harold's personal guard at Hastings, receive much attention from the historians. This is not true of King Edward's personal followers; at times of crisis, as in 1051, it is his earls who hurry up their hearth-troops. He was much more energetic than has been generally thought; he remained fond of hunting until the last months of his life; in northern legend he is pictured, during the sacred feast of Easter, listening to the sagas of Olaf Haroldsson, St. Olaf of Norway. But we do not hear of him with fighting men; he is, possibly deliberately, detached and remote. He breathed the rarer air of settled kingship, legitimate and above secular battles.

The emphasis on the picked retainers is slightly misleading. They were the men who fought at the lord's side in battle, to whom it was disgrace unbounded to survive a lord who had died in battle. At the end of their career they were rewarded with land and honourable maintenance, the heroes of epic poetry, the men of loyalty of the epic world. There remained a national army, a fyrd, which in England, at all events, was important. Originally it was the duty of every freeman to serve in the fyrd. By 1066 it was customary for peasant households to be grouped so that their resources could provide for one effective warrior. In Berkshire, for example, a five-hide estate contributed one soldier to the fyrd, and each hide contributed four shillings for two months towards his provision or pay. It is uncertain if this was the practice throughout the country, but there is enough evidence to suggest that such grouping was widespread. It may well be that there existed two 'fyrds', complementary and side by side: the general levy of all free men, still called out for defensive campaigning that involved one shire, and the select fyrd, chosen on the basis of one warrior from each five-hide unit, and levied for service or active royal campaign, by land or sea.[5] The warriors were not cavalry, though they rode to battle led by the thegns of a locality and commanded by the earl. They were summoned by order of the king or responsible royal officer. Their service was national, not personal to the thegn who led them. The fact that *fyrdwites*, penalties for failing to attend the fyrd, were common to the whole kingdom, inflicted as a consequence of royal declaration of law, is enough to confirm the existence of an army which, no matter how localized in practice, was in theory a levy of the whole kingdom.

Naval organization was even more elaborate. Part of the geld went to pay ships' crews who were expensive, and to some degree professional. King Edward, between 1049 and 1050, paid off part of his navy, Scandinavian by race, and threw extra responsibility on the Cinque Ports in return for the profits of justice. Geld for naval defence continued to be levied. The events leading up to the return of Godwin in 1052 show a royal fleet still active in the Thames. Inland shires such as Worcestershire and Warwickshire contributed, as well as coastal shires. In some areas three hundreds were joined together for fiscal purposes into one ship-soke, presumably to make provision for sixty oarsmen from three hundred hides. The bishop of Worcester in Worcestershire and the bishop of

Dorchester in Oxfordshire controlled such groups of hundreds.

Organization was on a national scale by sea as by land. It is sometimes difficult to bring Northumbria, busy with the northern border, into the picture, but south of the Humber there is much evidence of a national community gathered around a king of the English. Byrhtnoth at Maldon, at the head of the Essex fyrd, protected the *eard Ethelredes*, the homeland of Ethelred; the rival armies in Gloucestershire in 1051, as we have seen, had no wish to fight one another. Again in 1052, when Godwin confronted King Edward, the Anglo-Saxon Chronicle recounted that 'it was hateful to almost all of them that they should have to fight against men of their own race, for there were few men of any account except Englishmen on both sides; and they had no wish also to leave this land wide open to foreign invasion by destroying one another'. Social differences and racial differences persisted, but the realm which Duke William came to discipline did not lack unity.

(d) *The Old English church*

Finally, before we turn to the events of 1066, a word is needed on the Old English church. The problem that has vexed generations of historians concerns the supposed decadence of that church. It is easy to see why such decadence should be assumed. The most prominent churchman in England, Archbishop Stigand, was notorious throughout all Europe for his dubious title, his political nature, and his 'gross pluralism. By the side of the triumphs of the Anglo-Norman church under Lanfranc and Anselm the preceding period certainly looks black. There has been a tendency, which applies not only to ecclesiastical history, to attribute improvements general to the whole of European society to the merits of the Normans. A just reappraisal of the late Old English church is possible only by placing it firmly in its proper context of the early years of the reformed papacy. In that context epithets such as 'backward', 'sluggardly', 'out of the main stream', seem inappropriate.

Our view of the ecclesiastical situation has been distorted in the past by prejudice against the papacy. All are now agreed that contact with Rome should be taken as a touchstone of health not as a symptom of disease in an eleventh-century church. England had been consistently loyal to the papacy; Peter's Pence had been paid regularly, there was an English School at Rome, and a steady flow of Anglo-Saxon monks and pilgrims made their way, along a well-beaten route, through Rheims, Besançon, Aosta, Vercelli, and Pavia to Rome. The great change that came over Rome after 1046, when reform was forced upon it by the zealous Henry III, may be summed up in one phrase: as a movement from acceptance of a somewhat passive primacy to a struggle for an active supremacy. Full implications of this change of heart did not show themselves until the pontificate of Gregory VII, 1073–85. But under Pope Leo IX, 1049–54, Rome was very active, and this activity had important effects on English affairs. Leo held great Councils outside Italy as well as inside, and English churchmen were present at Rheims in 1049, and again at Rome and at Vercelli in 1050. In Lent 1051 Archbishop Robert (nine out of fourteen archbishops are known to have done so between 925 and 1066) visited Rome to receive the pallium. While he was there he was ordered to refuse consecration to the Englishman Spearhafoc, bishop-elect of London, and the Norman bishop, William, was consecrated in his place. There can be no doubt that Pope Leo had a very shrewd idea what was going on. His successors also played an important part in English affairs. Churchmen started to look to Rome for confirmation of their rights and privileges. A privilege to Chertsey Abbey was confirmed by Pope Victor II (1055–7); Ely claimed confirmation of her liberties from the same pope. Under Nicholas II a privilege was granted to Bishop Giso of Wells, and an appeal was heard by Dorchester against the encroachments of York. In 1062 a most important constitutional issue was settled when the papal legates demanded separation of York and Worcester, and saw to it that Wulfstan, prior of Worcester, was elected to the see. This awareness on the part of the papacy of affairs in England is a clue to the renewed vitality of Rome; it also adds weight to the papal support of William's claim to the succession.

The problem of the state of the English Church was complicated by the personality of an extraordinary man, Stigand. He was the type of political bishop against whom the advanced reformers directed their principal attacks. As an associate of Godwin and his family, he was promoted first to the see of Elmham in 1043, then to Winchester in April 1043, and then, on the flight of Robert of Jumièges, to Canterbury in 1052. This latter promotion caused a great scandal in the church. Robert appealed to Pope Leo, who condemned Stigand, a condemnation that was repeated by succeeding popes, except from a few precarious months when the insecure Pope Benedict recognized him in 1058. There are features of his career, however, which demand closer investigation. Not much can be said for him personally, except perhaps that the silence of his many enemies on his private moral life suggests that he was not a person of scandalous behaviour. It is the attitude of other Englishmen towards him that gives a slightly different view of their church. No other bishop was consecrated by him except during his few months of recognition. Harold favoured him politically, and yet Harold had his new foundation at Waltham Holy Cross consecrated by Cynesige of York. It seems certain that Harold was crowned by Ealdred of York. Representative opinion in England respected the papacy, and was uneasy at papal condemnation of the archbishop. It has been argued with some force that Stigand's career, far from showing that the English church was corrupt, merely proved that he was exceptional.

Such negative argument is not enough in itself, but a close examination of the existing evidence suggests that internal discipline was not lax for the age. The king controlled appointments to bishoprics and abbacies, but this was common practice and most of the appointments were sound. The ideas of a territorial church, with the profits adjunct to the altar a landlord's perquisite, were also firmly implanted, as was common in the Germanic north. Church-building was a sign of institutional health, and in this respect England showed to good advantage. Collegiate churches, serving a wide area, remained normal in the extreme south-west, and in other sparsely populated areas, but elsewhere England was well served with parish churches. In areas such as Hampshire and Berkshire parish churches were usually of landlord foundation; in East Anglia and the Northern Danelaw they were at times built by groups of free men of humble rank. For the administration of their churches, bishops had plentiful written material at their disposal to instruct them in the conduct of affairs. The writings of Wulfstan, the early eleventh-century archbishop of York, were exceptionally valuable. There are occasional hints of diocesan synods. Bishops sometimes held their own courts to discipline their clergy. Landed families were still in the habit of commending children to the care of religious houses; profitable estates often accompanied such pupils as a payment for their maintenance.

It is true, nevertheless, that the English church was ripe for reorganization. Pluralism was a fault which needed correction. Stigand held the two cathedral monasteries of Winchester and Canterbury; he also administered the abbey of Gloucester and, for a time, of Ely. The *Liber Eliensis* condemned his pluralism, but applauded his generosity to the house. Ealdred of York held his old diocese of Worcester in plurality for a short while after his elevation to the archbishopric in 1061 until the papacy intervened, although earlier there had been a long precedent for this combination of wealthy southern see and impoverished northern archiepiscopate. Ealdred had administered—at various times and in seemingly legitimate circumstances it is true—the sees of Hereford and Ramsbury and the great house of Winchcombe during his tenure of the see of Worcester (1046–62). Abbot Leofric of Peterborough, the nephew of Earl Leofric, directed four other monasteries, at Burton, Coventry, Crowland, and Thorney, though it is possible that these had become subordinate cells of Peterborough at the time. There was certainly some pluralism. The rules of celibacy were not strictly kept, and at least one bishop (of Lichfield) was married. These were abuses that needed firm handling, and Stigand was not a man of the stature, nor of the inclination, to cope with them. But it does seem too sweeping altogether to dismiss the church as corrupt and politically subservient.

In the monastic field there were signs of true vitality. The foundations at Westminster and at Waltham would have been conspicuous in any age; Peterborough, Evesham, and Worcester were all flourishing. In one respect England was ahead of the Continent. As an answer to the difficulty of providing the central see of a diocese with an efficient clergy, four of the chief bishoprics, influenced by the Benedictine reform of the tenth century, instituted clergy bound by the rigid discipline of the Benedictine Rule, in place of secular clergy. At Worcester, Winchester Old Minster, Christ Church, Canterbury, and Sherborne, monks, headed by a dean, guided the fortunes of the cathedral. The office of dean increased in importance to the diocese, as the bishops became more involved in royal and national affairs. Not only monks but missionaries were also active; contacts in the mission field to Scandinavia were strengthened by the reign of Canute and persisted until the twelfth century. In cultural fields there was a slackening from the Golden Age of Wulfstan and Aelfric (c. 990–1020), but the standard of literacy was high in the vernacular. The treasures of Rouen public library (where material from Jumièges is preserved) still bear witness to the assiduous collection of precious manuscripts in late Anglo-Saxon England. There were some good bishops and abbots. The work of Ealdred and Wulfstan at Worcester must be held in the balance against Stigand. William of Malmesbury, in gloomy vein, attributed to the Normans the revival of the rule of religion 'which had there grown lifeless'.[6] Most modern observers would declare his judgement harsh.

1 William of Poitiers, p. 102
2 *Vita Ædwardi*, pp. 61–2
3 F. E. Harmer, *Anglo-Saxon Writs*, Manchester, 1952, no. 30, pp. 184–5
4 G. Barraclough, 'The Anglo-Saxon Writ', *History*, 1954, especially pp. 211–13

5   C. W. Hollister, *Anglo-Saxon Military Institutions on the Eve of the Norman Conquest*, Oxford, 1962, especially p. 26
6   William of Malmesbury, *Gesta Regum*, p. 306; *E.H.D.* ii, p. 291

The Conquest

BY ANY historical standard 1066 is memorable. Contemporaries gave the disturbances of the year a cosmic setting, and modern astronomers record 1066 as one of the years in which 'Halley's Comet' made its appearance. Within twelve months three kings of mature age reigned over England, as was not to happen again until the very different circumstances of 1936. There is a shape to proceedings which resembles the setting of a tragedy; yet, possibly because of some inadequacy in the character of the chief participants, full tragic grandeur was not achieved. The year started with the death of an old king and ended with the coronation of a vigorous new king. Both men had their proper role to play—the Hamlet's father and the Fortinbras of the tragedy. But Harold himself would be grossly miscast, in stature and by temperament, for the part of Hamlet. Victor at Stamford Bridge in one of the sternest battles of the epic world, slayer of Harold Hardrada, the greatest contemporary hero of the North, and of Tostig, his own brother, Harold nevertheless fails to arouse, despite his death at the hands of the efficient William, those feelings of pity which tragedy demands. The Golden Warrior has been created in the poetic imagination; the historical record has little room for him.

The best account of Harold's reign is given by Florence of Worcester. The old king, Edward, died on 5 January 1066. He had held the royal court at Christmas, but had been too ill to attend the solemn dedication of his new church at Westminster to St. Peter on 28 December 1065. The king was buried on 6 January, and on the same day Harold, the *subregulus*, was elected king by the chief magnates of England, and was crowned with great ceremony by Ealdred, archbishop of York. The Northumbrians were slow to acquiesce in the succession, but the blandishments of Bishop Wulfstan of Worcester and Harold himself appear to have convinced them. His government was just, but harsh; the magnates as a body remained loyal to him; there is little positive evidence of disloyalty, even under stress of the immediate military situation, at Fulford, Stamford Bridge, and Hastings. His name continued to be held in honour among many English ecclesiastical houses. His queen, Ealdgyth, was the sister of Edwin and Morcar. The marriage in 1066 was a political step which necessitated the breaking of his union (*more Danico*) with Edith Swannehals, by whom he had had at least four and possibly six children. Queen Ealdgyth was well regarded and finished her days peacefully and honourably. The *Liber Eliensis* repeats the eulogies of Florence even to the exclamation of despair at the account of their king's fall: 'After many had fallen on both sides, alas, he himself fell at the twilight hour (*heu, ipsemet cecidit, crepusculi tempore*), and with him the nobler element in all England'.[1]

On the other hand the Norman sources were savage in their attacks on Harold's character. William of Poitiers, as we saw above, interpreted the agreement between Harold and William as the swearing and reception of an oath of fealty. This enabled the Normans to influence public opinion on the Continent, and to treat Harold as a violator of his oath. In praising Tostig, William of Poitiers referred to Harold as 'stained with vice, a cruel murderer, purse-proud and puffed up with the profits of pillage, an enemy of justice and of all good'.[2] Harold's accession was certainly interpreted by the Norman court as a serious breach of faith on his part. William lost no time in putting forward his claim, and in preparing the ground for its successful prosecution. We have already referred in general terms to the reasons for his success; his skill in harnessing the military ventures of the

North French nobility and his provision of an admirable outlet for Norman energy. In 1066 he exercised to the full his undoubted diplomatic ability. The two important monarchies in the West, Germany under Henry IV, and France under Philip I, were in the hands of minors; and both sets of regents were friendly to William. Flanders was in close alliance with him; Anjou, the hated rival of Normandy, was defeated and in a state of civil war. The church was favourable, and the vastly important support of the papacy was ready for William to exploit, a support that may most easily be understood in the context of papal monarchical policy in South Italy. William fought under the prestige of a papal banner, which strengthened his hand not only in his own duchy but throughout feudal France. Perhaps his greatest diplomatic triumphs of all, however, came in an area from which we have tantalizingly little written evidence —that is to say, from the North. Both Danes and Norwegians had some rights in the election to England. Edward the Confessor was the successor of Canute as well as of Ethelred and Edmund Ironside, and it is probable that his reign would not have been so successful had not the Danes and the Norwegians found themselves constantly at war. Even so, the Scandinavian menace remained in the background, with occasional irruptions, as, for example, in 1058 when a fleet menaced the western shores of Britain. The Danish kings had rights by blood to succeed Canute; their king, Sweyn Estrithson (1042–74), was Canute's nephew, the son of Earl Ulf and Canute's sister Estrith. Sweyn promised support to William, probably through fear of the more active Norwegian, but in fact he went on to provide a threat to William's kingdom after the Conquest. Much more serious in 1066 was the Norwegian threat. The Norwegian king was Harold Hardrada, one of the immense figures of the age, in prestige as well as physical size. A former captain of the Varangian Guard at Constantinople, he returned home in 1047 with great wealth, particularly in silver, to contend successfully for the throne of a Norway separate from Danish dominion. He governed Norway harshly but successfully, 1047–66, intermittently moving

against the Danish king. As king of Norway he inherited rights
to succeed to England, based on a formal pact made between
Harthacnut and Magnus. Harold Godwinson of England could
scarcely have found two rivals more formidable than those who
confronted him in 1066: William of Normandy in the south and
Harold Hardrada in the north.

Much was written about these events by contemporaries, and
much more by succeeding generations. In the net of intrigue that
spread from Normandy to Norway two facts stood out: Flanders
was the meeting-place of intriguers; Tostig of Northumbria was
the chief intriguer. Yet other important facts are still unknown.
For example, there is the question of collusion among the chief
actors. Norman sources suggest that William of Normandy
knew little of the northern preparation. This is exceedingly
unlikely; the men of Rouen knew much that went on in Flanders,
and news travelled fast from Flanders to Bergen. Tostig himself
was related by marriage to Duke William; his wife Judith was
either a daughter or a younger sister of the Flemish count. It is
possible, of course, that the Normans had no idea of the proposed
scale of Norwegian intervention. The most probable explanation
seems to be that William knew that Tostig was seeking help to
regain his earldom of Northumbria, and that he expected Tostig
to enlist personal support in Scandinavia. It would be quite in
keeping with William's future actions if he chose to welcome
immediate advantage—the distraction of Harold—and to leave
the final settlement of York and the northern earldom to a more
propitious time.

Tostig certainly provided a link between the claimants. He
broke with Harold, and departed into exile, probably before
Harold's succession. The Anglo-Saxon Chronicle (1065) implies
that he went overseas to Count Baldwin between the end of
October and Christmas, accompanied by his wife and 'all those
who wanted what he wanted'. He is said to have stayed in
Flanders all the winter. The *Vita Ædwardi* attributed later disaster
to the division between these brothers 'of a cloud-born land, the
kingdom's sacred oaks, two Hercules' who excelled all the

English when joined in peace. Both were said to be cautious and serious-minded. Both 'persevered with what they had begun; but Tostig vigorously, Harold prudently; the one in action aimed at success, the other also at happiness'. There was cause to lament the 'vicious Discord sprung from brothers' strife'.[3]

Tostig found refuge in Flanders, and Scandinavian sources tell in dramatic terms of personal expeditions in 1066 to seek support in Denmark and in Norway; it is more probable that these accounts dramatize authentic reports of missions of ambassadors from the exiled earl to the northern courts. In May Tostig had enough immediate support, from Flemish and possibly from Norman sources, to start probing the English defences. He ravaged the Sussex and Kentish coasts, and occupied Sandwich. In Kent he was joined by the enigmatic figure of Copsi, an old friend of northern campaigns, who travelled south from the Orkneys with seventeen ships. Copsi was afterwards favoured by the Norman William; one of the many personal ironies of these years is that it was Copsi who eventually succeeded to the earldom of Northumbria in 1067 at William's command, only to meet assassination at the hands of the indignant Northumbrians in a very short space of time. Tostig continued ravaging up the east coast, but was defeated by Earl Edwin and the Lindsey fyrd. Earl Morcar checked any attempt to penetrate Northumbrian defences, and so Tostig headed further north, spending the summer of 1066 in Scotland. It is probable that the final agreement between the dispossessed earl and the Norwegian king took place during this period, with the Orkneyingers acting as intermediaries. Harold Hardrada equipped a great fleet, estimated at three hundred ships, and collected a correspondingly vast company of fighting men from all over the north. Tostig bowed to him and became his man, receiving promise of his coveted earldom in exchange. In September they attacked, ravaged the Yorkshire coast, entered the Humber, and sailed their Viking ships up the Yorkshire Ouse as far as Riccall. At Gate Fulford, about two miles to the south of York, they crushed English resistance on Wednesday, 20 September, though at considerable cost. York capitulated on favourable terms, and Harold Hard-rada and Tostig withdrew to Stamford Bridge, probably to make their headquarters at the old royal manor at Aldby, in preparation for the reception of hostages from the whole of Yorkshire.

King Harold of England had spent the spring and summer in active preparation for invasion. There were some naval engagements in the Channel, presumably against Norman ships. The immediate defence of the North was left largely in the hands of his two brothers-in-law, Earl Edwin of Mercia and Earl Morcar of Northumbria. Harold kept the fyrd on service, until in early September, for financial reasons, he was forced to permit part of the defence force to return to their homes. He was still in the south, anxious for defence of the Channel, when news of the Norwegian invasion was brought to him. At remarkable speed he made his way north, entered Tadcaster on 24 September, and on the following day, Monday, 25 September, fought and won the Battle of Stamford Bridge. Later Scandinavian accounts made full use of the epic ingredients of the battle: the confrontation of the two brothers Harold and Tostig; the latter's faithfulness to his oath of loyalty and his new Norwegian lord over against the ties of kinship; the contrast between the mighty Harold Hard-rada (promised the traditional seven feet of soil) and Harold Godwinson (a small man though he stands well in his stirrups). Later accounts tend also to write the story of the battle in military terms intelligible to the readers of their day. When all embroideries are stripped away, the outcome of the battle remains a tribute to the victor's speed of action and power of decision. In late September Harold II of England proved himself the ablest warrior in the northern world. He was generous to the vanquished. Prince Olaf and the Earl of Orkney were allowed to limp home with the survivors; only twenty-four ships were allocated to take back warriors who had needed at least three hundred ships to bring them to battle. One of the survivors among the defeated, Godred Crovan, an Icelander, made a successful career for himself in later years as the conqueror and ruler of the Isle of Man. Later traditions reported that as Harold sat at the formal banquet at York to celebrate victory a message was brought to him, post-haste, to say that William had landed at Pevensey in Sussex on Thursday, 28 September.

The Norman duke had had an exceedingly busy spring and summer. Apart from his diplomatic efforts, he had chiefly concerned himself with military preparations for the invasion. He had to carry his council with him; many of the most experienced were opposed to what must have appeared a reckless scheme. England had submitted to the rule of an experienced and formidable warrior, and tales of English readiness probably lost nothing in their transmission across the Channel. But William's resolution and single-mindedness were enough to carry the day. A certain sympathy with the waverers does not come out of place. William had the confidence; he also needed and obtained extraordinary luck. Even the weather favoured him. There were delays—no doubt infuriating at the time—when adverse winds blew in the Channel, but when the favourable wind eventually came William's opponent was in the north, dealing decisively with Tostig and Norway.

In one respect the historian attempting to describe the Battle of Hastings and the events leading up to it has a great advantage. There has survived a compressed artistic view of the Conquest of England embroidered in wool on the linen strip, two hundred and thirty feet long and twenty inches broad, known as the Bayeux Tapestry. This record was probably made before 1082, the date of the imprisonment of Odo, bishop of Bayeux. It was designed by an artist of distinguished quality, working in a tradition well known and mature in England and the North. His object was to express dramatically the Conquest of England, and no one who has walked the length of the hall in Bayeux where the tapestry is at present displayed will deny his success. He relied on written sources to some extent, especially on William of Poitiers (or on material behind Poitier's work itself), and on a version of the Anglo-Saxon Chronicle. He also used oral traditions of his own, derived from the Anglo-Norman court, notably from Odo of

Bayeux and his entourage. He was probably an Englishman, and many have remarked that chief interest is focused on Harold rather than on William. The story is told as a tragedy, with attention drawn to the oath of loyalty sworn by Harold to William, to the breaking of the oath by Harold's reception of the English crown, and finally to the Battle of Hastings itself and the death of Harold. A short length is missing at the very end of the tapestry (otherwise in a remarkable state of preservation), and this may have portrayed William crowned and in triumph—a likely dramatic contrast to the opening scene which shows King Edward in royal majesty.

The evidence of the tapestry is of unique importance for the information it gives on eleventh-century dress, armour, arms, equipment, food, ship-building, and castle-building. There are no fewer than 626 human figures shown on the tapestry, 190 horses or mules, 35 hounds or dogs, 506 other animals, 37 ships, 33 buildings, and 37 trees or groups of trees.[4] In relation to the story exceptionally valuable information is given on the preparation for the invasion and on the battle itself. The energy and care which went into William's preparation are graphically portrayed: all is a bustle of tree-felling, carpenters at work, ship-building, and provisioning of ships with all manner of equipment, and especially with horses, men, and armour. The artist (resembling here William of Poitiers in the nature of his approach) was clearly fascinated by practical details. He gives a quarter-master's view of the invasion. He is selective. Some of the fine stories told by the chroniclers could not be portrayed in his medium. The tense moment, so well described by William of Poitiers, when Duke William's ship outsailed his companions, and the duke found himself alone in mid-channel, could not easily be shown. The chronicler illustrated William's calmness by telling of the splendid meal (with spiced wines) which the duke ordered to be served. The designer can do no more than show the ducal ship with the lantern on its mast, and transfers the meal from shipboard to successful landing. Again nothing is shown of William's reputed stumble, as he stepped ashore on the soil of

England. Instead all again is bustle and activity, the collecting of provisions, throwing up of defensive works, and the burning down of houses. The designer was a practical man, held by the detail of necessary arrangements. He shows a successful crossing, clearly indicates the enormous labours involved, and leaves us with William ashore, taking anxious care for the provisioning and safety of his troops. The Bayeux tapestry shows how the Conquest of England captured the imagination of the generation; King William's daughter Adela, countess of Blois, possessed a tapestry depicting the success of her father which was hung around her bed in an alcove of her richly adorned bedchamber.

Meanwhile Harold, as soon as he had heard of William's landing, collected what forces he could and hurried south in one of the best-known forced marches of English history. A voluminous literature relates to the events of the next three weeks. The outlines are clear and certain. Harold left York very early in October, probably on 2 or 3 October; he set out from London on his march into Sussex on 11 October. William moved from Pevensey to Hastings, and then out towards the hill ever after to be known as Battle, in the very early morning of Saturday, 14 October. Harold had camped during the night on this ridge, six miles to the north-west of Hastings, with the possible intention of delivering a surprise attack on the Normans. William's move forced him to adopt defensive positions, and so he drew his army up along a half-mile front, taking advantage of the rising ground so that the traditional shield-wall of the foot-soldiers could have its maximum effect. A conservative estimate of the number involved would be about five thousand men on each side. According to the designer of the Bayeux tapestry—and he was too intelligent an artist not to be fully aware of what he was doing—the equipment of the armies differed in two essentials. The Normans alone possessed cavalry (and the concern of the tapestry to portray the successful ferrying of the horses over the Channel is now explained); the Normans also possessed a pre-dominance, perhaps a decisive predominance, of archers. Otherwise there is little difference in arms and equipment. Both sides had conical helmets, swords, hauberks, and throwing spears. Both sides had kite-shaped shields with round tops, though some more antiquated round shields are shown in the English camp, notably among the following of the English earls Gyrth and Leofwine. Only the English are shown using (sometimes to devastating effect) the great 'Danish' battle-axe at Hastings—again a pointer on the part of the intelligent artist to the different military traditions of the English host.

William's forces were divided into three principal groups: the Normans in the centre, the Bretons on the left, and the 'French' on the right. William had two great advantages which he used to the full. First, there was the simple fact that no one in his army could have much doubt what his fate would be in case of defeat; it was literally a matter of conquer or die. Secondly, he was allowed to dictate the course of battle; the initiative throughout lay with the Normans. This was due to no fault in Harold's generalship, nor was it solely a matter of fresh and rested troops against an army of veterans weary after a set of forced marches. It was a simple consequence of mobility against immobility; cavalry and archers gave the Normans full freedom of movement and tied the English down. Even so, it was a near-run thing.

Fighting started at about 9.30 in the morning of Saturday, 14 October, with a somewhat ineffective attack by archers on the English positions. This was followed by an infantry attack which was repulsed; the Bretons on the left were defeated, but some English, too rash in their pursuit, were trapped and cut up by the Norman cavalry. There followed a full-scale cavalry attack (brilliantly pictured in the Bayeux tapestry), but this also failed against the solid shield-wall of the English infantrymen. Again, however, the English made the mistake of leaving their high ground to pursue the retreating enemy, only to be destroyed by the mobile Normans. At this stage, probably late afternoon, the battle was still fairly evenly poised. According to the evidence of the Bayeux tapestry, Harold's brothers, Gyrth and Leofwine, had fallen, but so had many Normans. Time was running desperately short for William. A so-called 'drawn' battle on the 14th would have been for him not a simple defeat but a disaster. His nerve and resource were equal to the occasion. The last Norman attack was made with the full force of archers, infantry and cavalry. The English shield-wall was broken, the royal hearth-troop fell around their lord, and finally Harold 'towards the twilight hour was slain'. There is a mystery about the exact manner of his death. The abbot Baudri of Bourgueil, writing at the end of the century, attributed his death to a shot in the eye by an arrow, and this may well represent the truth, or at least part of the truth. Scholarly opinion is hardening in favour of the view that Harold was first wounded in the eye and then struck down by a group of Norman knights, an interpretation which involves recognizing that the great scene of Harold's death in the Bayeux tapestry portrayed the English king twice, once wounded by an arrow and finally falling to his death.[5]

The selection of incidents made by the designer of the Bayeux tapestry as an illustration of the battle has an importance which is more than artistic, and yet the quality of his artistic insight gives special force to his evidence. Magnificent draftsmanship, notably of the convulsed horses, helps him to make the point that William's cavalry charge failed. He does not ignore the picturesque incidents: William raising his helmet to show that the story of his fall was false, or Odo of Bayeux encouraging the young warriors (the *pueros*) to battle. His finest achievement is the picture of the last stages in the battle. The very border of the tapestry—to this point used chiefly for ornamental or for symbolic purposes—now intrudes on the main story itself. The representation of what may well have been the decisive attack by the archers is astonishingly effective, so much so that the method of shooting with high trajectory into the air is made quite clear to the viewer. The borders of the tapestry also show, in a fashion not unworthy of comparison with Picasso's 'Guernica', that the designer was fully aware of the realities behind the abstractions of the poets and chroniclers who wrote about the battle. Mangled and mutilated bodies, and fragments of bodies litter the border. In the final scenes naked corpses are portrayed, stripped of their armour. The savagery and bitterness of the conflict were not lost on this amazing artist.

The traditional view of the battle as a whole has been that it was a triumph for up-to-date continental tactics and techniques, for mobile cavalry warfare and skilful use of archers against the inflexible shield-wall and battle-axe slogging of the infantry warfare of the North. The tendency now is not to underestimate the strength of the Old English army, nor to overestimate the importance of cavalry, notably the cavalry charge, either at Hastings or in subsequent warfare during the remainder of the eleventh century. Nevertheless, there is much to be said for the substance of the traditional view. Skilful use of mounted knights, notably in guaranteeing freedom of movement for the army as a whole, seems to have been a very important element in William's success. The military triumph was complete. William of Malmesbury, writing two generations later, said, with pardonable exaggeration, that the Normans had won all England in a single battle. The contemporary William of Poitiers expressed the same view: 'William in a single day so crushed the English that afterwards they never dared again face him in battle'.[6]

There are some difficult points in relation to Hastings on which general agreement appears to have been reached. The old view that the English earls deliberately held back from support is now discredited. Edwin and Morcar had borne the weight of battle at Fulford, and were not guilty of treacherous behaviour towards their brother-in-law. It is now agreed that Harold, though a good military commander, was probably mistaken in hastening south, and certainly mistaken in engaging in a pitched battle so soon with tired troops, indeed with, to all appearance, only a part of his army. It is further agreed that Harold met in William a commander abler than himself both in judgement of immediate tactical situations and in general strategic grasp. William had built up a reputation in Normandy as a patient wager of campaigns by attrition, as a man who used his head and avoided pitched battles. But in his perilous situation a quick victory was essential. His lines of communication with the Norman home-land were tenuous; and later legend reported (of somewhat dubious provenance, however) that he made them more so by a spectacular bonfire of transport vessels. The state of the country was uncertain, more likely to be hostile than friendly, particularly after the triumph of the English king in the north. It is probable that he deliberately provoked Harold, flushed from his northern exploits, in the hope that the English king would act rashly. If Harold had waited at London and built up the forces which would flock to the victor of Stamford Bridge it is hard to imagine what William would have done; the pro-Norman party at London does not seem to have been strong enough to cause serious trouble. Instead Harold undertook, a little contemptu-ously, to mass his army, roughly equal in number, against William. He had defeated and destroyed a king; now it was the turn of the duke. Harold paid for his rashness with his life and his kingdom.

On other problems in relation to the battle there has been much discussion but no agreed conclusion. The antiquated nature of the English army has been hotly denied, and it has been emphasized that Harold himself had found the military tactics of William's army in Brittany very much to his taste. Professor Hollister has ascribed the English defeat at Hastings primarily to an almost unbelieveable run of bad luck, and in-sists that military organization in later Anglo-Saxon England was far from obsolete.[7] The topography of the battle has received, and will continue to receive, much attention. Harold appears to have drawn up his army in too close array, with the result that very little space was offered for effective manœuvres. William's disposal of forces has been much praised; his own conduct of the centre, where his Normans predominated, was clearly imaginative and successful. William of Poitiers drew a telling contrast between Julius Caesar and William himself; William would have considered it dishonourable to have exercised the function of a general if he had not also equally well acquitted his duty as a knight, as had been his custom in earlier campaigns:

'But it would have seemed shameful and slack to William to take on the role of general in that conflict in which he crushed the English if he had not also done his duty as a knight, as had been his custom in other wars'.[8]

Chronicle reports of the battle were as episodic as the reports of any battle; more so in some respects, as contemporaries could not resist interpolating phrases and descriptive passages from classical authors into their accounts. The one fixed point was the later high altar at Battle Abbey, which is the spot where Harold fell; the one agreed conclusion that the English were out-generalled, out-fought, and that they suffered disastrous casualties. Three heavy battles, Fulford, Stamford Bridge, and Hastings, were fought in England within one month. They were all severe conflicts between forces relatively evenly matched. The Normans escaped comparatively lightly; the Saxons suffered heavily in their victories as in their defeats. At Hastings Harold, his brothers Gyrth and Leofwine, and most of his active personal retainers perished; an ominous entry in the Abingdon Chronicle referred to those men known as thegns (tahinos) who had perished in the Battle of Hastings, with the implication that to be a thegn of Berkshire in 1066 involved almost certain defeat and death at Hastings. The gaps in the ranks of the landowning class were so great that the task of the Norman reorganizer was made that degree easier.

The news of sweeping Norman success seems to have taken England by surprise. A strong commander, of assured position, might have rallied them even at this stage against the Norman duke. The key figure was Ealdred, archbishop of York. He, acting with Archbishop Stigand, and with the somewhat confused support of the northern earls and the Londoners, proclaimed the heir of the ancient dynasty as king of England. This young man, Edgar Aetheling, could not have been more than about fifteen years of age at the time. He was born in Hungary, the son of Edward Edmundson, who had died so mysteriously on his return from exile in 1057. If Ealdred had been sure of firm military support he would have proceeded to a coronation. As it was, with no strong representative of the Godwin interest left alive, he wisely held his hand, and, equally wisely, William moved slowly but steadily along the south coast into Kent through Dover and Canterbury towards and around London. William acted harshly on the early stages of this journey, and the trail of devastation can still be traced from the Domesday survey twenty years later. London was his objective, and divided counsels gave him the prize. In the ten weeks between Hastings and Christmas Day, 1066, responsible opinion, anxious for peace, turned to William. Ealdred, Edgar Aetheling, the Londoners, and many of the magnates came to terms at Berkhamstead, and William promised to rule as Edward's legal successor. He reaffirmed that promise in the most solemn fashion available at the coronation ceremony at Westminster on Christmas Day. There can have been little enthusiasm in the abbey except among the Normans. Even they were more ready for trouble than rejoicing, as their actions show. A noise as of a riot was enough to set the men-at-arms busy with fire, if not with sword. Grim-faced acquiescence is a fair description of the reaction to the conqueror. Yet the coronation marks the true end of a period, and the recognition of a man competent and able to govern the ancient kingdom.

1   *Liber Eliensis*, ed. E. O. Blake, London, 1962, p. 170; Florence of Worcester, i, p. 227
2   William of Poitiers, p. 167; *E.H.D.* ii, p. 222
3   *Vita Ædwardi*, pp. 31–2 and 37–8,
4   *The Bayeux Tapestry*, ed. Sir Frank Stenton, Phaidon Press, London, 1957, p. 42
5   The best modern discussion of the death of Harold is in the paper by N. P. Brooks and the late H. E. Walker 'The Authenticity and Interpretation of the Bayeux Tapestry', *Battle Conference 1978*, pp. 23–34. See also Sir Frank Stenton, *The Bayeux Tapestry*, p. 176; Guy of Amiens, pp. 34–6; and full discussion in R. H. C. Davis, L. J. Engels *et al.*, *Battle Conference 1979*, pp. 1–21; M. Ashdown, 'An Icelandic Account of the Survival of Harold

Godwinson', *The Anglo-Saxons* (studies presented to Bruce Dickins), ed. P. Clemoes, London, 1959, pp. 122–36.

6   William of Poitiers, p. 248

7   *Anglo-Saxon Military Institutions on the Eve of the Norman Conquest*, Oxford, 1962, pp. 151–2

8   William of Poitiers, p. 250

5

The Norman Settlement

(a) *The political settlement*

HASTINGS was a great victory, and chroniclers—as we have already seen—talked of the conquest of England in one battle. Caesar was compared unfavourably; the Britons attacked him many times in battle, William crushed the English in one day. The completeness of the successful result of the battle has been exaggerated, and so also has the smoothness of the rest of William's reign. To read the career of William I as an easy straightforward progress, a gentle course along a well-beaten track after the perilous ascent of 1066, is to be guilty of distortion.

William's career in England was extraordinarily successful, but it was not easy. Harsh, unrelenting effort was needed to maintain his authority, and to bring about his far-reaching changes in the organization of society. He remained duke of Normandy. The full measure of his achievement cannot be estimated unless we remember that the problems of his native duchy were still his to solve, made different but not lessened by the ducal success in England. He was in Normandy from February to early December 1067, in 1068, 1069 and early 1072, again in early 1073, between April and December 1075, for more than four years from spring 1076 to summer or autumn 1080, in the summer and autumn 1082, at Easter 1083, in the summer of 1084, and from summer 1086 to his death, 9 September 1087. His fatal injury in 1087, still no more than fifty-nine years of age, was received when on campaign against the Capetians in the Vexin.

In spite of all these absences and preoccupations William was able to impress upon the Norman Conquest and settlement a sense of purpose. The Normans were men who knew what they were doing. There is a simple explanation for this appearance of purpose. William emphasized the legality of his rule, the continuity with the Anglo-Saxon past and piety. These characteristics existed, and were no mere surface cover for tyranny. The complexity of the texture of William's England cannot be understood unless one grasps that in essentials he was the true successor to Alfred, Edgar, and Edward the Confessor. But he was also a conqueror, and the sense of purpose comes from the actions of a successful conqueror. His settlement of England was conditioned by military necessity; there could have been no settlement had he not achieved full military control. This meant especially control over strategic centres and the means of communication between them. William could give peace at a price. His method of doing so was to rely on the loyalty of feudal vassals, and to remain in full control of the royal wealth that was his by right. The wealth, in silver and in land, was used to buy mercenary service and to reward feudal followers; it gave the resources from which William could draw to confirm the superiority of the king over other feudal lords. Castle-building, the effective exaction of knight service, the skilful use of loyalties: to ensure these the Conqueror consistently followed the same policy. Concentration on the important strategic centres, and consolidation of Norman power in church and state in urban headquarters, are prominent, purposeful features of William's policy.

The military nature of William's rule is apparent from the very earliest days. His directions to his troops, as transmitted by William of Poitiers, read like the directions issued by any successful general with a sense of responsibility. The soldiers were to remember that they were in a Christian country, to restrain themselves from outrages that might provoke rebellion among those justly subjected to them, and not to disgrace the good name of their homeland in the midst of strangers. Brothels were forbidden, and taverns almost (*Potare militem in tabernis non multum concessit*), since drunkenness engendered quarrels, and quarrels, murder.[1] William withdrew after his coronation to Barking in Essex while his men built fortifications in the city. William was willing to recognize the rights of the Londoners; and sometime between his accession and the death of Bishop William of London in 1075 the king issued a writ stating that the burgesses were to be worthy of their laws as they were in the time of King Edward, and that each child should be his father's heir after his father's day. But above all in the early stages he recognized the need to coerce the Londoners. At Barking, Edwin, Morcar, and Copsi (who made a specially favourable impression) submitted formally to him. Edgar Aetheling was taken into full favour, and given extensive estates. William was generous to the English who won his favour, but he was more than generous to the men of proved loyalty he had brought from Gaul. They were rewarded with 'castles' and a multitude of horse and foot soldiers to garrison them. He gave them great fiefs (*opulenta beneficia*), but expected them in return to support great perils and labours. There was a vast amount of territory at his disposal after the disastrous battles of 1066. The early months of 1067 saw the beginning of the distribution of the spoils. Nevertheless the Norman chronicler was careful to tell us that a Frenchman (Gallus) never received a gift which had been taken from an Englishman unlawfully.[2]

The main lines of settlement must have been laid down in the vital month of January 1067, for in February William returned to Normandy. Descriptions of his return remind us again that although it was more than a successful expedition, it was precisely that. A heavy geld was laid on the country immediately; some of the proceeds—sheer booty—of conquest was sent back to Normandy in the January, in spite of heavy weather and tempestuous seas. When the Norman duke himself returned the Normans felt the pride and material satisfaction of successful conquest; the loot from England gladdened many a Norman church and many a Norman hearth. The duke himself appeared at Rouen in the finery of his new title and new vestments. The first taste of splendour and success must have been very sweet.

William left behind him in England two efficient regents, William FitzOsbern at Winchester and at Hereford, and Odo of Bayeux in Kent. Their task was to preserve order and discipline, to suppress rebellion, and to give freedom from outside invasion. There was still a Danish threat in the background, a threat that was to remain until the end of the reign. The government and administration of Edward was maintained and strengthened. Even the personnel was left virtually untouched. Regenbald, who had been an important clerk in the reign of King Edward, continued in office under King William; he may have been known as chancellor—a Domesday interlineation refers to him as *canceler*—though Herfast in 1068 or 1069, who was later bishop of Elmham (1070–85), is the first proven royal chancellor, *eo nomine*. Writs and charters continued to be issued in Anglo-Saxon. No bishop, not even Stigand, was dispossessed. Most of the abbots were left in office, though Abbot Aelfwig of the New Minster at Winchester, uncle of King Harold, died at Hastings, and two or three others were exiled or imprisoned, either immediately or in the first few years of the Conquest. The great house of Peterborough had to compound heavily for its folly—or misfortune—in supporting the wrong cause; Abbot Leofric fell at Hastings, and his successor, Abbot Brand, who first received recognition from Edgar Aetheling, had to pay forty marks of gold to reconcile himself with King William. Landowning and, in particular, military control of royal lands and royal rights were the chief concern of the Norman regents at this stage.

William prudently took back with him to Normandy the chief men who had promised to be obedient to him, Stigand, Aethelnoth, abbot of Glastonbury, Edgar Aetheling, the earls, Edwin and Morcar, and Waltheof, son of the old earl, Siward of Northumbria (who had died in 1055). This was a typical skilful and judicious move on William's part, as it enabled the new landowners to intrude themselves into their possessions and to take on their new duties at a time when there was no effective head and focus to discontent in the country. William returned to England late in 1067, and quickly and mercifully suppressed a revolt at Exeter, establishing a castle on the highest land in the city. Harold's sons were involved in this revolt. They withdrew to Scandinavian Ireland, and indulged in a series of raids on the south-west during the succeeding summers. These raids had the effect of stiffening support for the new order; the last representatives of the house of Godwin never rose above the stature of the leaders of an unsuccessful family faction. William was in sufficient command by the early summer to bring his wife to England, and she was crowned at Westminster on Whit Sunday 1068, a short while before the birth of her fourth son, the future Henry I of England. Unease at the extent of Norman success, however, led to a serious crisis. Edgar Aetheling and the earls Edwin and Morcar defected, and made their way towards Northumbria, which had erupted into sullen rebellion under the new earl Gospatric and the sheriff Merleswein. William showed his grasp of the situation in a spectacular progress north, which bore the appearance of a carefully planned move rather than an improvised reaction to English aristocratic disaffection. He extended his castle-building, setting up strongholds at Warwick (where Edwin and Morcar came to terms), Nottingham, and York—and at Lincoln, Huntingdon, and Cambridge on his return journey to the south. Edgar Aetheling fled to Scotland, which became the chief centre of his later political influence. The Scottish king, Malcolm Canmore, supported the ancient West Saxon dynasty, and about 1070 married Edgar's sister Margaret, one of the most influential women of her period, later known as St. Margaret of Scotland. Three of their sons became in turn kings of Scotland, 1097–1154, and their daughter Edith married Henry I in 1100.

The events of 1068 must have convinced many of the English aristocracy, well treated by the Conqueror to this point, that they could not live in the new Norman world. The active direction of affairs lay with the newcomers. The 'French' were the men to

whom William entrusted the new castles and fiefs, who led the
army and kept the peace. Discontent smouldered not at wholesale deprivation of estates but at the loss of political influence.
The Normans, engaged in perilous enterprise, were drawn
closely together, and the English found themselves squeezed out
of effective control. Norman policy and Norman success provoked rebellion, which, when crushed, hastened the process of
Normanization.

Open rebellion broke out in 1069, and for a full twelve months
the issue was in doubt. Northumbria had been particularly
restive. William appointed Copsi to the earldom in 1067, but he
was quickly assassinated by a private enemy. His successors,
unofficial rather than official, met with little fortune, and the
first effective Norman governor, Robert de Comines, established
as a consequence of William's expedition of 1068 in his newly
built stronghold on the site of Clifford's tower in York, suffered
an even worse fate. He was trapped and burnt to death with his
followers at Durham on 28 January 1069. General insurrection
thereupon broke out in Northumbria. Edgar Aetheling returned
and was well received in the earldom. From many other parts of
England came stirrings of revolt or active rebellion. Eadric Wild,
a Herefordshire thegn, allied to Welsh princes, was active on the
Marches of Wales. In Mercia, particularly in Staffordshire,
revolt was open. Harold's sons made troublesome raids on the
south-west. Danish threats became a reality when Asbjorn, the
brother of Sweyn, the Danish king, crossed the North Sea with
two hundred and forty ships to help the northern rebels. King
William had made one dramatic intervention in the summer to
re-establish himself at York, and to continue systematic castle-
building, but here at York, the decisive point, shortly after the
death of the influential Archbishop Ealdred, William's sheriff,
William Malet, was disastrously defeated by a combined force
of Danes and Englishmen on 21 September 1069. Waltheof, who
had defected from William, played a prominent part in the attack
on York. At this stage political observers must have considered
that the Norman Conquest would be lucky to complete its

third year, and that the Norman duke would be lucky to preserve his duchy. The Normans were saved by their own unity, discipline, and ruthlessness, by the leadership of William, by steady support from the prosperous south-east, and by the political ineptitude of their enemies. Barons and sheriffs and local levies held off pirates and bandits. The new castles proved their worth, notably on the Welsh Marches. William recruited mercenaries, English as well as Norman. He reserved his main strength for the critical area of the north. His advance was thorough and savage. A fearsome harrying of the north laid waste tracts of country in the winter of 1069–70. William held the grimmest of his Christmas councils at York, surrounded by devastation. New castles were built, notably on his journey south at Chester and at Stafford. William's 'scorched-earth' policy, which lay heavy on his conscience in later days, and even heavier on his reputation, fulfilled its political purpose. The will to resist was broken in both Northumbria and in Mercia. The countryside was made unprofitable to Danish pillagers. The Danes were virtually bribed to withdraw from active campaigning in the autumn of 1069, and again in May 1070 when the Danish king, Sweyn Estrithson, took command of the fleet. King William's forces were united. The rebels were disunited and scattered. The Danes lacked a practicable political objective, and degenerated into mere plunderers. William's ability to concentrate on the essentials, and especially his refusal to be side-tracked from the main theatre of rebellion at York, prevailed. He was able to treat with his enemies one by one, a skill learnt by bitter experience in Normandy. There was no leader capable of rallying all dissidents against William. Lack of a clear alternative prompted much support for the crowned king. Edgar Aetheling went back to Scotland and later to the Continent to an honourable exile. Waltheof was pardoned, and married Judith, King William's niece. Eadric Wild was also pardoned. William was not always vindictive in his political attitude to men who had opposed him. There remained one aftermath to the rebellion, greater in legendary than in political importance. The Danes had turned their attention south to the district of the Fens, and many English rebels, led by Hereward, had also been attracted to the safety of the lands around Ely and Peterborough. The earls Edwin and Morcar played no part in the insurrection of 1069–70, but in April 1071 they fled from William's court. Earl Edwin was killed by treachery on his way north. Earl Morcar joined Hereward in the Fens. The king took the revolt seriously, and in spite of the bravery of the English defenders crushed it decisively. The defeat of Morcar and Hereward was nevertheless essentially a postcript to serious rebellion. The Norman campaign against Scotland in 1072 was of similar nature, a necessary clearing-up after the issue had been settled. Already, by April 1070, William was confident enough to disband most of his mercenaries. York was the key to the whole situation. The 'Harrying of the North' (1069–70) placed the key firmly in William's hands.

The same year, 1070, witnessed the beginnings of the reorganization of the church in England, consequent upon the appointment of Lanfranc to Canterbury and his assertion of the supremacy of the archbishopric of Canterbury over York (Easter–Whitsun 1070). William's suppression of rebellion confirmed the durability of the Conquest. There could now follow an implementation of the policy initiated in 1067–9, the feudalization of England, and the Normanization of the aristocracy and the upper clergy.

After 1071 the political state of England was much improved from the Norman point of view, so much so that William was able to take positive steps to maintain the frontiers of England against the Scots and the Welsh. The Scottish king recognized William's overlordship after the campaigns of 1072, paid him homage, and gave him his eldest son Duncan as a hostage. None of the Welsh princes was a man of outstanding calibre. Rhys ap Tewdwr, who rose to prominence in South Wales after 1081, was the ablest, and he was content to accept William's overlordship, and to agree to an annual payment of £40. Apart from his Scottish expedition of 1072, and a dramatic show of force which led him through South Wales to Pembrokeshire in 1081, King William showed little direct personal interest in problems of the border. His main concern was with Normandy and with England south of York, the chief sources of his wealth and strength. He established three earldoms on the Welsh March with extraordinary franchises and with extraordinary responsibilities. Hugh of Avranches was made earl of Chester in 1071, and set up a powerful outpost at Rhuddlan under his cousin, Robert of Rhuddlan. Roger of Montgomery was made earl of Shrewsbury, and he set up his own powerful outpost at Montgomery. The earls and their followers proved fully capable of holding the native princes of Gwynedd and Powys. Robert of Rhuddlan was so powerful by the time of Domesday Book that he—a parallel to the native Rhys ap Tewdwr in the south—paid £40 to King William 'for North Wales'. In the south the earldom of Hereford fulfilled a similar function until the disgrace of the second earl, Roger, son of William FitzOsbern, in 1075. The earldom fell into abeyance, and it was left to a succeeding generation of Norman barons to overcome Rhys ap Tewdwr (in 1093) and to consolidate the Norman grip on the south from the lordships of Brecon and Glamorgan.

Evidence of William's success is to be found in the fact that he was able to spend rather more than half of the last sixteen years of his life in his Norman duchy. In the administrative field his absences contributed to the slow evolution of the early Norman justiciarship, though it was not until the work of Ranulf Flambard under William Rufus, reinforced by that of Roger of Salisbury under Henry I, that a great administrative officer could be referred to as 'second to the king'. In the political field William was able to rely for his regents on Archbishop Lanfranc, on Geoffrey of Mowbray, bishop of Coutances, on his own half-brother, Odo of Bayeux, and also on powerful support in the West Country from the English ecclesiastics, Aethelwig, the abbot of Evesham, and Wulfstan, bishop of Worcester. There were only two further serious threats to Norman peace. In 1075 three of William's earls flared up into a typical baronial revolt. The rebellion was planned at a wedding feast between Ralf, earl of East Anglia, and Emma, sister of Roger, earl of Hereford.

Waltheof, pardoned and made earl of Northumbria, after the revolt of 1069–70, was dragged into the rebellion, and Cnut, brother of the Danish king, appeared off the Northumbrian coast with two hundred ships. The regents easily suppressed the rebellion of the three earls; Ralf escaped to Brittany, and Roger made his way to Denmark—though on his return he was imprisoned and forfeited his fief. English support for William, together with the treatment meted out to Waltheof, alone elevated the incident above the ordinary revolt. There was some duplicity on the Conqueror's part. Lanfranc advised Waltheof to throw himself on his uncle's mercy (Waltheof had married Judith, the king's niece); William at first made light of the affair; but in May 1076 Waltheof was executed, the only Englishman of high rank to suffer that fate. Legends grew around him, even more so than around Hereward. He was a symbolic figure, the last of the great English earls. After 1076 the blanket of Norman uniformity covered feudal England.

The other threat to Norman settlement and stability came in the northern earldom. Northumbria was more backward economically and politically than the rest of the kingdom. Its social structure was antiquated; the machinery of royal government and territorial lordship was not so well developed. The Normans inherited problems that they could not solve in one generation. After the death of Waltheof, William tried the premature creation of a marcher-bishopric. He united an earl's power with a bishop's office in the person of Walcher, bishop of Durham. But in 1080 Walcher was assassinated as a result of weak handling of a private feud in which men of his own household were involved. William thereafter merely moved from expedient to expedient, the most successful being the building of a new castle at Newcastle-on-Tyne, the support of a strong Breton contingent in the great Honour of Richmond, and the fostering of Durham and of the Mowbray interest in the North. A contrast remained between the northern earldom and Wessex and Mercia where the Norman settlement achieved a much more uniform success.

(b) *The feudal and military settlement*

A convenient way of approaching this highly complicated problem of the settlement is by concentrating on its military nature. William was after 1070 universally recognized as king of the English. As such, he had the responsibility of ensuring good peace. Good peace depended upon a constant supply of reliable troops. William had his Norman precedents to work on; the use he made of them in England has the stamp of administrative genius.

The origins of feudal military service may on the Continent be traced back to Carolingian times. From the earliest times land, or more strictly the profits of land, had been the reward of the successful warrior. The feudal order went a stage further. A benefice, or a fief as it came to be known in the course of the ninth century, was granted to a vassal not as a simple reward but as an earnest of favour, valuable, profitable, and *conditional* upon the performance of future service. Such fiefs tended to become hereditary; loyalties were stronger from kin to kin than simply from person to person. In turn the great vassals of emperor, king, or prince granted fiefs to their own vassals. In its age the feudal 'system' offered a realistic means of preserving central authority, rewarding army leaders, maintaining a force competent to protect the community, and providing a formal, legalistic peace. The dangers of degeneration into 'anarchy' are obvious; a minority, or a weak and foolish ruler, could leave the barons with too free a hand. The positive achievements of feudalism, especially the maintenance of a state of society bound by rules and contract in which custom could develop into law, should not be overlooked.

England, as mentioned earlier, was not isolated. The growth of secular lordship was as prominent a feature of English social development in the tenth century as of the continental. The nature of military service was, however, very different. The English military hierarchy was not as specialized as on the Continent. There were straightforward, technical reasons why this should not be so. Thegns and housecarls were set apart by special legal protection, higher personal status, and a heavier wergeld. They were important military leaders and important local commanders. They were not cavalrymen. This is not to say that they could not manage horses, even in warfare; Harold had no difficulty in fitting in with the Norman army on the Breton campaign. One of the first aims of the Danish raiders in the Alfredian wars had been to acquire horses; horses meant mobility. But the thegns of England were not subjected to the long training in cavalry warfare that was the lot of young noblemen in France. Group consciousness and group exclusiveness on the part of the mounted warrior had developed further on the Continent than in England. There was greater fluidity in English society. In the eleventh century a simple freeman (a *ceorl*) could thrive, even to the point where he became an *eorl*. He could certainly make himself worthy to receive thegnship and the honour due to a thegn, by military prowess, by service, or by the sheer possession of wealth in land, in goods, or in ships.

The social implications of the technical difference between a land defended by cavalry and a land where soldiers were primarily infantrymen are great. The thegn, well equipped with sword, helmet, and byrnie, could be a splendid figure. But the sheer weight of expense of his equipment was less than that of the Norman knight with his war-horse, his accoutrements, and the servants necessary to his existence as an effective fighting unit. Even greater, however, were the social implications which stemmed from differences in historical development, in the way that political units were moulded. There is no need to mask the feuding violence that lay beneath the surface, subject to sudden eruptions, in Anglo-Saxon England. But organized military endeavour was a matter for the king and his chief advisers deliberating in the royal court. There was no private warfare on the continental scale. In spite of the undoubted strength and influence of Old English bishops—such as Wulfstan of York, for example, at the beginning of the eleventh century—no Peace of God was preached, and no Truce of God proclaimed, either in

Anglo-Saxon or in Anglo-Norman England. There was no need for such demonstration. The Peace of God and the Truce of God were the church's answer to the sporadic private warfare which racked feudal Europe. England had her full share of political problems. She had to face successful invasion from outside. But her state of internal peace was more highly developed than that of the Continent; the apparatus of government, shire-courts, reserved pleas to the king, the discipline of the hundred, the relative efficiency of the royal tax-collectors, even the useful expedient of the new earls, provided no scope for private war. It was in such private war that the Norman knights learnt their warrior's trade; it was the persistence and frequency of such battles which bred solidarity in the group. The continental knights were more proficient than the English thegns, and had more opportunity to practise their professional qualities.

William naturally wished to have such an efficient feudal army at his disposal in England. General and immediate precedents were at his disposal in Normandy. Military feudal tenure was the normal style of land-holding of his great vassals, lay and ecclesiastical. The concept of an honour, a fief with its complex of rights and duties, was well understood. Such an honour possessed a court at which the peers of the lesser vassals would be the doomsmen, retaining and adding to the custom of the honours. The incidents of the feudal world were also understood. A man, on entering into a fief, paid a relief to his lord. He would be responsible for the payment of free gifts (aids) at specified occasions: after the knighting of the lord's eldest son, the marriage of one of his daughters, or in case of need of ransom. On the man's death his heir paid homage to the lord; the lord in turn accepted guardianship of a minor heir, and took responsibility for the suitable marriage of heiresses. The lord would accept a reasonable relief from the heir of legal age, who would then enter into his inheritance. These incidents were understood in Normandy, though not always fully formulated or well observed. To the vassal possession of a great fief brought wealth, an honourable station in life, standing at court as well as in his own locality, where he enjoyed the tangible estates that made up the intangible 'fief'. It also brought duties. The ruler, duke of Normandy, or later king of England, expected in return for the fief, to be provided at regular intervals, for a clearly defined number of days, with the services of a specific number of well-armed, well-schooled knights. These knights were generally grouped in fives or tens according to the size of the fief; ten was the regular number in a Norman constabulary. The length of service came to be established at forty days, but this did not necessarily mean that the knights were employed on their business for only a short space of time each year, to be dismissed on, say, 1 September, at the end of a campaigning season, and to spend the rest of the year in rustic idleness, hunting, hawking, and squabbling. The great vassal himself would have demands on his domestic knights for escort duty, fortification guarding, and such tasks. The king could and did keep the feudal levies long after the forty days were passed. Some knights were unattached, professional mercenaries, *chevaliers du solde*. Money-fiefs played a more active role in the workings of feudal society than once used to be appreciated. In particular the early Norman kings treated the counts of Flanders as substantial pensionaries, who received three hundred marks in 1066, and as much as four hundred in the early days of Henry I's reign, in return for the provision of a company of professional 'knights'. A wealthy ruler such as William I could attract great numbers of mercenaries to his service, as he did in 1066, again in 1069, and in 1085, when, according to the Anglo-Saxon Chronicle, a 'larger force of mounted men and infantry from France and Brittany than had ever come to this country' arrived in such numbers that men wondered how the country could support such an army. Reception of knighthood was a formal act on the Continent from at least the late ninth century. The Normans rejoiced and his enemies feared when William received his knightly spurs. Subinfeudation, that is to say the division of the fief, quickly became a characteristic of most fiefs. The key men, the constables and the marshals, would expect to receive a portion of the overlord's estates. Only gradually, and probably not until the twelfth century was well advanced, did it become a commonplace for a knight to be rewarded with land. Only slowly did the term 'knight's fee' become common currency. Already in Normandy in 1066, however, the hierarchy of duke, baron, and knight was well established, more exclusive and different in function and principle from the nearest Anglo-Saxon equivalents of king, earl, and thegn.

Yet England, though not feudal, was well placed to receive the full feudal order. The bond between lord and man was as strict as in Normandy. Treachery to a lord was regarded as a crime without remedy. To talk of *mere* commendation is misleading. Hold-oaths bound the man with all the religious sanction available to love what his lord loved and to shun what his lord shunned. Heriots were paid to a lord on the death of his man, and these heriots, which varied according to rank, could involve heavy payments in horses, arms, and gold. The heriot was remitted when a man fell before his lord in campaign, whether within the land or outside the land. Each free man still owed military service to the fyrd, the 'national army', though in England, as on the Continent, specialization had already set in. Households were grouped to provide one warrior for perhaps five hides of land; the role of the thegn in the military forces grew more prominent. It is likely that the obligation of every freeman to fight was reserved to defensive campaigning, and that the 'select' fyrd provided the substance of the royal army when the king campaigned on an *expeditio*. On some ecclesiastical estates, such as the great nexus of rights and lands belonging to the church at Worcester, dependent tenures were common. Strictly defined feudal service, however, was not. There is no trace in the quite extensive English records of lands being granted by the king to a great tenant-in-chief in return for the military service of a stated number of soldiers on precisely defined conditions.

Perhaps the best indication of England's readiness for the institution of the feudal order is given by the existence of the five-hide units, notably in the West Country. Much argument, possibly too much, has revolved around the existence of this grouping of episcopal lands. Five-hide units before 1066 were not knights' fees. Yet they represent in clear form the grouping of estates for taxation purposes which could serve as an example to a feudal lord. Indeed, attempts were made at Worcester and elsewhere after the Conquest to equate five-hide units with knights' fees, and there can be no question of the importance of the survival of the select fyrd principle on the conditions of feudal service. But if the soldier whose service was due from five hides had been the equivalent of a Norman knight the figures of feudal 'service due' would reveal an unsuspected benevolence on the part of the Norman kings. Abingdon in 1066, held land assessed at a little over five hundred hides (equivalent to the provision of one hundred soldiers) mostly in Berkshire; its feudal 'service due' was for no more than thirty knights. It is at the deeper level of honorial organization that the survival of the Anglo-Saxon assessments had the greatest effect. The geld, governed by its elaborate assessment system, accustomed the community to territorial divisions and territorial grouping of responsibility, and the new feudal lords were naturally able to build upon such a basis of territorial administration.

William's reorganization after Hastings, and even more after the rebellions of 1069–70, was feudal, and, as such, an innovation in England. The effect on land tenure in the upper ranks of society was revolutionary. Feudalism is best studied (as has often been argued) in its strength and weakness, not in the communities which gave it birth, but in the communities to which it was introduced full-grown, notably in England, Sicily, and the Crusading states of the Holy Land. The situation in England was exceptionally favourable. William, legitimate king as he claimed to be, owed his political power to a Norman minority of skilled soldiers, occupying a subjected, though not completely hostile, country, distinct in race and language from the small group of conquerors. The group was small, and had to hold together. The 'Normans', even at the end of William's reign, constituted only a very small proportion of a total population of about one and a half million. In such conditions it must not be taken as especially remarkable that the group cohered, and that the community of interest between the king and his barons was rarely lost.

It has long been held that the best proof of the ideal circumstances under which feudalism was introduced consists in the fact that the tenurial revolution never degenerated into a mere scramble for lands. The king and his agents maintained control. In 1067 William was able to exercise the right to dispose of the lands of the many Englishmen who had fallen in battle in 1066. There were others, for the main part ecclesiastics, who bought their land back at a price. Forfeited land was granted out in *opulenta beneficia* to the victors of Hastings in return for continuing and permanent military service. As a consequence of rebellion and royal success more land passed under royal control, extending from the south (Wessex, West Mercia, and such districts of north-east Mercia which lay on Harold's path south on his way to Hastings) to cover most of Mercia and Northumbria. The Normans insisted that no Englishman lost his lands merely because he was English. To judge from the very full record of Domesday Book such action was unnecessary; and the distinction was fine between losing lands for racial and for other reasons. Many English landowners fell, many rebelled, many emigrated, or were exiled. Many found refuge in the Scottish court, and helped to Anglicize the Scottish royal house and government. Some English thegns were heard of in Norway, others in Denmark, and others again at Constantinople in the Varangian Guard, fighting for the Emperor against the hated Normans of South Italy. Even so, it is hard to account for the virtual political extinction of what had been a large and powerful class of some four to five thousand thegns. Norman feudal conceptions of the duties of a landowner were probably particularly important in this respect. The right of succession to land from father to son was recognized in general terms. There are examples of heiresses succeeding, to be married off safely to Normans. But it is likely that William deliberately applied the full rigour of feudal law to all landed estates. An Englishman could survive but only at a price which rendered him impotent politically. Some 'bought back' their estates at excessive rents; others succeeded to a mere fragment of their fathers' possessions; and some continued to enjoy a modest competence, often stripped of military and political aspirations, as sub-tenants of the new Norman lords. There were only two English tenants-in-chief recorded in Domesday Book as possessing land to the annual value of £100 or over; and it is exceedingly likely that exceptional circumstances alone accounted for what seems to be their rise rather than their survival.[3] More typical of the lot of the English landed class were the sad groups of royal thegns (*Taini Regis*) who appear at the end of the county surveys in Domesday Book, usually holding minute portions of land, and of little more than humble ministerial standing.

William's own position was strengthened by feudal concepts under which he was the owner of the land within his principality. This clear-cut view of landlordism was different from the more old-fashioned English custom, and its implementation must have helped to provoke the English into active rebellion. The greater part of England in lay hands in 1066 was reallotted to new tenants by William in the course of his reign, mostly before 1071; and the remainder was brought systematically into the new and alien feudal order.

William's object in the course of reallotment was to reward past loyalty and to ensure future service. His method of work was essentially simple: to grant a powerful fief with correspondingly large obligations. It is possible that some rough-and-ready bargaining was conducted early in 1066 at the outset of the expedition. The Normans were promised great endowments after William came into his own, perhaps in proportion to the number of ships and men they were able to provide for the expedition. His chief followers probably had a rough idea what they would receive: a large fee sufficient for the provision of several hundred knights for Robert of Mortain; a small fee sufficient to sustain twenty knights for a lesser man. The function of service demanded was more complicated. For example, castle-building and castle-protection played a great part in the initial settlement. Contemporaries stressed the introduction of castles (*munitiones*), which had up to then been virtually unknown to the English, as a prominent feature of the Norman Conquest. Castles multiplied more rapidly in William's new kingdom than in his native duchy, and English needs stimulated technical improvements in the construction of strong places. Castleguard became a heavy charge on many of the new baronies. The abbey of Abingdon and the barony of Pinkenys shared much of the responsibility for guarding the new royal castle of Windsor. The family of de Cioches later provided a garrison of fifteen knights at Northampton castle at ten shillings a fee. Rockingham became a charge on the barony of Warden at five shillings a fee. The estate of Hartwell in Northamptonshire owed two knights' fees to Dover castle. Such services are a reminder of the complexity of the settlement of England. The introduction of castles and of knights' service are interrelated. Many personal and local factors were involved in the detailed working out of allotment of fiefs and imposition of service. It is helpful, therefore, before we turn to examine the methods and nature of the distribution of land, to summarize what is known about the chief beneficiaries of the Conquest, who they were, where they came from, and when and where they settled.

It is generally accepted that the army of the Conqueror at Hastings consisted of about five thousand men, many of whom would expect to qualify either directly or at second remove for a substantial benefice in land. Domesday Book describes the holdings of about a hundred and eighty tenants-in-chief who possessed land to the value of £100 a year or more. There were altogether about fourteen hundred tenants-in-chief in 1086 and a further eight thousand sub-tenants, among whom there was an English element. Such figures are unfortunately not as straight-forward as they seem. Tenants-in-chief could also be sub-tenants. William de Cahanges, the founder of a family which flourished in Northamptonshire for over three hundred years, held only one hide in the county as tenant-in-chief, but twenty-five consecutive entries in Domesday Book were needed to describe the lands which he held as a sub-tenant from Robert of Mortain. Domesday Book was planned twenty years after the Conquest, and, although the survey set out to record the name of the owner of each estate at the time of King Edward, and when the first Norman lord took over, in only a few counties was this procedure systematically adopted. Twenty years was time enough for the son or even the grandson of the first Norman lord to succeed. Even so, we are remarkably well informed about the state of landownership in the England of William I; the care with which ownership is recorded in the survey is a clear indication of the importance of the tenurial revolution achieved.

Modern investigation has taught us to be very cautious on one score, and not to infer presence at the Battle of Hastings from honourable mention in Domesday Book. Great interest has always been shown in the 'companions of the Conqueror'. From at least the fifteenth century the construction of a plausible genealogy that would go 'back to the Conqueror' was a legitimate aim for local historians and genealogists. As late as 1866 a roll of four hundred and eighty-five names was solemnly incised in stone and placed in the church at Dives; even after the nineteenth-century scholars had done their worst, an almost equally formidable list was placed on a tablet erected at Falaise in 1931. In the critical air of modern scholarship fewer than forty names survive, and D. C. Douglas, who has investigated this problem thoroughly, has expressed the view that he will be surprised if the list ever passes fifty.[4]

The list of known companions of the Conqueror contains its surprises. Not all who took part in the Battle of Hastings reaped benefit from the victory. Some were killed, such as Taillefer, the minstrel, *Incisor Ferri*, who opened the battle, and who advanced, according to later authorities, singing songs of Charlemagne and of Roland and Oliver at Roncesvalles. Others who were prominent in the campaign decided that England was no place for them. Aimery, viscount of Thouars, helped to 'persuade' the duke to accept his royal title, but later returned to his Breton and Angevin interests. Geoffrey, son of Rotrou, count of Mortagne, was commended for his personal appearance and his skill, but he made no mark on English affairs. Humphrey of Tilleul had visited England during the reign of the Confessor, and seemed destined for a fine future in England under the Conqueror who entrusted the safe keeping of the new castle at Hastings to him during the campaigns of 1066. Doubts over his wife's fidelity in his absence caused his return to Normandy. Humphrey's brother-in-law, Hugh of Grandmesnil, went back with him for a similar reason, but wisely returned to England to his own great territorial advantage. There were others, however, who were masters not only of the battlefield of Hastings but of the settlement of England. Outstanding among them were William's two half-brothers, Odo and Robert, Geoffrey, bishop of Coutances, William FitzOsbern, Eustace of Boulogne, Ralf of Tosny, Hugh of Montfort-sur-Risle, William of Warenne, Robert, the son of Roger of Beaumont, Richard FitzGilbert, Pons, and Hugh of Grandmesnil after his return from Normandy. A leading member of the Breton ruling house, either Brian or Alan the Red, was probably also present at Hastings, and the Bretons played an important part in the settlement. But there were among the greatest beneficiaries of the Conquest men such as Roger Bigot who was probably not present at Hastings. Roger of Montgomery, Hugh Lupus (later earl of Chester), and William of Percy seem not to have arrived in England until December 1067.

The men responsible for the allotment of land comprised a very small inner group of the royal advisers, most of them related to the ducal house. Evidence is mounting that Odo of Bayeux, and possibly William FitzOsbern, were the strongest influences in determining the course of the settlement. Fitz-Osbern, however, died in battle in 1071, and the sequestration of his great fief shortly afterwards (in 1075) has left an awkward gap in our detailed knowledge of the settlement. Odo of Bayeux remained prominent until his disgrace in 1082; it is likely that dabbling in papal politics brought about his eventual downfall.

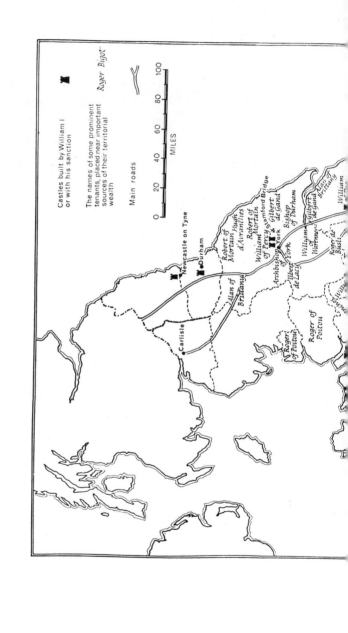

Castles built by William I or with his sanction

The names of some prominent tenants, placed near important sources of their territorial wealth

Roger Bigot

Main roads

0 20 40 60 80 100
MILES

Carlisle

Newcastle on Tyne

●Durham

Robert of Mortain, Hugh d'Avranches

Alan of Brittany

Robert of Mortain

William of Perry Stamford Bridge

Gilbert de Gand

Archbishop of York

Bishop of Durham

Ilbert de Lacy

William of York

Gilbert de Gand

Roger of Poitou

Roger of Poitou

William of Warrenne

Roger de Busli

Alan of Brittany

William

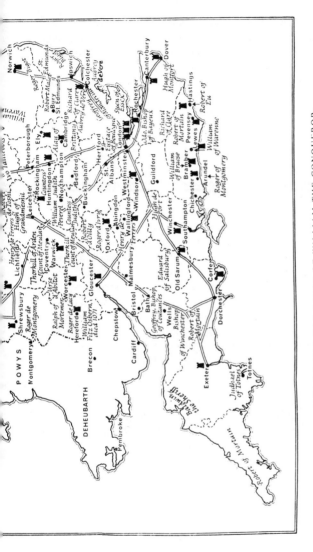

ENGLAND DURING THE REIGN OF WILLIAM THE CONQUEROR-

By that time his effective work had been done. To be closely connected with the Bayeux fief in Normandy, or to be a reliable subordinate of the earl-bishop, was the golden passport to success for many Normans in England.

The size of the effective inner group is occasion for surprise. D. C. Douglas has brought to our attention the fact that close on a quarter of the landed wealth of England, about half the land held by lay tenure, had been granted to only ten men, most of whom were related to the duke himself.[5] This is a fact of tremendous importance, but of almost equal importance is the meaning behind such a phrase as 'received a fief of eighty knights' service'. These men possessed their local interests, their heads of honour, a 'Clare' (FitzGilbert) in Suffolk, FitzOsbern in Hereford and Winchester, Roger of Montgomery in Shropshire and in Arundel. But they remained royal servants, bound to their overlord not only by the theoretical ties of homage and fealty, but also by the personal solidarity of a small, almost a family, ruling group. Their local interests were never allowed to detract from their central responsibilities; they were governors; they were in regular attendance on the king; their duties as members of William's inner council had first call on their energies. The sense of purpose which we have suggested as an outstanding characteristic of the Norman Conquest came in large part from the continued compulsory participation in central affairs of this wealthy group.

Participation in central affairs and attendance at the royal court were consistent features of the service of the top rung of the baronage in the first generation of the Conquest. Devotion to the duke was forced upon them in the sense that any slackness from active participation in immediate ducal affairs could lead to loss of influence and estates. This is not always quite so true of the second generation, nor of the slightly lower rung of tenant-in-chief. Some outlet for their energies was found on the frontier, notably in the Marches of Wales. But there were many important fiefs which from the earliest days of the settlement fulfilled a military purpose, concentrated specifically on one special area. Such baronial concentration, often focused on a castle as a *caput* of the honour, would possess other estates as sources of supply, or as refuges further afield again. The castles were normally simple but effective structures, consisting of a *motte*, or substantial mound, with wooden fortifications on its flattened summit, and a bailey, or larger enclosure, at the foot of the mound. Both *motte* and bailey were further protected by deep ditches, ramparts, and wooden stockades. The lordships dependent on them were sometimes called castleries, a term which gives the right military flavour to the settlement: Richmond in Yorkshire, the Rapes of Sussex, and a string of marcher lordships, Caerleon, Richard's Castle, Ewias Harold, Clifford, and Montgomery. Some great honours bore the character, though not the name, of castleries. A most interesting group of powerful baronies guarded the northern border of ancient Mercia. Roger de Busli held the honour of Tickhill, centred on the castle of Tickhill on the Yorkshire border; Ilbert de Lacy was in charge of Pontefract in South Yorkshire; Henry de Ferrers held Tutbury in Staffordshire. Between them the three men controlled the routes south. De Busli (famous in Domesday Book and nowhere else) had more than eighty antecessors, and his demesne ranged from Yorkshire to Devon. Yet the bulk of his estates lay in Nottinghamshire, where more than a hundred estates brought in over £170 a year, and contiguously in South Yorkshire, where most of his fifty-four manors were kept strictly in demesne—only one sub-tenant was recorded among this group in Domesday Book.[6]

In more settled parts of the country such concentration of wealth was familiar. In Essex, for example, nearly a half of the land held by lay tenure was in the hands of five men. Four of these men—Count Eustace of Boulogne, Geoffrey of Mandeville, Richard FitzGilbert, and Ranulf Peverel (Peverel of London)—were figures of national, or indeed of European, importance. The fifth, Suen of Essex, although he ranked third among the landowners of Essex with land to the annual value of over £250, held only a few parcels of land outside the county, and most of his estates were concentrated around Clavering (his father's, Robert FitzWimarc's, centre of interests) and his own new *castellum* of Rayleigh. In practically every county there were similar men of this important second rank, sometimes sheriffs or ex-sheriffs, whose interests, even at this early stage in the Norman settlement, were firmly localized.

In general, however, it is true to say that baronial estates tended to be scattered over many shires. Robert of Mortain, for example, held nearly eight hundred estates in no fewer than twenty counties, and it was quite common for barons to hold in four counties or more. Such scattering of estates should not be read as a masterstroke of political government on the part of a wily king. To be sure, it was useful for the king to have loyal men with strong interests in several shires. The scattering of estates, too, certainly helped to break down awareness of different backgrounds among the new baronage; they were 'French' as opposed to their English subordinates, rather than Breton, Flemish, or even Norman. Only the Bretons preserved something of a feeling of racial difference, in the Honour of Richmond in Yorkshire, and for a time around Totnes in Devon and further to the south-west; the conspiracy of 1075 was regarded by some as a Breton plot. The greatest advantage to the king resulting from the scattering of estates came in the legal rather than in the political field. Every lord had the right to hold a court for his tenants, but lack of geographical cohesion in estates lessened the efficiency of such courts. The weakness of feudal courts in England may be attributed in part to geographical difficulties. But it is wrong to suggest that these long-term advantages to the crown should be ascribed to conscious policy on the part of William and his advisers. Indication of royal strength comes from royal control of the distribution of estates, not from the pattern of distribution. There was no conscious 'anti-baronial' policy in the pattern itself. Indeed, it was scarcely possible in the circumstances of the Conquest for a baron to build up a consolidated block of political authority. The Norman baron was much more dependent on the king in England than he or his father had been on the duke in Normandy. There was probably little royal objection to the concentration of estates as such, and when the military need was apparent such centres of wealth and influence were fostered.

As for the barons themselves, they stood to gain positive economic advantage from diversity. It was not wise to have too many assets in one district. The estates of the king were often widely dispersed within the shire, and it is significant that those barons in closest attendance on the king tended to have estates most obviously scattered in nature. Lower down in the feudal scale many of the most loyal honorial barons also had estates scattered over several counties. Convenience entered into the question. The Normans at times succeeded Anglo-Saxon thegns who had possessed land in various parts of the country. Ralph Paynel, the ancestor of the Luttrells of Dunster, took over extensive estates in Lincolnshire and Yorkshire, as well as in Devon, Somersetshire, and Gloucestershire, all of which had belonged to Merleswein, a great thegn and sheriff under the Confessor and in the early years of the Conqueror. The Normans intensified processes already at work in Anglo-Saxon England. Estates provided an income as well as a source of political power. An industrialist in the modern world with business interests in Newcastle-upon-Tyne may have considerable influence in the north-east; that influence is not lessened if he has extra sources of income in Barnsley, Bristol, or South Wales.

For if we must be cautious in applying modern parallels we must also be cautious not to make the barons the low-browed military morons of historical fiction. William of Poitiers, admittedly partisan, declared that with the support of ducal counsellors 'the Roman Republic would not have needed two hundred senators', and Ordericus added expansively that they did not yield to the Roman senate in strength or maturity.[7] King William's chief barons were able men, bearing a heavy role in the difficult task of governing a conquered country. They were wealthy men. The tenants-in-chief consolidated estates which had been in the charge of several thousand thegns before the

Conquest, and most of this landed wealth passed into the hands of fewer than two hundred men. Normans predominate in the wealthy group, notably those from the district around Rouen. William and his regents showed much skill in preserving the integrity of this group. The great Councils, the successors of the Witenagemot, held three times a year at the time of the chief ecclesiastical festivals of Christmas, Easter, and Whitsun, helped to keep the king in touch, and to avoid unrest. Quarrels which might have flared up into private war were there brought to the light of day.

To keep the group together was one thing; to ensure that they helped provide the king with an army was quite another. The service demanded from baronial lands was heavy, certainly heavier than the corresponding service in the duchy. In Normandy before 1066 many, indeed most, of the great vassals could have acquitted their service to the ducal host merely by drawing on their domestic knights. The assessment of service in England was fixed by the king, presumably on the occasion of the grant of the honour to the new tenant. The amount of service bore no exact relationship to the extent or to the value of the lands granted, though it would be folly to deny some correlation. On economic grounds alone a rough correspondence of value to the holder of the land and of service laid on that land was desirable. The means by which the knights were recruited and maintained was largely a matter for the great baron, though not in England exclusively so. There were two methods open to the baron by which he could provide for his knights. He could maintain them at his own expense in his household, provide them with food, keep, equipment, and general maintenance; or he could extend the feudal hierarchy by carving off estates from his own demesne, on which they would accept the status of enfeoffed knights, bearing a similar relationship to the baron in respect of feudal oaths and incidents as the baron himself bore to the king. Much depended on the wealth, nature, and distribution of estates, and on the temperament of the baron. There were men, particularly the most active, constantly engaged in perilous border warfare, who liked to be surrounded continuously by a troop of knights, paid and maintained directly by them. These energetic barons were to be found among ecclesiastical lords—such as the abbot of Glastonbury—as well as among the secular. But on all great fiefs sooner or later the process known as subinfeudation, that is the division of the estates of the great fief, was put into effect. The fief was held together personally and territorially by a court presided over by the baron, the honorial court, which busied itself with feudal matters, such as title, and the terms and the rewards of service. The honorial courts were a direct innovation of the Normans. Some fiefs quickly became highly organized. Roger of Montgomery, the only one of William's tenants-in-chief to give his name to a modern county, possessed an administration that was quite elaborate, particularly in the financial field. There is evidence that he even appointed his own sheriffs in Shropshire and in the Rape of Arundel. It is likely that subinfeudation applied first to the responsible officers of a fief, at times kinsmen of the baron, at times his most skilled and trusted fighting men, his constables, or marshals, or seneschals. These officers would be entrusted with land capable of sustaining four or five knights, and would themselves take the responsibility of levying that number. They were not tenants-in-chief, but they were men without whom the fief could not function. In the baron's absence they would lead the feudal contingent; if the levy from the fief were needed at two points the lord might lead one group, the seneschal the other. These men were probably the 'land-owning men of any account', that is to say the *feudati homines* of substance, who were specially summoned to take an oath of allegiance to King William at Salisbury in 1086.

The 'Oath of Salisbury' illustrates both the nature of early Norman feudal society in England and William's skill in asserting his royal dignity and strength within a feudal framework. The king had faced grave political problems in the last years of his reign. In 1085 Danish threats, reinforced on this occasion by support from Flanders, led him to recruit mercenary soldiers on a large scale. Elaborate preparations for the making of Domesday Book were well advanced by the summer of 1086. In August the king summoned a great council at Salisbury, attended by his counsellors and by 'all landowning men of any account' throughout England, no matter whose men they might be. They performed homage to the king, and swore oaths of loyalty to him that they would be loyal to him against all other men. It is true that such men owed allegiance to William without any need for special oaths, but it is a characteristic of feudal society that a state could be strong only when the head, the king, clarified and freshened his contact with the second rung of the feudal hierarchy.

These key men are often known as 'honorial barons', and some of them later developed into tenants-in-chief themselves. Their activities were not necessarily confined to one fief. The complexity of the feudal world was such that already by 1086 tenants-in-chief are found as tenants of other great men. Roger Bigot, Roger Blunt, and Peter de Valognes, for example, held land and proferred service to the abbot of Bury St. Edmunds, and men such as Hamo Dapifer, the count of Eu, and Hugh of Montfort, were answerable for military service from quite modest estates held of the archbishop of Canterbury. A fief did not stand in England of itself. Below the barons and the chief men of the barony were the knights, who were occasionally in the eleventh century men of modest social position: corporals of horse, not Guards officers. Yet they too in time, and quite early in many fiefs, received their reward in land. In the first instance it was customary to group such men at estates near the *caput* of a lord's honour; traces of such settlement exist in the place-names Knighton (that is to say cnihta-tun, or 'settlement of the retainers'). There is a good example in the Honour of Rayleigh in Essex, where subsidiary estates grouped around the new castle of Suen at Rayleigh seem to have been allotted to the military retainers. But others, possibly after a period of service well understood in their generation but lost to us, were settled, at times to receive as reward land formerly held by a Saxon thegn, at other times to receive endowments which corresponded to the revenue from whole villages. This reward was often a matter of hard bargaining. The idea of a standard knight's fee did not become general until the end of the Anglo-Norman period.

(c) *Feudalism and the church: some general conclusions*

The feudal army was recruited not only from lay tenants but also from great ecclesiastical tenants, and it is from their more extensive records that we have here the best chance of discussing the nature of feudal service in the early days of the Conquest, the extent to which the knights were enfeoffed, and allied problems. In the eleventh century bishops and abbots were landowners on a large scale, as well as heads of ecclesiastical establishments or pastors of souls. As such, they were subject as were the laity to the obligations and duties of landlordship. Military service was imposed on their lands. In one sense this was no innovation, and there was no resistance to it; the military obligations of a great church such as Worcester could be heavy in Anglo-Saxon days. The earliest writ of summons to survive was directed to an Englishman, Abbot Aethelwig of Evesham. It enjoined him to attend King William at Clarendon with five knights, fully equipped, which he owed in respect of his abbacy, and commanded him to summon all subject to his administration and jurisdiction to perform their own knight service, duly equipped.[8] Detailed information concerning the amount of service demanded was collected in the course of Henry II's inquiry into the state of the baronial honours in 1166. He obtained statements of the service due in 1135, and there is enough corroborative evidence to suggest that the figures relating to the ecclesiastical fiefs represented substantially the services demanded by the Conqueror. Military service was undoubtedly a heavy burden on the church. The English church alone was responsible for the attendance of some seven hundred and eighty knights to the royal host, roughly the figure which the Norman duke could expect from all his tenants-in-chief in Normandy. Some churches were heavily assessed; others lightly. Christ Church, Canterbury, Winchester, and Worcester, among the cathedral monasteries, owed sixty knights apiece. Lincoln came to be responsible for the same service. Among the abbeys, Peterborough, and probably originally Glastonbury, owed sixty knights, though Glastonbury's assessment was later reduced to forty. Bury St. Edmunds owed the heavy service of forty knights, and Abingdon thirty. But the wealthy house of St. Albans owed only six knights; Evesham, another wealthy house with strong political interests, owed only five; and Ramsey, a very wealthy house with a gross income in Domesday Book of more than £350 a year, owed only four. There has been much discussion of the great variation in assessment. It was not related directly to the wealth of the house, nor to its political leanings. Bury St. Edmunds was close to the new Norman rulers; its abbot, Baldwin, was a link with the world of Edward the Confessor and a loyal supporter of King William. Perhaps local reasons, strategic position of the house, and the warlike or non-warlike nature of the abbots, were the chief determining factors in the assessment. Peterborough was very much in need of protection against Hereward and the Danes; its abbot, Turold (who comported himself more like a knight than an abbot), had one hundred and sixty men-at-arms under his command in 1070; service of sixty knights would not trouble such a commander of men. The abbots of Peterborough were content to keep a standing force in their households; even in 1100 there were fewer than fifty enfeoffed, although by 1166 this number had reached sixty-five.

The new Norman bishops and abbots were accustomed to the exaction of military service from their fiefs. Later evidence suggests that they were generous in their enfeoffments. By 1133, for example, the great see of Bayeux, which owed only twenty knights' service to the duke, had no fewer than one hundred and twenty military tenants; Coutances had eighteen, answerable for a debt of five, and Évreux one hundred and eleven for a debt of twenty. The Norman situation was complicated by the institution of the arrière-ban by which the duke reserved the right to summon extra forces in times of special peril, but even with this reservation the figures remain impressive. England was more conservative, and enjoyed a better internal peace. Fear of permanent alienation of church lands provoked a cautious approach to subinfeudation. Bury St. Edmunds had thirty-two *feudati homines* on its estates by 1086; during the succeeding century the abbey relied on a similar number of feudal tenants to perform its service due of forty knights. Abingdon appears to have enfeoffed tenants responsible for slightly more than thirty knights' service before the death of Abbot Athelhelm in 1084, but increased very little after that. Abingdon was a special case in one respect. Its military service was closely connected with castle-guard at Windsor. Thirty-three knights of the old enfeoffment were settled on Abingdon lands in 1135, and the same number in 1166, according to the returns made to Henry II's inquiry.[9] Abingdon traditions are particularly illuminating in that they record the variety of purposes to which knight service could be put, from garrisoning the new royal castles, to protection of the monastic household, to active campaigning in the field against the Scots (presumably in 1072, a point corroborated by independent Ely evidence), and against the Welsh.

Lanfranc at Canterbury had less hesitation than most in setting up knights' fees on his estates. It may be that in return for his other great services he had received favourable treatment from the Conqueror. Service of sixty knights was not disproportionate to the financial resources of Canterbury. By the end of Lanfranc's archiepiscopate there were nearly one hundred knights' fees on Canterbury lands, and the objection made by Rufus to the contribution made by Anselm to the Welsh wars suggests that quality had been sacrificed in the process. The superplus, as it is known in feudal terms, above what was demanded is proof of Lanfranc's vigour. There were even some Englishmen among his knights, including Aethelwine, the son of Brihtmær, a member of a prosperous London family which had survived the Conquest with no loss of social standing. The number of fractional holdings on Lanfranc's fief gives proof of the financial importance of knights' service.[10] Fractions such as a quarter of a knight's fee appear only when the equivalent in hard cash to military service is well understood. Scutage was

commonplace before 1100, when a royal charter expressly
exempted Lewes priory from the burden.

Some of the most interesting and exact work on the imposition of knights' service has been done on the Bury St.
Edmunds records. Abbot Baldwin was asked to provide forty
knights, that is to say four constabularies of ten knights apiece.
The king took an active interest in the process. He addressed a
writ in English to the abbot in which he instructed the abbot to
hand over the land belonging to those men 'who stood in array
against me and were slain', who belonged to St. Edmund's
soke. It is probable that some of this land was reserved in royal
hands until a suitable military tenant was found. A precious
charter of enfeoffment, preserved in a later copy, shows William
introducing a knight into the great fief, a proved soldier who will
hold land of the abbot on condition that when duly summoned
on behalf of the king and abbot he will serve within the kingdom
with three or four knights at his own cost, and that he will provide
a knight for the abbot's service within and without the kingdom
when the abbot shall wish. He performed homage to the abbot
(*manibus iunctis fore feodalem hominem*), reserving the fealty due
to the king.[11] The importance of this document is that it shows
the king interfering in a subordinate fief. It is a matter in part of
common sense. William knew his soldiers well. The Bury St.
Edmunds contingent was important to him; it was also important to the abbot. When a good man appeared, not of
tenant-in-chief status, what better reward than a fat subordinate
fief on the abbot's lands? The new tenant was responsible for
supplying three or four (the vagueness of number is odd, and
suggests an early date) knights to the host; he thus became a key
man in the military organization of the fief, one of a new class
intruded between the abbot and his sub-tenants.

Not all religious houses were wealthy enough to sustain such
burdens without apparent strain. At Tavistock, a relatively poor
house, regional factors, a heritage of consistent contribution to
local defence, and a series of warlike abbots conspired to raise
the levy of knight service to fifteen. H. P. R. Finberg has sug-

gested in a picturesque and accurate image that this is 'as if one of the least wealthy colleges were ordered to find the whole pay of fifteen cavalrymen in perpetuity'.[12] He shows that some twelve manors had to be alienated in consequence, yet a further reminder that knight service does not necessarily mean the static placing of a soldier on a piece of territory, but is a convenient and spectacular symbol for what was often a complicated financial transaction.

Finally a word should be said in general about the feudal settlement of England. There can be little doubt of its success in the military field. The land was so organized that its resources could provide for defence. The tenurial revolution was complete. English landowners could not adapt themselves to the new feudal world. Yet in one sense the tenurial revolution itself was superficial. All tenure was not military tenure. On even the most warlike of the great fiefs there were men, some English and some Norman, who held land on other than military service. Some of these tenures, it is true, would be semi-military. The proceeds of an estate would be given to a man in return for castle-guard, as for provisioning the army, or for entertaining the lord and the lord's servants. All apparent military tenure was not what it seemed; at times a simple buying of the services of a knight was important. F. W. Maitland warned us long ago that in some of our books 'military tenure has a definiteness and a stability never possessed elsewhere'. The general principle that a great man should be responsible for his quota of knights to the royal feudal army was vastly important. But the fief itself was both more and less than military service. Domesday Book does not even mention the military service due from the lands it described so minutely. The abbot of Bury St. Edmunds was more than a landowner whose chief function was to provide his overlord with forty well-equipped knights at the right time for the right period with the right equipment. He was also lord of ancient sokes and liberties and the man of an ancient monarchy. Emphasis on feudal innovation is necessary. It brings out the quality of the Normans as efficient, practical innovators. Emphasis must not be excessive, lest it blind the student to the reality of the continuity of the monarchy and of the English state.

1   William of Poitiers, p. 232
2   Ibid., p. 238
3   See below, pp. 171–2
4   D. C. Douglas, 'The Companions of the Conqueror', *History*, 1943; also J. F. A. Mason, 'The Companions of the Conqueror: an additional Name', *E.H.R.*, 1956, pp. 61–9.
5   *E.H.D.* ii, p. 22
6   F. M. Stenton, *The First Century of English Feudalism* (2nd ed., Oxford, 1961), pp. 195 ff., and (on scattered holdings and sub-tenancies), pp. 64–6, and 97–101
7   William of Poitiers, p. 148; *Ordericus Vitalis*, ii, p. 140
8   *E.H.D.* ii, p. 895
9   D. C. Douglas, *Feudal Document from the Abbey of St. Edmunds* (Brit. Acad.), London, 1932, p. lxxxvi; *E.H.D.* ii, pp, 903 ff., especially p. 910 (Abingdon)
10 *E.H.D.* ii, pp. 898–9; D. C. Douglas, *The Domesday Monachorum of Christ Church, Canterbury*, London, 1944, p. 105 and pp. 63–73
11 D. C. Douglas, *Feudal Documents*, p. xcvi. *E.H.D.* ii, pp. 896–7
12 H. P. R. Finberg, *Tavistock Abbey*, Cambridge, 1951, p. 227

Norman Government

(a) *The government of the realm*

THE changes brought about by the Norman Conquest were spectacular. Feudal innovations have been discussed in the last chapter, but these were only some of the many changes that came about in English affairs within one generation. The attempts in the opening years of William's reign to create an Anglo-Norman government in the strict sense of the word failed. Normans gradually replaced Englishmen in key positions in church and state. At the court Norman-French took the place of Anglo-Saxon as the language of current use. In administrative matters Latin had long been the favoured language for permanent record; it now began to prevail over Anglo-Saxon as the language for current business. Writs in Anglo-Saxon became increasingly scarce, although isolated examples are known as late as the third decade of the twelfth century. Some monasteries, in spite of Norman abbots, remained centres of Anglo-Saxon learning. Two great cathedral churches, at Worcester and at Exeter, encouraged the preservation of the English past. At Canterbury until at least 1118, and at Peterborough tenaciously to 1155, the Anglo-Saxon Chronicle continued to be kept in the English tongue. In general, however, historians, biographers, and hagiographers wrote in Latin; in the first half of the twelfth century the works of Florence and John of Worcester and of William of Malmesbury show the old skills productive in new Latin channels.

Yet Norman language, Norman customs, Norman skill in building, and Norman feudalism with its knight service and castle-building should not obscure the continuity between Anglo-Saxon and Anglo-Norman England. This should not be matter for surprise. The Normans came to rule, not to settle, to use existing institutions, and not to innovate except where innovation was unavoidable. In the military and aristocratic field change was essential, and bore the character of a social revolution. For most of the inhabitants of England, Norman rule did not achieve so revolutionary a character. The Norman kings merely did rather more efficiently what the Anglo-Saxon rulers had attempted with varying success.

The Norman kings governed strictly, and on the whole well. They observed traditional forms, not for any sentimental reasons, but because traditional forms gave them the authority they desired. Under the sons of the Conqueror, William Rufus and Henry I, there was a distinct danger that royal government would become too arbitrary. The kings were strong in theory, as well as in practice. William I, in spite of his notorious illegitimacy, fostered the ties of blood which linked him with the mother of Edward the Confessor. He also observed the formality of election, a ceremonial act which, divorced from modern 'electoral' implications, signified public approval, or perhaps strictly approval of the chosen. Designation by the old king helped to give sanction to the new ruler, and William I, who laid great weight on his designation as heir by the Confessor, attempted a similar service on his death-bed to his son William Rufus. Most important of all, at the public level, was the coronation. William I dated the opening of his reign from the coronation, not from the death of the former king. In a sense coronation was secondary. The king was chosen before he was crowned. The coronation ceremony was nevertheless a great public symbol of kingship; mystical elements were strong around the consecrated king. Legends sprang up in England of the sacred crow of St. Oswald (corresponding to the sacred dove of the Merovingian kings), which was reputed to have brought holy oil for the unction. The early Norman age gave classic expression to general Germanic ideas. There was intense belief in the virtues of a special royal kin. The ablest, or the most conveniently placed, of the kin could act with his personal followers so as to ensure succession on the death of a king. Approval by election and consecration brought popular and ecclesiastical sanction to a resolute candidate. The succession of both William I and of Henry I may justly be interpreted in these terms.

Theoretical factors were helpful in the establishment of the king, and in ensuring continuity of rule. The Anglo-Norman kings successfully asserted their right to rule. In so doing they showed themselves in the direct line of descent from the Anglo-Saxon past, and such continuity is yet more recognizable in their methods of ruling. The key institutions were undoubtedly royal councils. Such councils should not be interpreted as in any way a direct check upon royal authority. They had no life without the king, and were not regular in summons or in session as of right. It is nevertheless true that no king in the eleventh century could act without advice, and full accounts that have survived of William Rufus in council show (after all allowance has been made for the artistic sense of the historians who first recorded them) that deliberations were hard argued and sincere. Decision rested with the king; the function of barons and of churchmen was to give counsel. The only limitations imposed on him as king were those of his coronation oath: he was to protect the church, to rule justly, and to suppress thieves and other malefactors. He engaged himself to rule under law; his counsellor, particularly the great ecclesiastic, had a moral obligation to see that the coronation oath was obeyed. To argue that there were firm institutional checks would be unwise. It is wrong to see the councils as imposing or implying a limitation on the royal right to govern. The councils, like the witenagemots before them, were royal councils.

A set of problems of great complexity surround the question of the composition of royal councils under the early Norman kings. Both in fact and in terminology the conciliar position was a matter of ambiguity. It is doubtful if a differentiation of court and council was consistently made. A plurality of royal councils is a concept more familiar to modern historians than to William I or any of his contemporaries. But some great assemblies were specially marked out. We mentioned in an earlier chapter William's skill in keeping in touch with the compact baronial class by means of three special assemblies on the occasion of the great ecclesiastical feasts. These were the three solemn crown-wearings of the Norman kings. They were not held quite as regularly as the Anglo-Saxon Chronicle tells us, nor at such fixed points. But they were held with sufficient regularity for us to be sure that they were accepted as part of the normal procedure of government, and the Anglo-Saxon Chronicle itself carefully recorded the time and place where the kings held their councils, especially their Christmas councils, from 1090 to 1126. All important tenants-in-chief were expected to attend. Absence without excuse would be interpreted as suspicious. Political decisions were taken there; campaigns were planned, and administrative matters of importance, such as the preparation for the Domesday survey, were inaugurated at these great councils. The *Magnum Concilium* of William I has been described as a feudalized witan, and also as the ancestor of the House of Lords. It was a court—the presence of the king was sufficient to make that so—an assembly of vassals which was competent to form judgements. These great councils were also great feasts, an element in the social life of the community which our prosaic, record-minded generation has tended to underestimate. The idea of a king surrounded by his hearth-troop persisted into the feudal world. Precious glimpses of the colour and vitality of such assemblies are given in the works of the poets who used contemporary courts to illustrate their accounts of King Arthur or Charlemagne. The Normans inherited a strong tradition of rich ceremonial from their Anglo-Saxon antecessors. In this, as in so many aspects of government and social life, they brought their own peculiar powers of definition and regularization to bear on ancient institutions.

The great councils were, however, extraordinary occasions, social, legal, political, and feudal. The administrative decisions taken at such assemblies concerned matters of high moment. Government business did not halt because the ecclesiastical feasts came to an end. How was English government carried on, how were decisions reached, on the ordinary occasions of the early Norman world?

Any important matter beyond that which could be settled in the locality at a shire court or at the meeting of a group of shires had to be referred to the king. If the king were in England he would consult directly with his court, his curia. If he were absent, and the matter grave, recourse might be necessary to his curia in Normandy, or in the field on expedition. If the matter were not so grave, his viceroys in England, perhaps Odo of Bayeux, or Geoffrey of Coutances, would hear the plea and settle the dispute in the royal name. The *curia regis*, which dealt with routine business, normally consisted of his accustomed companions; the term *curiales* could be used even of the boon companions of the young William Rufus. It was the court in constant regular attendance on the king, the people to whom the king would turn naturally for counsel, some of his kindred, some barons, bishops, and household officers. From charter evidence it has been possible to reconstruct William I's inner council, in that close, intimate sense. Membership fluctuated; the only constant factor was the king or his immediate representative, but —for example—from 1067 to 1071 one would expect important formal business in England to be transacted over the subscription of William FitzOsbern, Geoffrey of Coutances, Odo of Bayeux, and some other prominent Norman barons such as Richard FitzGilbert, Henry de Ferrers, Roger of Montgomery, or William Malet. Geoffrey, bishop of Coutances, held a position of outstanding importance as adviser throughout the reign; the names of some important men who also held office as sheriffs, such as Robert d'Oilly, Peter de Valognes, and Roger Bigot consistently recur. The directing group of men was strongly baronial; only the chancellor and some of his special chaplains came from outside the upper rung of Norman feudal society. It became a complaint against Henry I that he raised men from the dust, the Clintons and the Bassetts, to participate in the council.

All thoughts of neat institutional outlines become blurred, the closer the evidence is examined. Archbishops and some great men expected to be consulted on matters of moment. On extra-ordinary occasions, it was customary for the consent of the barons to be obtained; the Coronation Charter of Henry I stated that the laws of King Edward were to be restored 'together with such emendations as my father had made with the counsel of his barons'. But it is a question of a king taking counsel, not of a council possessing the right to be consulted. How the counsel was to be obtained was a matter for the king, for common sense, and for tradition, probably in that order.

Concern with government has to this point been very much with the higher aspects of government, with the taking of decisions. Great interest has been aroused in the last generation on other aspects of government, on routine administration which is in many respects a surer test of the growth of a com-munity. A modern state begins to emerge in recognizable form when routine acts multiply; the modern historian tends to be much happier with the twelfth century than with the eleventh for the simple reason that the clearer definitions of the latter century enabled the apparatus of government to be better under-stood—by later investigators as well as by contemporaries. The eleventh century was still essentially the age of the undifferentiated royal household. Later medieval development is clear in outline, though complicated in detail. From the household rudimentary departments of state developed; the departments in turn built up their own traditions of office, with the royal household re-maining a prolific, and almost inexhaustible, source of growth. The royal court itself, the Exchequer, the Wardrobe, and the Chamber, at different times took the lead in financial affairs. The complicated clash of new and old is a constant reminder of the astonishing flexibility of medieval institutions.

The immediate post-Conquest period witnessed only the

beginning of division into departments and of differentiation between them. Even so, royal administration was clearly operating in the overlapping but separate fields of general secretarial activity, finance, justice, and local government. The absences of the king in Normandy, and later royal preoccupation with Norman and continental problems, facilitated and hastened the process of differentiation. No justiciar could exercise the full authority of the king. The essential agency of government was the royal household, though household itself was a term of wide scope. A distinguished local thegn, enjoying extensive local interests, could be as much part of the household as a chaplain. All great households, lay and ecclesiastical, appear to have developed in similar ways in tenth and eleventh centuries Western Europe. Offices that were necessary and domestic became honourable and quite divorced from their nominal function. Marshals, butlers, stewards, simple stallers (place-men) had little to do with horses, drink, and food, though the origins of their offices were remembered at great ceremonial occasions, such as, for example, the coronation of Otto the Great of Germany in 936, when the dukes performed their menial tasks symbolically as a sign of subjection. The Norman ducal court in this respect was not unlike the late Anglo-Saxon, except that the military functions of the great officers were more pronounced. It is probable that we have consistently underestimated the influence of such great officers not only as advisers but also as administrators. It is likely that their function, particularly when the king was a warrior, was analogous to that of active staff-officers, and that they were responsible for the safety of the royal court on its frequent journeyings, for the arrangements of great ceremonies, and for the executive implementation of important decisions. Our immediate concern is, however, with other aspects of the household, the humbler but well-recorded ministerial elements.

Under Edward the Confessor there existed a body of clerks in constant attendance on the royal court, responsible for the construction of records and the routine business of government.

With William's coming business increased and at a very early stage signs appear of a greater specialization. Regenbald has already been mentioned as an important clerk under Edward who continued to subscribe to early documents of the Conqueror. His successor, Herfast, known as 'the illiterate', was referred to as chancellor before he was elevated to the see of Elmham in 1070. The next chancellor, Osmund, became bishop of Salisbury in 1078. During his term of office he seems to have been responsible for very important developments. He initiated the change in language for writs from Anglo-Saxon to Latin and to judge from his surviving writs (though other factors, such as the greater chance of survival, have to be taken into account) he was also responsible for an extension in function of the writs, which are now used more freely as governmental orders. Sheer pressure of business brought about increased complexity in organization. By 1085 the administration was confident enough in its own powers to carry through a survey that remains to the present day the best testimony to William's efficiency: the survey which resulted in the production of Domesday Book.

The making of Domesday Book was an extraordinary achievement, and William's own reputation as a statesman is derived to a great extent from the fortunate survival of the two large volumes which have been known from the twelfth century onwards as Domesday Book. The Anglo-Saxon Chronicle recorded that at Christmas, 1085, William had deep speech with his counsellors at Gloucester about the land, how it was peopled and with what sort of men, and that he sent his men all over England into every shire to ascertain how many hundreds of hides of land there were, how much the king had, and what were his rightful annual dues. The king also ordered that a record should be made of all that the other landowners had in land and livestock, and what it was worth. The chronicler lamented (*sub anno* 1086) that the task was done so thoroughly that scarcely an ox, or a cow, or a pig escaped notice ('it was shameful to relate but he thought it no shame to do'). Robert, bishop of Hereford, writing shortly after the inquest, added the information

TABLE 3—THE MAKING OF DOMESDAY BOOK

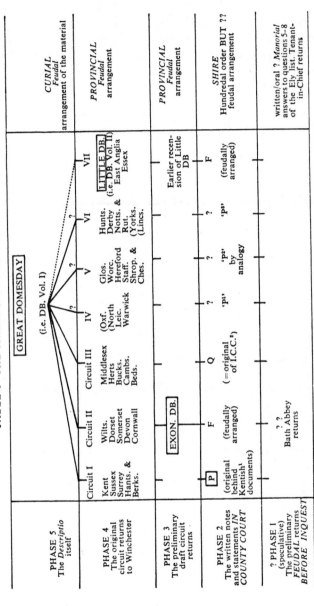

GREAT DOMESDAY (i.e. DB, Vol. I)

	Circuit I	Circuit II	Circuit III	IV	V	VI	VII	
	Kent Sussex Surrey Hants. & Berks.	Wilts. Dorset Somerset Devon Cornwall	Middlesex Herts Bucks. Cambs. Beds.	Oxf. (North Leic. Warwick	Glos. Worc. Hereford Staff. Shrop. & Ches.	Hunts. Derby Notts. & Rut. (Yorks. (Lincs.	LITTLE DB (i.e. DB. Vol. II) East Anglia Essex	
PHASE 5 The *Descriptio* itself								*CURIAL* Feudal arrangement of the material
PHASE 4 The original circuit returns to Winchester	?	?	?	?	?	?	Earlier recension of Little DB	*PROVINCIAL* Feudal arrangement
PHASE 3 The preliminary draft circuit returns		F (feudally arranged)	Q (= original of I.C.C.²)	?	?	?	F (feudally arranged)	*PROVINCIAL* Feudal arrangement
PHASE 2 The written notes and statements *IN COUNTY COURT*	P (original behind Kentish¹ documents)			'P'	'P' by analogy	'P'		*SHIRE* Hundredal order BUT ?? feudal arrangement
? PHASE 1 (speculative) The preliminary *FEUDAL* returns *BEFORE INQUEST*		?? Bath Abbey returns						written/oral ? *Manorial* answers to questions 5-8 of the Ely list. Tenant-in-Chief returns

EXON. DB

¹ *Excerpta* (St. Augustine's Canterbury), *Domesday Monachorum* of Christ Church, Canterbury, *Textus Roffensis*, Rochester
² *Inquisitio Comitatus Cantabrigiensis*—possibly a careful copy of hastily written court notes

that the inquiry was connected with troubles over the collection
of royal money, and that the inquiry was conducted in two stages.
A second group of *inquisitores*, who had no personal connection
with the districts in which they operated, checked the work of the
initial inquirers.[1]

Modern research of great subtlety and some complexity has
succeeded in reconstructing an intelligible account of the
Domesday Inquest. It is now generally accepted that the tenants-
-in-chief themselves played a more active part in proceedings,
and that much more written evidence was made available to the
royal commissioners than would have been considered likely or,
indeed, possible a generation ago. The country was divided into
seven, or just possibly into nine, circuits. A group of royal commissioners, presumably the second set of *inquisitores* referred to
by Robert of Hereford, made a solemn progress through each
shire in their several circuits, holding their formal meetings at the
shire-court after extensive preliminary inquiries had already
been made. These commissioners were great men, and possessed
very full powers to hear, and in some circuits to all appearance
to settle, questions concerning ownership of land. Among the
known commissioners were Remigius, bishop of Lincoln, Walter
Giffard, Henry de Ferrers, and Adam, brother of Eudo Dapifer
(all members of a circuit which included the shire of Worcester),
the bishop of Durham (for the south-west), and possibly Suen,
lord of Rayleigh, sometime sheriff of Essex, though it may be
that his special function concerned the initial sorting out of
factual material for the eastern circuit. Within each circuit a full
record of the inquiry was prepared, arranged shire by shire, but
within each shire according to royal lands, ecclesiastical lands,
and lands of lay tenants-in-chief. The record incorporated
elaborate statistics relating to the assessment of each estate, the
population, the wealth, and the value. Attempts were made, and
these varied from circuit to circuit, to give the value in 1066
(when Edward was alive and dead), when the new Norman
lord took over, and in 1086. The full surveys were then sent
to Winchester, and there (except for the eastern circuit of

Essex, Norfolk, and Suffolk) they were abbreviated by a scribe or scribes of high administrative capacity into the form that is now known as Domesday Book, Volume I. For some reason—and the death of King William in September 1087 has been adduced as a possible reason—the return from the eastern circuit was not abbreviated, and in its elaborate detailed form, bearing the marks of the relatively unpolished circuit return, it still survives, and is known as Little Domesday, or Domesday Book, Volume II. The two volumes, which in their differences give vital clues to the original construction of the record as a whole, are the greatest treasures today of the Public Record Office in London.

The original purpose of the survey has been hotly disputed by generations of historians, and there are those who say that its purpose has been more evident to later historians than to contemporaries of the early Norman kings. The view has even been put forward, perhaps with more vigour than power to convince, that Domesday Book was something of an administrative mistake, respected but unused. Certainly if it was used—and if it was prepared in the elaborate fashion suggested above—a well-developed clerical administration is implied. Modern investigation has gone far to suggest the existence of such a developed administration, and it is possible to see how Domesday Book, as we know it, served a very important purpose to the early Norman kings. A financial purpose is apparent in practically every entry; Maitland called Domesday Book a geld-book, and it certainly does supply a very detailed account of the assessment to tax laid on the landed estates of England. More attention has been paid, since Maitland wrote, to other aspects of the survey of equal, indeed in some respects of greater importance than the financial, that is to say to judicial and to feudal affairs. Domesday Book needs to be examined in the light of the judicial pleas of William's reign; the Domesday Commissioners bore some of the characteristics of later judges on eyre. V. H. Galbraith, who has done much to unravel Domesday problems, has described Domesday Book as 'the formal written record of the introduction of feudal tenure, and therefore of feudal law into England'.[2]

Domesday Book provided the Norman kings with an authoritative index to the tenurial revolution which had been accomplished by the Conquest; it satisfied royal curiosity concerning the English kingdom. It also remains as a permanent testament to the efficiency of the royal servants, from the great men who served as commissioners to the humble ministers who created the record in final form at Winchester.

Other documents have survived which show that William's clerks were as good at their craft as his soldiers. His charters and writs were normally written in Latin, and show a high standard of competence in the use of a clear, legible Caroline minuscule. At this stage there is little distinction between the function of bookhand and courthand, but the ambitious use of abbreviation alone demonstrates the technical competence of the Domesday Book scribes. William liked things to be committed to writing. When on his death-bed he is said to have summoned notaries to write down his wishes concerning the distribution of his property.

It is no accident that the skill of the clerks expressed itself particularly in financial affairs. The 'Treasury' succeeded, as always, in attracting the ablest of the civil servants. The English kings were rich, and their Norman successors were grasping. William was a complicated character and there are many different accounts of his reactions to situations and people. The consistent quality present in most accounts is avarice; like many others who have had a hard time in their youth, William the Norman duke was fond of money. He could be splendid, magniloquent, richly apparelled, every inch a king; but a full treasury was essential to successful kingship, and he knew it. The Anglo-Saxon Chronicle (1087) held among his greatest faults:

> Into avarice (*gitsung*) he fell
> And loved greediness (*grædinesse*) over all.

We are told further that William Rufus went on his accession to the treasury (*madme hus*, treasure-house) at Winchester, and that it was impossible to recount how much treasure was there in gold, and silver, and vessels, and costly robes, and jewels. Such accumulation of wealth at a time when royal armies were constantly on the move is proof both of the wealth of England and of the skill of the Anglo-Norman financial agents.

Yet all credit should not go to the new men. The Anglo-Saxon financial system had been advanced and efficient in its age. Anglo-Saxon kings drew wealth from regalian sources. The geld was, to all appearance, an annual tax levied on the landed wealth of the country; and land-taxes imply skill in the construction of written records. The assessment system was elaborate and flexible. It was handled freely by William. The geld was collected, probably largely by landowners, and handed over to the royal officers at the shire-court. Many villages obtained reductions in hidage, that is to say reductions in the equivalent of modern rateable value. A geld-roll for Northamptonshire, undated, but of about 1072–8, has survived, which provides a careful record of land which paid geld, of land which was in demesne (and therefore exempt), and land which was waste. Similar accounts have also survived for some of the south-western counties in the Exeter Domesday Book. The geld tended to grow antiquated, particularly as more and more exemptions were granted. It was obsolete by 1162, though revived as an emergency measure in 1194 when the Domesday Book figures were used to calculate the carucage; but in the late eleventh century it should not be neglected as a substantial regular item of royal revenue. Royal officers also drew extensive revenues from the ancient dues of the shire, and from the composition of royal rents and rights. In England the majority of the boroughs were royal, and large sums in the shape of the farm of the borough passed to the king; indeed with the disappearance of the Old English earldoms (two-thirds of such revenue passed to the king and one-third to the earl under the Old English custom) and with the more limited field of activity of the Norman earls royal revenue from such sources substantially increased. The administration of justice, as always, was profitable; great pleas, bearing some resemblance to reserved pleas later to evolve into the pleas of the sword of the Norman duchy, were reserved to the English king, and again substantial sums of money passed to the royal agents in each shire. The Norman introduction of a harsh law of the forest increased further revenue from judicial sources.

The main source of royal wealth was, however, land. In terms of annual values recorded in Domesday Book the king personally owned about a seventh of the land of England in 1086. There was scarcely a shire in which his interests were not prominent and looked after either by the sheriff or by a special *custos regis* appointed for that purpose. If the lands of the king's immediate family and followers is added to the specific *Terra Regis*, close on a quarter of the landed wealth of England lay directly in the royal grasp, a shade more than was possessed by the church, and close on two-thirds of the land held by all the rest of the baronage. Most of the manors were farmed, and royal agents were notorious for the high farm they succeeded in exacting from such estates. The Anglo-Saxon Chronicle (1087) recorded of the king himself that he granted (*sealde*) his land on very hard terms, as hard as he was able, 'then came some other and offered more than the one had given before; and the king let it to the man who had offered him more; then came a third and offered yet more, and the king gave it to the man who had offered most of all. And he paid no heed how very sinfully the reeves got it from poor men, nor how many illegalities they did'.

Royal profits from the farm were increased naturally by profits from estates which had escheated or been forfeited. Although these were normally granted out afresh, there was often an interim period when the profits went direct to the king. A great deal of hard cash must have changed hands, possibly more than in the England of Edward the Confessor. The men mainly responsible for handling this money and bringing it safely to the fixed treasury at Winchester were the sheriffs. In the new circumstances of the Conquest the sheriff's office became increasingly important; he was the royal man in the shire. In Norman times men of high rank, such as Suen, lord of Rayleigh, or Peter de Valognes in Essex, Roger Bigot in East Anglia, or Hamo the

Steward in Kent, were content to accept office as sheriff; their military co-operation was needed, not least in the safe transport of royal revenue from the shires to Winchester. King William kept a stern eye on them, powerful as they were, and a commission headed by Lanfranc and Geoffrey of Coutances held an inquiry into the depredations of all the sheriffs in 1076-7.

The main treasury was fixed at Winchester. The English were experienced in the techniques of currency, in the striking of dies, and the regular issues of types. They could test the purity of the coins by an effective process of blanching. Methods of accountancy were still primitive; split sticks with notches of varying shapes were used in calculating. But knowledge of more advanced methods, from the Moslem world, came to England during the reign of William I. Robert, bishop of Hereford, 1079-95, for example, was a mathematician and something of an astronomer in his own right. Not until the reign of Henry I was the new knowledge applied to financial matters. In 1110, for the first time apparently, an aid was assessed at the Exchequer (the *scaccarium*); and the first recorded roll for receipt of revenue to survive comes from 1129-30. The Exchequer was in some respects a court, the *curia regis ad scaccarium*; it did not control all expenditure and check all revenue: indeed for long it continued to bear the nature of the royal household acting as a specialized financial bureau. Yet the work of Roger of Salisbury, in particular, was well done, and the Exchequer persisted as an advanced system of government accounting. The institutional prestige of the Exchequer should not, however, blind us to the fact that the Normans inherited from the Anglo-Saxons an elaborate system of coinage, assessment, and collection and storage of revenue, upon which stable institutions could be built.

The king's government was markedly active in the financial field, and equally energetic also in judicial matters. There was little formal legislation. Later compilations give an account of the laws of William I, but in fact a general acceptance of the good laws of King Edward seems to have been enough for the Conqueror. Only in the institution of the *murdrum* fine, that is to say the imposition of a specific fine on a neighbourhood if the neighbourhood proved unable to produce for punishment the slayer of a Frenchman, does the Norman king appear to have enacted a significant piece of legislation. This was a necessary precaution for an occupying military force, and it is a symptom of the sullen unrest below the surface that a murdered man was presumed to be French, unless the hundred could prove otherwise. There were important changes in organization, in the use of the sworn inquest, and radical changes in the treatment of ecclesiastical offences. But of formal legislation there is surprisingly little trace, a symptom of the sufficiency of Anglo-Saxon regal authority and Anglo-Saxon legislation.

The Normans, however, though reticent on the principles of law, excelled in the administration of law. Full records have survived of several great pleas held by the representatives of the Conqueror. Geoffrey of Coutances, for example, presided over an extraordinary shire-court for the county of Kent, at which Lanfranc made good in law, if not in fact, his claim to extensive estates which were alleged to be held illegally by Odo of Bayeux from the see of Canterbury. The same Geoffrey presided over a special assembly drawn from Worcester and the surrounding counties to decide in favour of the bishop of Worcester, in a land plea against the abbot of Evesham. This cause has a special interest, as it was inaugurated by a royal writ to Geoffrey which has been interpreted as the ancestor of the writ of right. Geoffrey was instructed so to make concord (sake and soke) between the bishop and the abbot, 'as it had been on the day when the geld for the building of a ship was last taken in the reign of King Edward'.[3] Geoffrey also presided at Kentford, probably either during 1081 or 1082, over the critical hearing in a very complicated set of pleas, held before royal barons and a large assembly drawn from Suffolk and Norfolk, and surrounding shires, at which the Abbot of Ely defended his lands and liberties. These formal pleas are best known, but they are only few among many which are alluded to in Domesday Book and elsewhere. Indeed the Domesday Inquest itself was held in part to avoid uncertainty over the ownership of land. The activity of the king in such matters is conspicuous, and equally noteworthy is the respect shown for the shire court as the institution in which such matters should be heard, and the great respect shown for the state of affairs in 1066. At the Kentish pleas referred to above, the aged bishop of Selsey was brought from retirement in a cart, so that he could testify to the rightness of the land-holding position in the days of King Edward.

In local government generally continuity is the principal theme. Great men became sheriffs, but they or their subordinates perambulated the hundreds, taking the view of frank-pledge which ensured that the tithings were full and the law-worthiness of the freemen made manifest. More hundreds passed into private hands, and exemption even from the shire increased. Nevertheless the folk courts were not feeble at the end of the eleventh century. The use of such courts by William I and William II is a foretaste of their increased vitality in the twelfth century, when innovations in procedure and increased use of royal writs brought about that blend of royal central control and ancient local institution that was to be the principal bulwark of medieval English administration. Already in the land pleas, and throughout the whole country in the Domesday survey, the Normans used extensively the sworn inquest for administrative purposes. These inquests, the sworn company of neighbours, were royal processes in origin, as Maitland said 'not English but Frankish', though precedents are also to be found in late Anglo-Saxon England. To decide a matter of fact by the sworn testimony of neighbours was infinitely more rational than trial by ordeal or compurgation. In the twelfth century such inquests became instruments for legal reform. The administrative capacity of Henry I and Henry II led to the multiplication of original writs, based in the first instance on a request to the king to do right. But it is the early Norman kings who established the jury as a regular part of the machinery of royal government.

(b) *The government of the church*
Activity in the arts of secular government was mirrored by

similar activity in the church. William's chief agent was the formidable and experienced Lanfranc, appointed archbishop of Canterbury in 1070. The accepted generalization is that the English church was reformed according to the royal will, with the close co-operation of the archbishop. From the papal, curial point of view, it was all rather old-fashioned; Lanfranc remained throughout all his career 'something of a pre-Investiture man', closer in temper to the spirit of the 1030s and 1040s, in which he had spent his young manhood, than to the 1070s of Hildebrand's day.

The king and the archbishop busied themselves in two principal fields: the internal reorganization of the church and its relationship to the papacy. William's position in England was curious. His desire to reform the church was genuine; his desire to maintain control of the church was equally genuine. The suggestion that there was any doubt in his control, implied or expressed, is misleading; control of the church was proper to a prince. A bishop was expected to be active on the king's business. Gundulf, bishop of Rochester, was placed in charge of work at the Tower of London by command of the great King William (*regis Willelmi magni*). Yet William's approach to English ecclesiastical affairs was cautious. It might be expected that a conqueror who owed so much to papal support would have acted abruptly, particularly in the matter of Stigand. Nothing of the sort; we even find a Norman bishop, Remigius of Dorchester, going to Stigand for consecration, a step which Anglo-Saxon bishops had succeeded in avoiding. There have been many attempted explanations of this delay in action; the most likely is simply William's preoccupation with secular affairs. As long as Ealdred of York lived, William knew that he had a respectable and compliant metropolitan on whom he could rely. After Ealdred's death in September 1069 reorganization became imperative, and William now looked to the papacy, which must have furthered the belief at the curia that England was a vassal state. In April 1070 an important Council was held at Winchester, presided over by Ermenfred, bishop of Sitten, a trusted papal legate, assisted by two cardinal priests. The bishop of Lichfield resigned before the Council met, which was not surprising, as he was married, and had children. Stigand at long last was deposed, apparently to his own surprise, and his brother Aethelmær was removed from the see of Elmham. A little later the bishop of Selsey was deprived of his see, though under somewhat kinder circumstances. On their return journey to Rome the legates laid a solemn penance on the Normans for the part they had played in the conquest of England. The document which states the terms of the penance is interesting in its own right; it draws a distinction between those who fought merely for gain and those who fought in a public war (*in publico bello*); it also distinguished the weight of penance laid on those who killed men before the consecration of the king and after the royal consecration. Papal support of the established order is conspicuously strong in this document; those who killed men after the consecration of the king were to do penance as for homicide wilfully committed, unless the slain were rebels in arms against the king when a milder penitential scale applied. The imposition of a penance also has its interest in showing how the reformed papacy would act on absolute moral grounds even against the secular interests of which it approved; to slay a man *in publico bello* was none the less an act worthy of penance.[4]

After some persuasion, which included a direct command from the Pope, Lanfranc accepted the vacant see of Canterbury, and so started one of the most fruitful periods of office ever enjoyed by an English archbishop. His formal nomination on 15 August was followed a fortnight later by his consecration on 29 August 1070. He had first the difficult task of asserting the supremacy of his see in England. This was by no means easy. York had been well governed for twenty years; Canterbury had been in disgrace. Ealdred of York had taken the lead on great national, religious occasions. Archbishop Thomas of York, nominated to office as early as 23 May 1070, but not consecrated (this vital act of consecration was deliberately delayed) until 25 December 1070, objected strongly to Lanfranc's demand for a written statement of obedience. Eventually he acquiesced, but with reservations, and Hugh the Chantor records that the profession was avowedly personal ('I shall be subject to you, as long as you live, but not to your successors, unless by the judgement of the supreme pontiff').[5] In 1071 he brought the matter before a papal court, in itself a significant step. The matter was referred to a council held at Winchester in 1072. The outcome of the council was a tremendous triumph for Lanfranc. Great dispute has surrounded the means by which this triumph was achieved; a parade of papal documents seems to have been less effective, and much more limited in scope, than an earlier generation of scholars believed, and much dispute over whether Lanfranc or the monks of Canterbury were responsible for the forgeries appears to have been unnecessary. It is now generally believed that Lanfranc's autocratic temper, royal support, and the traditions of the see of St. Augustine, St. Theodore of Tarsus, and the martyred Aelfheah were enough to win the day for Canterbury. The issue was not finally settled; York was left with authority over Durham and such of the Scottish sees as would recognize its authority, though its claims to Lichfield, Worcester, and Dorchester were discounted. In the 1120s the case was reopened at the papal curia, when it appears that many of the forgeries (which scholars formerly considered the work of Lanfranc) were produced, only to be laughed out of court. The immediate success was none the less real, and Lanfranc was given the authority to make his active, conciliar reforms effective throughout the whole kingdom where King William's writ ran. Fear of separatist tendencies in the north contributed much to this unitary solution. Lanfranc is said to have argued that subjection of York to Canterbury was essential for the maintenance of the security and integrity of the realm, and in this argument he surely echoed the king's voice, who was not as *novus* or as *credulus* in such affairs as Hugh the Chantor would have us believe.

In the meantime, probably in 1072 and certainly before 1076, William and Lanfranc between them made a most important innovation. The Conqueror issued an ordinance which had the effect of withdrawing pleas relating to the episcopal laws from the hundred court, and of forbidding any matters concerning the cure of souls to be brought to the judgement of secular men. In Anglo-Saxon days most ecclesiastical causes had been settled in public courts. England was now brought, by royal writ to the shire-courts, into line with more advanced continental practice. On the continent of Europe separate ecclesiastical courts were commonplace, with a growing body of written law to sustain them, the canon of the church. The introduction of non-English speaking prelates must have hastened the need for such reform in England. There are features of some ambiguity and complexity in relation to the ordinance. It is clear enough in its statement that bishops and archdeacons were to withdraw spiritual pleas from public courts, and that such pleas were to be heard at a time and place nominated by the bishop. But the secular authority of the sheriff was specifically mentioned as the instrument of discipline by which the new measures could be enforced. The writ (or ordinance) did not inversely forbid churchmen to participate in the workings of secular courts; certainly many ecclesiastical dignitaries continued to take part in 'secular' judicial affairs. The laws of Henry I, a private compilation of c. 1118, assumed that bishops will still be very busy in the popular courts. But the ordinance of William I represented a contrary move on the part of the church of reformers, though it prepared the way for later dispute.

It may well have been the council of 1072 which prompted the issue of the writ. Two more of his councils, one at London in 1075, and the other at Winchester in 1076, give proof of Lanfranc's energy. He was himself a considerable ecclesiastical lawyer. Indeed, he introduced into England an abridged, working collection of the canons of the church, which was a product of his scholarly inspiration at Bec, and which in part at least may have been a product of his own pen. Lanfranc was especially concerned not so much with general reform as with reform through emphasis on metropolitan rights and duties. Reform through provincial councils and episcopal authority was this great ecclesiastical statesman's ideal. At the councils he provided the theoretical basis of reform. Good bishops were needed to implement reform, and with William's help he was able to ensure the appointment of a creditable bench of bishops and group of abbots. Of the eighteen men appointed to the other English sees from 1070 to Lanfranc's death in 1089, at least sixteen were Normans by birth or by training; and at least eight of them were clerks of the royal chapel. They were competent but overshadowed by Lanfranc, who dominated his bishops much more so than, for example, Becket dominated his in the succeeding century.

At his 1072 council he deposed Abbot Wulfric of the New Minster at Winchester, and accepted certain canons, the most significant of which concerned diocesan order. All bishops were to appoint 'archdeacons and other ministers of the holy order' in their churches, a step which marks formal recognition of what had been customary in at least the more advanced sees. It was also laid down that each bishop was to hold a synod twice a year. Three years later further decisions were taken concerning episcopal order, and decisions were made which resulted in the transfer of the central church of the sees of Lichfield, Sherborne, and Selsey, to Chester, Salisbury, and Chichester. As early as 1050 a similar arrangement had been reached in the south-west with the transfer of Crediton to Exeter. In East Anglia the main church of the see had been moved from Elmham to Thetford before 1072, and ultimately to Norwich. Before the end of William's reign the great eastern Midland see had shifted its main church from its southern tip at Dorcester-on-Thames to its northern extremity at Lincoln. The great churches were urbanized, a step fully to the Normans' taste. Castle, cathedral, and eventually the walled town became the typical product of Anglo-Norman order. Further declarations at the London Council brought England into line with continental moral reform: decrees were published against simony and vagrancy.

In 1076, a year of great crisis in the affairs of the Western church, Lanfranc held at Winchester the best-known and most thorough-going of his ecclesiastical councils. There is a certain irony in the situation. Lanfranc and William put forward an effective programme, in somewhat old-fashioned terms, paying full respect to papal wishes on moral questions and on questions of discipline, in the very year when, in Germany and Italy, the greatest dispute of the Middle Ages between Church and State was in progress. Reform by provincial synod under direct royal patronage was not the Hildebrandine ideal. The reforms attempted, realistic as they were, bore a theocratic stamp of the type that would have been fully approved by Charles the Great, or Otto the Great, or their successors. The separation of courts was tacitly reaffirmed, and detail was given of the discipline, royal discipline, in the way of fines, by which episcopal jurisdiction was to be made effective. Very important clauses dealt with the protection of priests, and here again royal discipline was essential. Priests were to be secure in their benefices against intrusion by vagrant monks, and also against abuse by landlords. An attempt, which probably succeeded, was made to uphold the status of a priest by insisting that a priest should give only accustomed service (i.e. that which had been paid at the time of King Edward) for his benefice. The most interesting feature of this reforming council was its actions relating to moral reform. These actions indicated the realism of the council, and indicated also the limitations imposed by that too zealous royal co-operation, against which advanced papal thinkers were agitating. Lanfranc attempted to impose the Christian marriage law, and to make the blessing of the priest necessary for a lawful marriage; but he was not successful. It was decreed that no man should give his daughter or kinswoman in marriage without priestly benediction. Much more remarkable was the council's attitude towards celibacy. The law of the church made provision for a celibate priesthood, but, particularly in the Germanic countries, the legal prohibition of marriage was ignored—or merely evaded. It is likely that most parish priests had their *focariae*. Responsible opinion was turning more to reaffirmation of celibacy, in part as the separation of function of the priesthood became more pronounced. Lanfranc conformed in prohibiting expressly (if not altogether effectively) the future marriage of priests; but he also ordained that there was to be no compulsion for parish priests to put aside their wives. 'For priests with wives, whether they live in towns (*castellis*) or in villages, are not to be compelled to put them to one side; those without wives are to be forbidden to take them; and henceforward let bishops take care not to presume to ordain priests or deacons, unless they first make sure they have no wives.'[6]

Much was left to the individual initiative of the bishop. An energetic moral reformer such as Wulfstan of Worcester had no hesitation: he gave his clergy the clear choice of their wives or their churches.

Norman reorganization of the secular church was on the whole effective. Diocesan administration was tightened, and the bishops were kept in close touch with the metropolitan and with each other. As in the secular field the smallness of the inner group tended to produce efficiency. Norman work for the regulars, the monastic churches, was also notable. Lanfranc introduced new customs for his monks at Christ Church, Canterbury, which were widely quoted and copied in other English monasteries. He took harsh action against monks who were disobedient to their abbot, and was particularly harsh towards the end of his archiepiscopate to the monks of St. Augustine's, Canterbury, who tried violently to resist the appointment of a new Norman abbot from Christ Church, Canterbury. Lanfranc also brought order into a sphere that affected monastic establishments directly, in pruning the list of English saints, perhaps with more vigour than discretion. But in the moral sphere his concern with monasteries was not as great as might be expected from the 'father of the monks'. It was in the field of organization that Lanfranc again excelled. Appointments were carefully scrutinized and, although there were no wholesale deprivations, there was a gradual Normanization of abbatial office. It has been estimated that of the twenty or so known abbots in 1073 no fewer than twelve were English; by 1083 there were still eight, but by 1088 one and by 1089 none, though Englishmen trained in new schools were later appointed to such offices. The greatest influence was Lanfranc's monastery of Bec, which under his guidance had developed into a reformed Benedictine house with emphasis fairly placed on intellectual achievement and organizing ability. It is odd to learn that King William (possibly in the later rather than the earlier years of his reign) looked to Cluny for support and asked for six of their best men, a request which fortunately was turned down; and that the one substantial royal foundation, Battle Abbey, set up on the site where Harold fell, was sponsored by Marmoutier-on-the-Loire and not by a Norman house. Lanfranc (who refused the archbishopric of Rouen) may have suffered a temporary loss of influence in 1067 when the critical decisions were taken. However, the practical help needed in England was available in Normandy, and especially at Bec.

The new 'Norman' abbots seem to have possessed one quality above all others, and that is the quality of energy. They did not breed saints among their numbers, but scholars, builders, and administrators, such as Abbot Gilbert Crispin of Westminster, Abbot Paul (Lanfranc's nephew) of St. Albans, and Abbot Serlo of Gloucester. There were occasional bad appointments. Abbot Thurstan turned his men-at-arms loose on the Saxon monks at Glastonbury, an outrage which provoked his temporary suspension from office by King William, though he was returned to some favour under Rufus. On two counts it is probable that the general Norman settlement had a deleterious effect upon the pastoral qualities of the abbots. Norman abbots were men of business, and their concern with secular affairs tended to take them away from their houses, to the scandal of the orthodox Benedictines. The acceptance of full feudal obligations involved an abbey and its administration in earthly, not to say earthy, considerations.

Lanfranc clearly discovered one peculiar English arrangement very much to his taste. The problem of finding suitable clergy to serve the cathedral church of a diocese had been solved in some of the greatest English sees by the organization of the cathedral on monastic lines. At Christ Church, Canterbury, Winchester,

Worcester, and Sherborne the cathedral clergy were, to all intents, monks bound to the strict observance of the Benedictine Rule. The Normans encouraged such development. Rochester copied the Christ Church example. The great house of Ely, after many vicissitudes, became the chief church of the new diocese of Ely in 1109. It seemed reasonable to the Norman business mind to extend this process, and to unite a rich abbey with a poor cathedral see, wherever possible. Successful unions were arranged between Bath and Wells, and Lichfield and Chester; unsuccessful attempts were made to join the abbey of Bury St. Edmunds to an East Anglian see, and Norwich eventually became the centre of the East Anglian diocese.

There were not a great number of new foundations as a result of the Conquest, although Chester (direct from Bec), Selby, Shrewsbury, Cranborne, and Tewkesbury all had great influence in their districts. Battle Abbey was peculiar; very much under the special protection of the ducal house, it was treated as the personal territorial church of the Conqueror, his profitable act of penance for Hastings. In its day it represented a quite amazing expenditure; masons and even some of the stones were transported across the Channel from Normandy and Tournai. Cluny's influence was not great in the first instance; but the most important private foundation, that of de Warenne at Lewes, was of a Cluniac house (1078–82). Cluny, because of its strong monarchical constitution, did not fit well to the needs of the conquerors; the example was followed and Cluniac priories were set up, but not on an extensive scale. A wealthy Londoner, Alwine, known as the Child, established such a priory at Bermondsey (1082–9). By 1160 there were thirty-six such foundations, some very small.

The question of alien priories demands some attention. The Normans found in their English possessions convenient resources for the endowment of their monastic houses at home. Some twenty Norman monasteries had received lands in England by the time of the Domesday survey. Intensive recent work on these endowments, notably by Mrs. Chibnall (*née* Morgan), enables some general conclusions to be made.[7] There was a natural tendency for lands on the south and south-east coast to be granted, and there was precedent for such grants from the reign of Edward the Confessor. Often churches or the revenues from churches would be sequestered for the use of alien houses. At times extensive manors, such as the great estates at Deerhurst Gloucestershire, would pass to foreign houses, in this instance to St. Denis, near Paris. The sheer weight of financial business involved in such transactions was considerable, and led to the foundation of small priories in this country. A house like St. Denis needed trusted agents who would look after the revenues drawn from its extensive endowments. The Norman house of Bec, as might be expected, was especially well favoured. Soon after the Conquest, Bec was munificiently endowed with land, first by Hugh of Chester, and then by Gilbert de Brionne. Under Henry I the Clare family proved great benefactors, and the shape of truly extensive holdings became apparent. Demesne was concentrated especially in the dioceses of Winchester, Salisbury, London, and Lincoln. Important priories were set up at St. Neots (Huntingdonshire), Stoke-by-Clare (Suffolk), Ogbourne (Wiltshire), which seems to have been the chief priory, Cowick (Devon), and Goldcliff (Monmouthshire). These dependent priories remained a permanent feature of the English medieval scene; the English loss of Normandy in 1204 made little difference; the priories contributed greatly to the universal European sentiments of the central Middle Ages. Bec did not lose her endowments until the last stages of the Hundred Years War; Cowick and Goldcliff both passed to Henry VI's new foundation at Eton.

Of almost equal importance to Bec in English affairs was the abbey of Jumièges. Its contact with England was strong during the reign of the Confessor, and remained so under the Norman kings. It has been estimated that between 1066 and 1130 about forty abbots or priors of cathedral monasteries were recruited directly from one or other of the twenty-six Norman abbeys, and that no fewer than fifteen of these (a number equalled only by Bec and her daughter-houses) came from Jumièges and the

daughter-houses of Sées and St. Évroul. William looked to
Jumièges for resolute men capable of dealing with difficult situa-
ations. In the first nine years of his reign he appointed Jumièges
men to the three critical abbacies of Westminster, Ely, and
Abingdon. Geoffrey of Westminster was not a success, and was
deposed in 1075; the other two were among the strongest abbots
in the country, Abingdon taking on special responsibility for
castle-guard at Windsor. Jumièges itself gained property in
England from the Conquest. Its chief priory was set up at Hayling Island, which was probably granted to it in 1067 when
William was present at the consecration of the new church at
Jumièges. Some English estates remained in its possession until
the early fifteenth century.

Norman monastic enterprise was particularly active in this
first generation of the Conquest in the South and the East, in the
prosperous lands from London to Winchester and Salisbury, and
in the group of houses on the fringes of the Fens. Stimulated by
Norman example, the English themselves were far from idle.
They were at their busiest in two areas; the West Midlands and
the North. Success in the West Midlands was largely the product
of the work of two extraordinary men: Wulfstan, bishop of
Worcester, and Aethelwig, abbot of Evesham. Wulfstan (of whom
a revealing biography has survived) was in a difficult position
immediately after the Conquest. He sensibly concentrated on his
diocesan work, particularly on his cathedral church at Worcester,
where the monastic community flourished under his direction.
There were only twelve monks there at the beginning of his
episcopate in 1063; there were fifty at the time of his death in
1095. Although some later writers gave him a reputation for holy
ignorance, Old English scholarship flourished under his direction;
the greater part of Heming's Cartulary was prepared, and the
background work done which made possible the chronicle
achievements of John and Florence of Worcester in the twelfth
century. Aethelwig of Evesham was a more formidable figure
politically, and indeed at one stage, Englishman as he was, acted
as a virtual viceroy in English Mercia. But he also increased the

number of monks from twelve to thirty, and stimulated contact overseas, including one fruitful and slightly exotic contact with the monastery of Odense in Denmark.

These two men appear to have provided the principal force behind the reintroduction of the monastic observance into Northumbria. There had been half-hearted attempts at Ripon and at Durham before 1066, but all that remained after the Conquest was the strong tradition of Bede, and the even stronger tradition of St. Cuthbert. Pilgrimages were still paid to St. Cuthbert's tomb. In 1073–4 Aldwin, a prior of Winchcombe, Reinfrid, a *conversus* of Evesham, and a monk, Aelfwig, re-established a monastic house at Jarrow; other small houses were set up at Tynemouth, Wearmouth, Whitby, and Durham. Helped by the fantastic Turgot, another knight turned ascetic of the type of Herluin of Bec, they extended the monastic revival to Scotland, to Melrose, and St. Andrews. A small house was set up at York. These new, unpretentious Benedictine houses were firmly established in Northumbria by 1100; they provide the context in which the later, dramatic, Cistercian movement could succeed. They also provide a somewhat neglected example of effective Norman and Anglo-Saxon co-operation in the first generation of the Conquest.

It remains to say something of the relationship of this active Anglo-Norman church to the papacy. In general King William and Archbishop Lanfranc were favourably regarded by the papacy; there were long years when they must have seemed to the papal curia the only respectable rulers in Western Europe. Friction came, however, on the matter of fealty. The papacy had a good case. William had to all appearances submitted his cause to a lord's court early in 1066 when he appealed to the curia. He had received a banner from the hands of papal legates. The customary payment of Peter's Pence from England was interpreted as proper tribute to the pope as overlord. This view was not weakened by events between 1066 and 1072. William left the delicate question of Stigand to papal legates. He showed great deference to the legates; he seems to have let himself be crowned a second time by them in 1070. Even after Lanfranc's election full respect was paid to Rome. The most difficult political question, the matter of the primacy of Canterbury, was submitted to the pope, and thence to the papal legates. There was much justification for the view that Norman England was a dependent fief. The Norman situation in South Italy must have appeared exactly similar to Pope Alexander II and to Hildebrand.

Yet the king also had a case, and his attitude towards the formal payment of fealty, always dubious, stiffened into absolute refusal, once Lanfranc's primacy was assured. Z. N. Brooke gives the best insight into William's attitude when he states that William, in appealing to the Pope in 1066, had appealed to 'an independent moral tribunal'. To many thinkers of the eleventh century the papacy was the source of authority and law, 'the hinge on which the whole church turned', but it was not the active master'[8] The pope was an arbiter, indeed the final arbiter, on earth. Direct government of the church was still matter for the archbishops and the episcopal order: provincial councils provided the unifying administrative force.

It is wrong to regard such councils as in any way an attempt to create a 'national' church. The moral authority of the pope was greatly respected. William was anxious to consult the papacy on all important ecclesiastical affairs, but in matters of government he continued to act in the tradition to which he had been accustomed in Normandy. He appointed to bishoprics and to abbacies. He treated papal legates as legates to the king. Papal decrees were not to be published without the royal consent; no investiture decrees were published in England until Anselm's return from exile early in the reign of Henry I. William continued to invest his prelates in England, as he had in Normandy—possibly an innovation on the English scene.

A crisis developed in the year 1079–80. Pope Gregory VII, at the height of his quarrel with the emperor, wanted to feel that he had a unified church behind him. He had already shown anger at Lanfranc's failure to visit him. He now summoned two bishops from the Norman and English provinces to attend his

Lenten Synod of 1080. Their failure to do so had to be seen to by a special embassy. Possibly arising from this immediate issue came a precipitation of the fealty crisis. In the famous letter of 8 May 1080 Hildebrand used the image of the sun and moon in referring to papal and royal authority; the one reflected the other. The letter may well have been accompanied by a request, verbal or in writing, for fealty. The request was refused shortly and sharply. William rejected the claim to fealty because he never promised it, and his predecessors never paid it. He promised to bring the payments of Peter's Pence up to date, and apologized because the money had been negligently collected during 'the past three years when I was in France'. He finished with the somewhat forbidding salutation that 'we always loved your predecessors and it is our earnest desire above all things to love you most sincerely'.[9] Hildebrand, who had just proceeded to his second, and politically injudicious, deposition of the emperor, could not afford to lose the royal love. The issue was, for the moment, settled.

Gregory continued to be indignant at Lanfranc's failure to visit him. A fresh crisis developed in 1082, probably because of Odo of Bayeux's ambitions, and some believe that Lanfranc may have visited the papacy at that stage. There could be no question of serious dispute, however, during the later years of Hildebrand's pontificate. The emperor had established his own antipope. Hildebrand had his hands full with Italian affairs. It is pleasing to note that he continued to be treated with respect by William and Lanfranc, in spite of a certain amount of imperial pressure on the Anglo-Normans to recognize the anti-pope.

For various reasons, therefore, the crisis of the Investiture Contest was delayed in England. Not until the early twelfth century did the struggle between church and state for effective control break out, to be settled by compromise. In the meantime the English church, secular and regular, was reformed along authoritative, traditional lines by the most fruitful co-operative effort of king and archbishop known to English history.

(c) *The government of the duchy*

William was by reputation and in fact one of the most active monarchs to have occupied the throne of England. He nevertheless remained a Norman, Duke William II of Normandy, and no account of his skill as a statesman would be complete which did not pay some attention to his work in the duchy. He spent much of his time there after 1066; interest in his new kingdom did not lead to neglect of his native duchy.

William faced a very difficult political situation in the north of France; indeed, his difficulties in later years underline both his good fortune and his capacity to take advantage of it in 1066. If Philip I of France had been more capable the Norman duke might well have been led to regret his cross-Channel adventures. As it was, William did not find it easy to maintain the successes of his early years. Brittany was restive, but his one full-scale attempt to settle the Breton problem was only partially successful, and his forces had to withdraw on a threat of Capetian movement from the south. His main troubles came from inside his own family, especially from his eldest son Robert Curthose. William had early made arrangements for him to succeed to the duchy, but the relationship between father and son was turbulent. A crisis occurred in 1078 when, to the scandal of all, Robert confronted his father in battle and wounded him. The reconciliation which followed was hollow, and Robert spent the last years of his father's life in active opposition. It is a reminder of the personal nature of the political scene to discover that William still honoured the pledge he had given 'before the Battle of Senlac', and conceded on his death-bed the duchy of Normandy to Robert 'because he is the first-born', and also, probably more significantly, because he had received the homage of practically all the barons of the 'patria'.[10] William rightly prophesied trouble for the duchy. He had no high opinion of Robert, whom he described as both proud and stupid. In the event Robert almost ruined the duchy, and it needed the best efforts, first of William Rufus, who held the duchy in pledge for

three years when Robert was away on Crusade, and then of
Henry I after his victory in 1106, to repair the damage caused
by their generous, feckless, elder brother. Robert himself survived as Henry's prisoner, first in Bristol, then in Cardiff, until
1134. He was well treated. Later stories of blinding and mutilation are false, as are also the stories in more pleasant vein of
Robert's reputed mastery of the Welsh language.

The political disasters which attended Robert's weakness—
similar in some respects to those which were to confront his
nephew Stephen of Blois in England a generation later—have
reflected back on William's own achievements in the duchy. In
the political sense it must be admitted that William's own testamentary arrangements destroyed the unity of England and Normandy, and that it needed the military and political skill of his
youngest son Henry I to re-establish the link, which was then
to survive, though not in unbroken form, for the greater part
of the twelfth century. One must be careful, however, not to
read modern ideas into medieval arrangements. The duchy and
the kingdom remained separate units. Yet within the duchy
there is evidence enough, though not as much as in England, to
suggest that William was successful in creating peace-giving
institutions.

There were parallels in the development of the two communities, and there were also natural differences. In ecclesiastical
affairs the Council of Lillebonne in 1080 provided an effective
statement of moral reform under ducal direction. This council
was so influential that more than eighty years later King Henry
II could use its decisions as an example of authoritative legislation in matters concerning ecclesiastical justice, and the limits
of jurisdiction of ecclesiastical courts. In secular matters there
is a danger in being too abstract. In the first generation of the
Norman Conquest there was much interaction and interchange.
The key men in William's council were the same on both sides
of the Channel. Experience gained in England undoubtedly
strengthened the duke's household, particularly in financial
affairs. But the greatest advance in modern scholarship has been

the realization that permanent advantage came to the ducal government in practical matters, relating to castle-building, control of the viscounts, or local government agents, and control also of judicial processes. It would be uncritical to relate all advance to direct copying of English institutions. The process is more complicated. Ultimately ducal institutions benefited most from the increased experience gained by numerous Norman agents who played a part in the strenuous task of governing the new acquisitions in England.

In Normandy, as in England, control of strategically placed castles was an outstanding feature of William's rule. It appears that knowledge of advanced techniques in the construction of substantial stone *donjons* had only recently reached the duchy on William's accession in 1035. There was much fortification building during the troubles of the minority, but stone castles remained few in number. Possession of such castles may indeed have been associated with the possession of comital rank. Count Guy certainly proved troublesome in his castle at Brionne, but it is worthy of note that the decisive engagements of the minority, and of the period of ducal recovery, were fought in the open field, at Val-ès-Dunes, at Mortemer, and at Varaville. Stone castles were fewer relatively in the duchy than in conquered England, but none the less important. Private, adulterine castles were the exception. William in his strength was able to insist on the obligation of his vassals to perform castle-guard and garrison duty for the ducal overlord. The troubles of Robert's early years as duke have obscured the strength of William's administration in this respect. Control of all important castles, and with them control of communications in the duchy, was very much a ducal preserve.

In legal affairs there are some interesting parallels with England. It was well said of William that if he controlled the people with arms he controlled the arms with laws. The duke retained the monopoly of higher justice. Some pleas were never granted to a subject, notably offences committed in the ducal host or within a week of setting out or coming back from it, offences concerning assault in the duke's court, or on the way to or from it, offences relating to coinage (the minting was limited in Normandy to Rouen and Bayeux), and offences against pilgrims. The count of Eu, a royal kinsman and one of his chief vassals, possessed in part at least of his very extensive estates in northeast Normandy all forfeitures except those relating to the duke's army and the coinage. Other offences were sometimes granted to the supervision of barons: *hamfara* (an attack on, or forcible entry into, a man's house), arson, rape, and murder. But the principle of delegation was stressed; such grants were grants from the duke. Similar delegation was known in England, but there is one important difference. Such offences appear to have been settled in Normandy in dominical courts. In England there was a survival of shire courts and hundred courts which was without parallel in Normandy. The viscounts, efficient as they might be, were expressly ducal officers; the English blend of popular and royal, of shire court and sheriff, was lacking.

There are other indications, too, of the turbulence and relative backwardness of Norman social development. In 1075 William issued decrees that attempted to limit the exercise of the blood-feud to those cases where a first cousin or nearer kin was concerned. Private war continued to be a scourge, though the duke's success in limiting both its outbreak and its results was considerable. Quite apart from the effect of his ordinances, his actions served to keep the Normans quiet. He provided the leadership in perilous enterprise needed to gain prestige and to keep the peace. And yet a comparison of William the duke with William the king points to one sure conclusion. There was more than mere legal abstraction to the mystery and sanction, popular and ecclesiastical, which surrounded eleventh-century kingship. William was a strong duke of Normandy; his reign was decisive in the establishment of public order and of a peace which was properly ducal; in England—with no reservations concerning outside overlordship—his actions were to that degree more confident, and his achievements more permanent.

1 W. H. Stevenson, 'A Contemporary Description of the Domesday Survey', *E.H.R.* 1907, p. 74; discussed fully by V. H. Galbraith, *The Making of Domesday Book*, Oxford, 1961, pp. 52–3
2 Galbraith, op. cit., p. 160
3 *Monasticon Anglicanum*, i, pp. 601–2; F. M. Stenton, *Anglo-Saxon England*, p. 642
4 *E.H.D.* ii, pp. 606–7
5 *Hugh the Chantor, History of the Church of York, 1066–1127*, ed. and trs. C. Johnson, London, 1961, pp. 3–4
6 Wilkins, *Concilia*, p. 367
7 See below (bibliographical note) p. 201
8 Z. N. Brooke, *The English Church and the Papacy*, Cambridge, 1931, particularly pp. 34–5 and pp. 132 ff.
9 *E.H.D.* ii, pp. 646–7; F. M. Stenton, *Anglo-Saxon England*, p. 667
10 *Ordericus Vitalis*, iv, p. 92; *E.H.D.* ii, p. 286: also William of Jumièges, p. 146; *E.H.D.* ii, pp. 279–80

Note: Table 3, p. 143 (*The making of Domesday Book*), was prepared by Mr Frearson, and is based on the work of Professor Galbraith, *The Making of Domesday Book*, Oxford, 1961. For further information on the construction of Domesday Book and its 'satellites' the reader is directed to Professor Galbraith's book, and to the relevant sections in *E.H.D.* ii, pp. 854–93. Recent work of great value on the 'satellites' includes P. H. Sawyer, 'Evesham A, a Domesday Text', *Worc. Hist. Soc. Miscellany*, I, Worcester, 1960, and R. Welldon Finn, *The Liber Exoniensis*, London, 1964.

The Effects of the Conquest

(a) *Some general effects*

WITHIN the scope of the present volume it is not possible to attempt a full analysis of the state of society in England in the late eleventh century. Yet no account of the Norman Conquest could pretend to be adequate if it failed to say something of the social changes, for most part accelerated rather than caused by the Norman triumphs. In the upper ranks of English society there was an almost complete revolution. Few Englishmen of the first order survived in positions of trust or great wealth, and those few, we may reasonably suggest, only by proving more Norman than the Normans. Thorkill of Arden possessed a huge fief in Warwickshire in 1086, consisting in part of lands of dispossessed fellow Englishmen. It was valued at more than £120, was assessed at over one hundred and thirty-five hides for the geld, and was calculated to be capable of supporting nearly two hundred and twenty ploughs. The value of the lands of the fief increased by almost exactly a third between 1066 and 1086. Thorkill had won a place for himself, presumably by zealous service as sheriff, in the new feudal world. Even so, his heirs did not continue to occupy his exalted position. The bulk of Thorkill's estates passed to the Norman, Henry of Beaumont, to augment the resources of the earldom of Warwick. Thorkill's heirs achieved modest fortune as military tenants of the great Warwick fief. Coleswain of Lincoln was the only other Englishman of comparable wealth and status at the end of the reign of the Conqueror, though some English merchants of London did very well for themselves financially. Coleswain was a complex character; he seems to have thrived on skilful building schemes in Lincoln, and to have extended his net from his urban headquarters. He did not found an enduring dynasty in contrast to Thorkill of Arden, and in contrast to the modestly endowed Eadnoth, father of Harding, and grandfather of Robert Fitz-Harding from whom the modern lords of Berkeley in Gloucestershire are descended. In the world of the church there were survivals. Leofric, bishop of Exeter, appointed in 1046, lived on to 1072. Acthelwig, abbot of Evesham, survived to 1077. Most famous of all, St. Wulfstan of Worcester, outlived the Conqueror himself, exercising his office for over thirty years, from 1062 to 1095. These men favoured the Conquest, and worked well with the Normans; they were exceptional, and by 1087 there were very few Englishmen prominent in the upper ranks of the English church.

This is no matter for surprise, as all students of the Normans will agree. They were skilled men at distributing the spoils, no doubt legally, but none the less completely. Norman control of the authority inherent in the possession of great estates, ecclesiastical or lay, was essential if the Norman settlement was to be secure. Further, it must be allowed that to many of the inhabitants of England, Norman bishops, abbots, and soldiers were to be preferred to the miseries of civil war and riot which were involved in the activities of an Eadric Wild or of a Hereward, though it is interesting to note that William of Poitiers, a well-informed witness to the early years of the settlement, complained that neither kindness nor severity sufficed to make the English prefer a quiet life (*quietam serenam*) to turbulent revolt.[1]

A clue is given to the general effects of the Norman Conquest by the influence of French upon the English vocabulary. This is a clue which has to be interpreted with caution. Many of the borrowings did not occur until well into the twelfth century. Social convention must be taken into account in any discussion of language evidence. Language and race are not synonymous.

The 'Dialogue of the Exchequer,' written late in the twelfth century, declared that English and Norman were so intermingled that 'it can scarcely be discerned at the present day—I speak of freemen alone—who is English and who is Norman by race'. William of Malmesbury had earlier recorded that the Normans intermarried with their subjects.[2] But the difference in intensity in the nature of the borrowing from French into English tells much of the social patterns imposed by the Conquest. There is very little borrowing in agriculture and fishing. There is heavy borrowing in administration, government, and law. 'Outlawry' and 'gallows' become pitiful English survivors in a legal vocabulary almost exclusively French. Heavy influence is also felt in matters concerning the social organization of the upper class, and in literary and cultural fields—a predominantly French feudal, literary, and architectural vocabulary. The language of commerce and of town life becomes predominantly French. It must be emphasized that these changes were not sudden, and yet the impression given by vocabulary that the changes brought about by the Norman Conquest were more marked in the upper reaches of society, in council, court, and town, than in village and field, is surely correct.

Language evidence concerns the long-term effects of the Conquest, and tells of the permanence of the settlement. It is convenient now to examine the immediate effects of the Conquest upon the inhabitants of England, perhaps one-tenth of whom were dwellers in towns, the remainder consisting of small-holders, lower clergy, cottagers, and slaves.

(b) *The towns*

The problem of the towns is the most clear-cut. Any notion that the Anglo-Saxons had no towns must be rejected. It is erroneous to suggest a sharp contrast between the rural Saxon and the urban Norman. Saxon towns had been developing steadily from the days of Alfred and his immediate successors. Some centres, such as Canterbury, London, Lincoln, and York, had indeed enjoyed continuous life as habitation sites with comparatively little break from the days of Roman Britain. As early as the seventh century, in the different context of early Anglo-Saxon England, these centres might properly be called towns. It would be unwise, however, to look for general urban development before the end of the ninth century and the beginning of the tenth. Active royal policy combined with genuine economic need led to a proliferation of towns in the course of the tenth and eleventh centuries. Communications had to be protected, fortifications (*burhs*) erected and maintained, and markets safeguarded. Anglo-Saxon kings and their advisers attempted unsuccessfully to control all trade through boroughs, where good witnesses could be found, royal officials established, and efficient mints set up. The safety of silver, the life-blood of commercial activity, was probably a very significant factor in provoking royal interest in the continued protection of the boroughs.

In 1066, therefore, roughly a century and a half of continuous, though at times precarious, urban development lay behind English town life. London was respected as one of the great towns of the northern world. Its population exceeded ten thousand, its governmental organization was elaborate, traders converged on it and were proud to win trading privileges within its walls. Rouen was small in comparison with it. To the north of the Humber York stood alone. Its numbers were swollen by constant movement across the North Sea, up the Humber and the Ouse. Its population cannot have lagged far behind London's, but the special position of York owed much to strategic, political, and administrative development, and the city was to suffer much as an immediate consequence of the Norman Conquest. More significant in many respects is urban development to the south of the Humber. In the Danish districts, to the north and east of Watling Street, there were a number of thriving mercantile settlements, notably the centres used originally by the Danish armies, the Five Boroughs of Lincoln, Nottingham, Derby, Leicester, and Stamford, together with Northampton, Thetford, Norwich, Cambridge, Bedford, and Colchester. In 'English' England urban development was more elaborate. A regular network of royal boroughs covered the country, from towns of great importance such as Chester, Worcester, Hereford, Gloucester, and Exeter to obscure little sites where a mint could be established and a safe place set up at the end of a day's journey from a bigger centre. Each shire had its shire town or towns. In the south, for different reasons, Winchester and Canterbury were especially conspicuous. Winchester was the favoured home of the West Saxon dynasty, and retained its importance as a centre of government in Norman times. Canterbury, with the long centuries of archiepiscopal prestige behind it, continued to be of the first importance in affairs of the church. Both enjoyed easy access to the Continent; Canterbury through Dover and the Cinque Ports, and Winchester through Southampton.

We must not, therefore, underestimate the importance of town-life in late Anglo-Saxon England. But neither should we underestimate the contribution the Normans were to make to its development. The Normans found towns much to their taste. Military necessity prompted concentration on control of roads and towns. Norman administrative efficiency also demanded the securing of centres at which officials could live in safety and to which great officers could come on their peregrinations of the country. Ecclesiastical reasons, the building of great cathedrals and abbeys, urged the further development of town life. Many Normans from their own background at home were also fully aware of the wealth and social importance of town-dwellers.

The immediate consequences of the Norman Conquest were not, however, uniformly helpful to English towns. In some places the heavy Norman hand did positive damage. York provides a good example. As a result of the unsuccessful risings of 1068–70, great physical devastation was caused in the city. Houses were destroyed, and two castles were built, one on each side of the river Ouse. The castles themselves were in the thick of the fighting, and were both reduced, though quickly rebuilt. William was at his most severe in the north. In 1086 the population of York appears to have dropped to only half of the 1066 figure, but King William demanded nearly twice the render made to

King Edward. Divorce from continuous contact with Scandinavian markets probably contributed to the decline of York. Not until the end of the reign of William Rufus did the city show signs of permanent recovery. Similar evidence of urban decline appears elsewhere in Domesday Book, especially in its accounts of tenements destroyed to make room for the new castles. At Lincoln no fewer than one hundred and sixty-six tenements were waste 'on account of the castle', and similar devastation is recorded elsewhere, for example, twenty-seven houses at Cambridge, twenty at Huntingdon, sixteen at Gloucester, and five at Stamford. It must not be assumed too readily, of course, that such destruction of tenements involved a substantial reduction in population; castles themselves were not uninhabited. Such destruction did involve a reduction in total rateable value, and either a loss in custom or an increased burden of payment for the survivors to bear. In some areas (such as York) a drop in the number of inhabitants between 1066 and 1086 is certain. Lincoln, for example, lost close on a sixth of its recorded inhabited houses between 1066 and 1080, the number falling from eleven hundred and fifty to nine hundred. Economic factors may well have applied here and elsewhere on the east coast. As a result of the events of 1066 and the succeeding years there was a slackening of trading contact with Scandinavia across the North Sea. Some of the towns of the east and the north-east Midlands suffered what would now be called a slight recession as a result of the swing of English interests south to the Romance world.

The absence of figures for London and for Winchester from Domesday Book makes it more difficult to estimate the immediate consequences of the Norman Conquest on the south and the south-east of England. Winchester, to judge from an early twelfth-century survey, was not then at the height of its prosperity. Yet it is likely that both centres, and particularly London, were stimulated by the Norman Conquest and the resulting centralization.

In some respects the Normans undoubtedly furthered urban

development. Immigration of traders was deliberately fostered, and many Normans quickly found an opening for their activities in England. In Norwich so many *Franci* were introduced that reference is made to the 'new borough'. Elsewhere there are numerous references to similar intrusions. When it came to framing customs and defining rights and dues, Normandy often provided the inspiration. Particularly in the West Country, along the border between English and Welsh, the laws of the little Norman borough of Breteuil provided the basis for the new borough charters in which the lord set out the concessions and liberties he was prepared to accord to his burgesses.

The framing in legal form of borough charters was mostly a matter for the second and third generation of the Norman conquerors. In late Anglo-Saxon England borough charters were unknown, and the mediatized borough was a rarity. Direct royal control was the outstanding characteristic of the Anglo-Saxon borough. Apart from the Kentish examples of Sandwich, Hythe, Seasalter, and Fordwich, only Durham and Dunwich were in non-royal hands in 1066. The earls were closely connected with the boroughs, and they normally shared the profits of the borough with the king, one part, the famous 'third penny', to the earl, to two parts to the king. As a result of the Conquest and the consequent rebellions the earl's share often passed also to the king. Only in special cases was this not so. On the Marches of Wales the earls of Chester and Shrewsbury, Hugh Lupus and Roger of Montgomery, appointed after the great rebellion of 1069–70, enjoyed palatine powers in their counties and over their county boroughs. William FitzOsbern enjoyed similar privileges in Herefordshire, and apparently in parts of Gloucestershire and Worcestershire, until his death in 1071. His son, Roger Fitz-William, succeeded to most of this great inheritance, only to lose all by his ill-judged rebellion in 1075. The special privileges accorded to the earls of Hereford were not renewed, but in the north similar palatine powers were granted to the bishop of Durham from 1080 in an attempt to stabilize the perilous northern frontier. Elsewhere the earl's title did not necessarily carry such privilege, and many shires were left without earls. Even in Cornwall, where the king's half-brother, Robert of Mortain, possessed very extensive estates, it is almost certain that Robert was not known as the earl of Cornwall. In Wiltshire and in Somersetshire the earl's third penny was accounted for by the sheriff to the king, and the boroughs were entered on royal land.

The retention of royal rights over boroughs, and notably over county boroughs, was countered to some extent by an increase in mediatization of smaller boroughs. This development was fully in line with continental feudal practice. At times old urban settlements passed under the effective control of a lord, perhaps a bishop or an abbot, such as the abbot of Bury St. Edmunds. At other times new settlements sprang up around the chief dwelling of a lord. At Tutbury, the *caput* of the great Ferrers fief, there were in 1086 forty-two men who lived by trade alone. As a sign of the growth and complexity of social life it became possible for such settlement to be dignified with the name of borough. This is partly a constitutional question. In Anglo-Saxon days the borough was distinguished by a special peace, a special legal protection, a *burh*-right that stood apart from the land-right which surrounded it. Gradually the idea grew that a special charter was the best way of defining borough rights. The London writ of the Conqueror, to which reference was made in an earlier chapter, represents a groping after a more systematic definition of custom. Most interesting and fruitful of all experiments were those which occurred in the West Country. These new Norman lords, faced with a body of customs which they and their officers could only partially understand, tended to introduce customs which were known to them on the continent. It is an indication of parallelism in development between England and Normandy that such customs could be introduced into the conquered territory, though in the first place the new customs were sometimes meant to apply to the Frenchmen alone.

What in fact did such customs involve? A practical example at this stage might be helpful. The borough of Hereford had suffered severely during the Welsh wars of the reign of the Confcssor. Even so, in 1066 there were one hundred and three tenements established within and without the city wall. The customs were set out in great detail.[3] The city was treated as royal demesne over which the king had three special forfeitures of one hundred shillings from all men guilty of breach of peace, of assault within a house, and of assault from ambush. Arrangements were made so that anyone wishing to sell a tenement could do so without loss of service to the king. Landgable was fixed at sevenpence halfpenny within the walls, and at fourpence halfpenny without the walls. Miscellaneous regulations dealt with the conditions for performance of reaping service, escort duty, hunting duty, guarding the king's person, military service, and the payment of heriots. The services of brewers, smiths, and moneyers (responsible men exercising rights of jurisdiction themselves) were enumerated. Most significant of all for our immediate purposes, we are told that different conditions applied to the foreigners (*francigeni* as opposed to *anglici burgenses*) who were burgesses. They were treated differently from the native burgesses, enjoying the privilege of a modest twelve-pence penalty for all forfeitures, apart from the special royal pleas. Similar arrangements, with specific reference to the customs of Hereford and Breteuil, were made by Earl Hugh of Chester and Robert of Rhuddlan for their new borough at Rhuddlan. According to a twelfth-century compilation which preserves some of William the Conqueror's laws, a distinction was made between the Normans who settled before the Conquest and those who settled afterwards:

'And each Frenchman who, settled in England in the time of King Edward, my kinsman, was subject to the customs of the English (which they call lot and scot), shall pay (or "be paid for" in some manuscripts) according to the law of the English.'[4]

Attractive conditions were established with the direct intention of encouraging Norman tradesmen and artisans to set themselves up in English towns, old and new. In two respects Norman discipline and organization proved very effective in relation to institutions already mature in Anglo-Saxon days: the market and the mint. Marketing was a complicated process. A great city such as London needed an elaborate system of courts in order to keep check on transactions which could range from large-scale marketing of foreign produce to the sale of butter by market-women on the quayside. Anglo-Saxon kings, after their unsuccessful efforts to confine marketing to boroughs, had endeavoured to bring order into the processes by insisting on the presence of good witnesses to all important transactions. Supervision of these witnesses and of the taking of the testimony of the witnesses became a very valued perquisite. The Normans carried the whole system to its logical conclusion. The lord guaranteed the market; in return he received a substantial profit from the market. It was simple then to extend the legal aspect of the situation to the point where a lord could set up a market. Subject to an over-riding royal supervision, and often to reservations implied in that royal right, the lord would grant a charter to the inhabitants of a township, setting out their privileges and duties. About 1100 Robert Fitzhamon granted such a charter to Burford, placing the inhabitants of that obscure rural community on the same footing as the burgesses of the proud borough of Oxford; they were to have the guild and customs which the burgesses of Oxford had in their guild-merchant. The great charter of Henry I to London in 1130 (though it had force only for a single decade) was the first to grant some measure of self-government. Exemption from financial and judicial impositions was the common privilege accorded a borough, and early Norman charters did little more than define a state of affairs implied in late Anglo-Saxon England, and brought to fruition after the Norman Conquest. On the Marches of Wales there was further elaboration of the burghal pattern. The establishment of a new lordship led automatically to the setting up of a borough at its chief seat. Robert Fitzhamon in Cardiff and Bernard of Neufmarché in Brecon both founded such dominical boroughs. Fitzhamon's successor, Earl Robert of Gloucester, later granted to the burgesses of Cardiff rights and customs identical to those of his burgesses at Tewkesbury. As an example of the intensification of urban life in the west, Tewkesbury is a good instance to note; in the Gloucestershire folios of Domesday Book it is recorded as a 'new' market, recently set up by Queen Edith, the wife of Edward the Confessor.

It became commonplace for relatively small markets to pass under the control of one lord. In some parts of the country the typical pattern of lord's castle, protected borough, and important church was drawn in the first generation of the Conquest. The complex borough was a different proposition. Already before 1066 the big boroughs were notable for what F. W. Maitland described in an informative but unhappy phrase as heterogeneity of tenure; that is to say, men of many lords lived in the borough. Heterogeneity of jurisdiction followed as a matter of course, and in the days of the Norman definer London, York, Norwich, Oxford, and other boroughs of similar rank presented an elaborate honeycomb of rights and jursidictions. Simplification came in the course of time from the source of authority, namely from the reserved royal power. The golden road to municipal freedom lay through the farm of the customs of the borough, the extension of the farm to the citizens themselves, the acquisition of charters, which slowly came to incorporate some of the principles of self-government, and finally in the advanced boroughs the stirring of aspirations towards the status of a commune. In parts of Western Europe such communes were accepted into the feudal hierarchy, bearing in somewhat incongruous fashion the characteristics of a corporate tenant-in-chief. The immediate consequence of the Norman Conquest in England was to increase (at times to a great extent) the farm of the borough, that is to say the lump sum paid to the lord of the borough for his financial rights. Oxford in 1086 was paying a farm of £60, almost double the figure paid in 1066, and other boroughs, both bigger and smaller, were paying farms often twenty or twenty-five per cent greater than the sums paid in 1066.[5] Emphasis in the early Norman period is on regularization, definition, and exaction. Struggle for charters of liberty and enhanced status came in a later age.

One aspect of urban life has received a great deal of attention in recent years: the problem of mints, moneyers, and the striking of coins. It is likely that in late Anglo-Saxon days possession of a mint, at which current silver pennies could be struck, was an attribute of every royal borough. The safeguarding of silver, the striking of coin, and the protection of the standard of the currency, may indeed be seen as among the most important of burghal duties. The Norman Conquest had no effect on the technical processes of minting; methods of blanching and assaying, familiar in England before 1066, continued to be operated. The weight of coins was somewhat increased, but moneyers continued to be drawn from the same class, and English and Danish names predominate among them to at least the end of the eleventh century. Some differences may, however, be ascribed in part to the Normans. A few of the smaller mints of the Anglo-Saxon period disappeared, although the range of minting was extended to some new areas from which coins were previously unknown, such as Cardiff, Rhuddlan, and possibly St. David's (*Devitun*). The most interesting innovation was the imposition of a regular tax known as *monetagium*. This may well have been a composition paid to the king, a general levy to make sure that the king did not lose over the exchange of coins from type to type, a makeweight to cover the cost of the somewhat heavier coinage. By 1100 this levy had come to be regarded as an abuse, and Henry I's Coronation Charter made specific mention of it. Henry I forbade the *monetagium commune* to be levied in the towns and shires on the grounds—probably accurate—that it had not been so levied in the days of King Edward. Coinage remained a regalian privilege, in marked contrast to the situation in France.

In general the main characteristic of eleventh-century English towns was continuity in development. Only in its military aspects did the Norman town differ substantially from its Saxon predecessor. The establishment of castles, partly to overawe the urban inhabitants, partly to act as administrative headquarters for royal and feudal officers, was the most conspicuous change in urban organization and in urban appearance.

(c) *The countryside*

Similar continuity is also the theme of those who attempt to analyse the impact of the Norman Conquest upon English rural society. Peculiarities in the structure of rural society in the late Anglo-Saxon period persisted, and the freedom of the Kentish and East Anglian peasants, the old-fashioned tenures of Northumbria and the Northern Danelaw, and the greater coherence of the manors in South and West England—to mention only the clearest examples—can be traced through medieval English history, and can still be identified as late as the sixteenth century. Over much of England the plough was king, and, where topographical conditions allowed, the 'typical' settlement was of a nucleated village with the great open fields, more often two than three, radiating out from the village centre. It is possible that we have consistently underestimated the non-arable elements in the rural economy. It is bookish to attempt to separate too clearly the corn-grower from the stock-raiser, as any farmer knows. Meadow, pasture, and rights in woodland are essential to the cultivation of the arable. The oxen which pulled the plough had to be fed and looked after. It is likely that sheep were very important, and there are many who think that the apparent lack of concern of the Domesday commissioners with sheep in many areas has led to a distortion of the true agrarian situation. In East Anglia and in Essex, to be sure, the high values of some Domesday manors with relatively little arable are best explained as the product of sheep-raising and wool production.

A relative economic uniformity was not accompanied by a corresponding social uniformity. Kent, as always, retained its special characteristics. Apart from the considerable ecclesiastical estates attached to Christ Church, Canterbury, and to St. Augustine's, and to a lesser extent to the cathedral church at Rochester, the estates of Kent were organized on a much more compact family basis. Gavelkind, partible inheritance, was the normal form of peasant tenure; smaller fields privately owned with partible rights to pasture in the Weald (sometimes quite remote from the main holding) was the outstanding rural characteristic. The main lines of social division in England, however, lay along a relatively recent political border—Watling Street and the river Lea, the dividing line between 'English' England and the Danelaw. Either directly or indirectly as a result of the Danish invasions, social differences were pronounced between the two regions. Church, state, and secular lordship were more highly developed in the south and west. Manorial organization was also more highly developed. The manor tended to correspond more exactly with the village, and the hold of the manorial lord on his officers was more personal, immediate, and presumably more effective. In the Danelaw it was possible for as many as ten so-called 'manors' to exist in one village, and the incomplete manors, where the village community itself retained rights and duties, were much more frequent and obvious in the north and east, notably in East Anglia and in Cambridgeshire. We must remember that the manor is essentially the super-structure to the agrarian community. But it would be wrong to neglect the social importance of the manor. For many of the peasants social discipline, social cohesion, was no more than vague generalization until the discipline of the lord made itself felt in the manorial court.

Now it is true that this great regional difference persisted in spite of the Norman Conquest. Yet it is also true that the coming of the Normans had a considerable impact on the rural com-munities of England. Their coming brought changes, partly in-direct, and a consequence of their new sharpened authority, but none the less real for that. These changes were derived from two principal sources: the Norman attitude to land and the Norman desire to exploit the land successfully. We have touched on both these matters in an earlier chapter, but it is as well now to bring them together in this final survey.

The Norman attitude to land was much more clear-cut than that of their Anglo-Saxon predecessors. William claimed an ownership of land so different in degree as almost to be different in kind from that enjoyed by the Anglo-Saxon kings. He was the successor of Edward, but he had won his right to succeed by the sword. His initial actions show that he intended to assert a control of land-holding, which was an extension of Anglo-Saxon royal privilege. He permitted those who had fought against him to buy their lands back. No simple right of lordship over land was involved; it was direct royal ownership that was being asserted. Many were guaranteed a certain right to succeed to their father's inheritance; it was a qualified right to be exercised in a context of landownership which was new. As head of a feudal hierarchy, William was accustomed in Normandy to the idea that all land depended upon him as effective feudal overlord; he proceeded to apply that idea to England, where it was unfamiliar. There was a strong tendency for personal lordship over men to be transformed into lordship over land.

It was also in part from feudal ideas that a difference in attitude to the exploitation of land stems. This is not a simple matter. The Normans were, it is true, happy to take what they could from their new kingdom; they were also prepared to give. Resources were available; resources were also used. Norman peace and Norman discipline were expensive; and ultimately the peasant paid.

Some of the most valuable modern investigation has discussed the methods by which this canalization of resources was achieved. It is undoubtedly true that much more land was leased than used to be thought. There was indeed a much stronger commercial attitude towards land than an earlier generation considered likely. The royal court dispensed patronage by the grant of estates, but these estates were no mere abstractions. Only a part of the estates so granted, possibly roughly a half of many lay fiefs, was kept in the lord's demesne and farmed by his officers directly for the production of food. Some land was leased out to military tenants in return for military service; much more was farmed in the financial sense, that is to say let out to other men who would try to make a profit on the transaction. At the highest level very important men would be only too pleased to obtain a lease on royal estates in return for a fixed sum, the farm of the manor. In some counties the sheriff, in others an officer known as the *custos regis*, took over the responsibility for farming the royal manors. In Huntingdonshire, for example, many royal manors were in the hands of Ranulf, brother of Ilger, who performed a similar function elsewhere, notably in Essex. Ranulf was also a considerable tenant-in-chief, who held land direct from the king in eight Domesday counties. Such transactions were commonplace also on the lands of the tenants-in-chief, particularly the ecclesiastical tenants-in-chief. Some of the greatest families of the twelfth century acquired their position by successful handling of other men's estates. The real puzzles emerge when we consider what happened a further stage down in the social scale. Plumberow (a manor in Hockley, Essex) was held of Suen by Ascelin; it was worth, in 1086, forty shillings, presumably the sum received by Suen. How did he receive his forty shillings, and in what form? We know that the formidable Suen, who had been sheriff of Essex and may have been the chief Domesday commissioner for the Eastern Counties, never turned his hand to the plough; presumably the money was paid in hard cash to him by Ascelin. But, then, how did Ascelin in his turn take his profit? Here again it is exceedingly unlikely that he busied himself with agrarian matters; he was a prominent and active subtenant, and though there were such who showed a flair for estate management (R. Lennard has shown us one splendid example of an improving landlord at work in the person of Ernulf de Hesdin, a tenant-in-chief at that), such men were rare.[6] Ascelin would put in a reeve to administer the estates, to look after the dominical rights, and in the absence of Ascelin, the immediate lord, to preside over any court that might be held to settle disputes over service, stock, or agrarian routine. It is exceedingly difficult to discover who were the reeves, what their race, or what their status. Reeves had a bad reputation, but they were, for all the complaints, our first experts in estate management. There is a high probability that they were local men who knew local conditions and who knew what was possible; it was considered right and seemly that a village should be represented by a reeve, a priest, and six men before the Domesday commissioners.

The fullest evidence concerning the reeves occurs in an Anglo-Saxon document, composed at latest in the generation immediately preceding the Norman Conquest. It is a little tract on the duties of a reeve, known as *Gerefa*, probably written as an appendage to the important survey of ranks and conditions on a late Anglo-Saxon estate, which appears under the forbidding title of the *Rectitudines Singularum Personarum*.[7] The reeve was especially enjoined to look after his master's interests, and also to respect the custom of the community. The Normans used such men, and where possible intruded men of their own choice. Like all new masters they no doubt used their rights to the full. It may well be believed that, where ambiguity existed, ambiguity was resolved in the lord's favour. The Normans had a tough and more flexible instrument of coercion at their disposal in their military arm. They were better placed to insist on manorial discipline than their Anglo-Saxon predecessors, though it is true that the well-ordered Anglo-Saxon manors, where they existed, gave them all that they needed in the way of legal right.

What effect had this increase of manorial discipline and efficiency upon the men who actually worked the land, upon the peasantry itself? Efficiency, as well as tyranny, can lead to hardship. In some areas marked increase in rents exacted seems to signify exploitation. It is generally agreed that there was some depression of the peasantry as a result of the Conquest. The evidence is not clear-cut; the great hurdle faces the inquirer of distinguishing between social and legal depression. Particularly intricate is the problem of peasant freedom. To be free meant different things at different times, and the Domesday survey itself, full and valuable as it is, recorded only imperfectly the elaborate gradations of English society. A high percentage of the peasantry in 1066—over ninety per cent of the recorded population—was legally free; an even higher percentage was free in this strict sense in 1086. At first sight this is somewhat surprising. Should we modify our views on Norman discipline, organization, and manorialization? Is William I no more than a benevolent despot, encouraging emancipation, suppressing the slave-trade, by policy and action moving to check what Anselm later referred to as the iniquitous practices of the Anglo-Saxons, when men were sold like brute beasts? Difference in stages of social development rather than personal humanitarian scruples provide the best reason for the relatively enlightened Norman attitude on this matter. The more Romanic and feudal world of ducal Normandy drew a strong line of social distinction between noble and simple but a much weaker line between simple and unfree. The more Germanic world of Anglo-Saxon England drew its line of social distinction firmly between free and unfree. A freeman possessed a wergeld, was oath-worthy, was justicable at a public tribunal, and could be answerable for the payment of his own taxes. In parts of England some men of modest estate, simple *ceorlas*, held land with a freedom of tenure that was hard to reconcile with the demands of the feudal world. They could go with their lands whither they would. All these were matters of great moment, and continued to be so for the first two generations after the Conquest. Freemen continued to pay their dues, their hearth-pennies, their church-scot, even as a freemen ought. The author of the compilation known as the *Leges Henrici Primi*, an anonymous clerk, probably of Winchester, who wrote towards the end of the second decade of the twelfth century, reproduced in the course of his extensive survey voluminous extracts from Anglo-Saxon law, notably the secular laws of Canute, as matters for guidance to doomsmen in contemporary local courts. The compilation was, however, already in its days somewhat antiquated. The new concentration on efficient royal justice, extending downwards into popular courts, was making unnecessary an ineffective older insistence on personal free status, or the possession of a wergeld, or the right to receive compensation (*bot*). In criminal matters emphasis was thrown on punishment rather than on compensation; thus prompting Maitland's graphic comment that 'the gallows is a great leveller'.[8] Matters concerning freehold land came to be decided on the evidence of a sworn jury of neighbours before a royal justice; in civil affairs generally the final stages were reached in a process already clearly foreshadowed in the last centuries of Anglo-Saxon England—the authority and sanction of free kindreds diminished as the power of the lord and the range of activities of the king increased.

It is true already in 1086 that if the absolute number of 'freemen' was high and the percentage of 'freemen' higher than in 1066, nevertheless the significance of the freedom was less. The peasants were classified into five main groups: *liberi homines*, sokemen, *villani*, bordars, and cottars. The *liberi homines* were almost exclusively confined to East Anglia, were responsible for the payment of their own geld, and were practically free from manorial jurisdiction; at most they had commended themselves to a lord who would help them at legal need. Their number dropped significantly between 1066 and 1086, and there are a number of specific references to their absorption into existing or newly formed manors. But their presence persisted, and even as late in the thirteenth century the East Anglian peasantry exhibited a marked independence. The sokemen differed from the *liberi homines* only in that their legal obligations to the lord to whom they had commended themselves were more exact and exacting. In large numbers they were concentrated in the Anglo-Danish counties, notably in Lincolnshire and in Leicestershire. Again there was a marked diminution in number of this group of peasants. The *villani* were a different proposition. They were by far the most numerous group, nearly two-fifths of the recorded total, which is not surprising when it is realized that the term itself was not technical, but was rather the equivalent of the Anglo-Saxon villagers (*tunesmen*), and that a *villanus* was recognized, with inevitable variation, as the typical member of a group of peasant cultivators. In many districts a *villanus* would hold about thirty acres of arable. Bordars and cottars were also numerous—nearly a third of the recorded population. They were probably the craftsmen, the general handymen, who also possessed their cottages and modest shares of the arable. No appreciable difference in their distribution or number appears to have occurred as a result of the Norman Conquest, except in Essex, where some of the *servi* of 1066 were upgraded to bordars.

All these men, no matter how poor in economic resources, were free in law. The slaves, the *servi*, were recorded carefully in some districts, possibly not so carefully in others, but were always kept separate from the free peasants with their share in the arable. They were not without rights. Very rarely, as in some curious Somersetshire entries, they were said to have a share in the plough beasts. But generally speaking their subjection was marked in both the legal and the social spheres. They had no rights of access to public tribunals. He stole alone, who stole accompanied by a slave. The slave did not possess arable on which he could feed his family. He had no rights in meadow, pasture, or woodland, the normal privileges of the free villager. His work was at will. Only custom and common sense protected him. At law there was little suggestion of compensation, though a small wergeld was sometimes paid to the kindred of a slave. He was a man from whom no right could be had save his hide, subject to the harsh discipline of the lash and mutilation, the outsider in rural society. Servile status could be transmitted by blood, though it was possible for a man to free himself of the servile taint. Economic conditions had more to do with social mobility than has always been recognized. It had been regarded as possible for a slave to own property; such ownership would lead to rapid amelioration of personal status and condition.

A notable improvement in the position of the slave took place as the consequence of the Norman Conquest. There was no out-and-out suppression of slavery, though it is clear that some responsible opinion, especially among the Anglo-Saxon and Norman clergy, was opposed to the institution. But slavers were still operating from Bristol during the episcopate of Wulfstan of Worcester. The importance of the Scandinavian world, and in particular of the Scandinavian colonizing expeditions to the islands around Britain and to Iceland, have not been thoroughly appreciated in relation to what seems to have been something of a revival of slavery, at least in the north, in the tenth and early eleventh centuries. A Scandinavian thrall was not the same as a classical slave. The former was bound in an extra-legal relationship to a master who had virtually power of life and death over him; the latter was bound in some respects more strictly in a legal relationship. The former was in an immediate relationship to his master, subject to household discipline; the latter could be subjected to the discipline of the state. Slaves in late Anglo-Saxon England seem to have been found predominantly on great estates; the *ceorl* in the eleventh century, no matter what might have been the position earlier, was not normally a slave-owner. But a great church, or a powerful lay lord, particularly if their estates lay to the west, could well record the presence of a dozen slaves or even more on a single manor.

The distribution of slaves in Domesday Book possesses features of interest. There were few in the north; generally the Anglo-Danish counties had markedly fewer, either because not recorded or more likely because they did not fit easily into the economy. It was more profitable to have a subjected peasant who could feed himself than a slave who had to be fed. Slaves were especially numerous in the counties bordering the Celtic communities, and there may be a racial reason for this: captives in war could be enslaved. Altogether more than twenty-five thousand *servi* were mentioned in the Domesday survey in 1086. The most substantial reduction in numbers appears to have occurred in the Eastern Counties. Essex is a particularly interesting example; as was mentioned above, some of the *servi* of 1066 were entered in the survey as bordars: the functional occupation of ploughmen, presumably on the lord's demesne, was of more interest to the new Norman masters than were any fine distinctions of personal status. For many reasons the distinction between free and unfree peasant became less important in early Norman England. By the end of the reign of Henry I slavery had virtually disappeared as a significant social institution in England.

All, however, was not gain. The general effect of the Conquest on the peasantry was not of amelioration as much as a general levelling. Over much of the country rents increased and the imposition of labour services grew more onerous. The process was slow. Not until the end of the twelfth century can it be said to have been completed. But the direction towards a more uniform serfdom was evident from the earliest days after the Conquest, and can clearly be disentangled from the complicated statistics provided by Domesday Book. By 1200 *servus* and *villanus* were virtually interchangeable words. Men subject to labour service on the lord's demesne, answerable for misdeeds at the lord's manorial court, were indiscriminately serfs or villeins.

Yet one is left at the end with the feeling that the great achievement of the Normans was to systematize, and in some respects to accelerate, changes which were already implicit in the Anglo-Saxon social structure. The manor was perfectly familiar to the Anglo-Saxon; it was for its day the most efficient method of wresting sustenance from the soil. Norman internal peace and concentration on the production of a proper surplus merely provided the means by which the process could be completed.

(d) *Conclusion*

On Thursday, 9 September 1087, in a year notorious for fires pestilence, and famine, King William I died at the priory of St. Gervais, near Rouen. The Anglo-Saxon chronicler praised him for his good peace, and for his political triumphs. Wales was subject to him and his castle-building; Scotland had been subdued; and we are assured that Ireland would have been his, by astuteness and without the use of weapons, if he had been granted another two years. The dark side was not concealed: avarice, oppression, and especially the protection of game by savage penal laws:

> For he loved the stags as much
> As if he had been their father.

Norman witnesses, who wrote when he was still in his prime, glowed with their set-pieces of praise. Those who wrote after his death were more critical. Ordericus Vitalis, using the device of a long death-bed speech to give an account of the reign, portrayed a complicated character, aware more of the sins of doing than of the joys of things done, 'stained with the rivers of blood' which he had shed, and especially sensitive of his harrying of the North, where 'innumerable multitudes, particularly in the county of York' had perished through his actions by famine or the sword. His piety was represented as more than skin-deep, a theme dwelt on by an anonymous monk of Caen, who gave, in a series of sentences drawn mostly from Einhard's *Life of Charlemagne* but partly from personal observation, a forceful impression of the Conqueror which stressed his physical strength, his piety, and his moderation both in eating and in drinking. The monk's variations from Einhard are as revealing as his borrowings. Einhard described Charles as fluent (almost to the point of garrulity), but referred to his voice as clear though not as strong as might be expected. The monk of Caen gratefully borrowed the phrases referring to fluency but added that William's voice was harsh.

'In speech he was fluent and persuasive, being skilled at all time in making clear his will. If his voice was harsh, what he said was always suited to the occasion. He followed the Christian discipline in which he had been brought up from childhood, and whenever his health permitted he regularly, and with great piety, attènded Christian worship each morning and evening and at the celebration of mass.'

'Being skilled at all time in making clear his will' (*poteratque quicquid vellet apertissime expellere*) is a splendid phrase, which gives a clue to William's extraordinary success in the public, oral, world of the eleventh century. This harsh, dignified soldier rarely failed to make known his purpose, whether in his native duchy or in his new kingdom of England.

He was succeeded in his kingdom by his second surviving son, William Rufus, 1087–1100, then by his youngest son Henry, 1100–35. The sons of the Conqueror completed the work of their father. Normandy, for a period left in the perilous care of the feckless Robert, 1087–1106, was restored to the fold of the Anglo-Norman monarchy after the Battle of Tinchebrai, 1106. Norman enterprise in the Mediterranean and in the Near East was helped by recruits from England as well as from the duchy. The Norman conquest of Sicily was completed by 1091; attention has recently been drawn to surveying techniques in the island which may have some relation to the great enterprise of Domesday Book itself. A contingent from Normandy, led by Duke Robert himself, played a prominent part in the First Crusade, side by side with the glamorous Normans from South Italy and Sicily, led by Bohemund and his nephew Tancred. Among the company that set out from the Holy Land was Robert's uncle, Odo, bishop of Bayeux, one of the principal men behind the Norman Conquest of England, and—as many believe—probably the chief architect in detail of the settlement. He died at Palermo in February 1097. The sons of Count Eustace II of Boulogne survived: Eustace III, the eldest, to play a somewhat undistinguished part in Anglo-French affairs, and in the Crusade, before retiring to the cloister in 1125; Godfrey to become first advocate of the Holy Sepulchre; Baldwin to be crowned first king of Jerusalem (1100–17). A new, cosmopolitan flavour was given to the Anglo-Norman aristocracy. King Canute, Earl Godwin, Earl Tostig, and Earl Harold were given splendid welcomes on their continental journeys, but they were treated, for all the respect paid to their generosity, as men from a distant, Christian yet different, world. With men such as Odo of Bayeux, Geoffrey of Coutances, Eustace of Boulogne, Lanfranc, and Anselm we are at the heart of Christendom. They belong to Europe; their place is central in European history. The Europeans would say of them 'they are one of us'.

In England itself the whole period was notable for the building up of royal institutions of government. Under Henry I, youngest son of the Conqueror, the process went far, and provoked some reaction during the troubles and unrest of Stephen's reign. It seems a far cry indeed from the efficiency of Henry's justiciars, and of the Exchequer, to the heavy gelds and the occasional ravagings in the name of discipline which occurred spasmodically in the first half of the eleventh century. It is a far cry also from the subtleties and logical refinements of Anselm's thought to the straightforward and simple homilies of Aelfric, or from the massive achievement of the Tower, Durham, or St. Albans to the finery of Earl's Barton or Barton-on-Humber. Yet, as we said earlier, it would be wrong to attribute all growth to the Normans alone. The eleventh century brought about a solid increase in absolute wealth in Western Europe, probably the product of more effective agrarian techniques and of more effective means of maintaining peace within a community. Ultimately freedom from barbarian invasion may be taken as the root cause of the progress of the eleventh century. Feudalism in this respect was a constructive force.

In the field of institutions continuity is the essential theme of English history. The monarchy, the shire courts, the hundreds with their courts, the towns, the geld system of assessment and collection were all products of Anglo-Saxon experience and skill. The principal means and instruments of royal administration, the royal chapel, the solemn charter, and the sealed writ were familiar in late Anglo-Saxon days. The very coinage and system of weights and measures were convenient and fostered by the Norman conquerors. Only in their feudal attributes do the Normans appear as conspicuous innovators. Elsewhere it is as constructive builders on solid Anglo-Saxon achievements that their principal virtues find expression.

1   William of Poitiers, p. 264
2   *E.H.D.* ii, p. 523, and p. 291
3   *D.B.* i, 179; *V.C.H.* Herefordshire i, pp. 309–11
4   Willelmi I Articuli, c. 4; Liebermann i, p. 487; *The Laws of the Kings of England from Edmund to Henry I* ed. and trs. A. J. Robertson, pp. 238–9
5   J. Tait, *The Medieval Borough*, Manchester, 1936, p. 184
6   *D.B.* ii, 45; R. Lennard, *Rural England, 1086–1135*, Oxford, 1959, pp. 210–12
7   *E.H.D.* ii, pp. 813–16; *Gerefa* in Liebermann i, pp. 453–5
8   F. W. Maitland, *Domesday Book and Beyond*, Cambridge, 1897, p. 32; reprinted (Fontana Books, 1960), p. 58
9   *E.H.D.* ii, p. 280; appendix to William of Jumièges, p. 149

BIBLIOGRAPHICAL NOTE

This selective note is intended for those who wish to carry further their studies of the Norman Conquest. For the most part it follows the arrangement and order of the present volume. Full bibliographical information is to be found in the second edition of D. C. Douglas and G. W. Greenaway, *English Historical Documents*, vol. ii, *AD 1042–1189* (London, 1981; first ed. 1953), a volume which also contains excellent critical comments on original sources. An outstanding addition to easily available primary evidence comes from the new edition of *Ordericus Vitalis* by Marjorie Chibnall, *The Ecclesiastical History of Orderic Vitalis* (six vols., Oxford Medieval Texts, Oxford, 1969–80).

Much of this note will be concerned with recent, or relatively recent, work. D. C. Douglas has given a masterly account of William I and his period in *William the Conqueror* (London, 1964), an authoritative book which is particularly strong on early Norman history. Commemoration essays issued in 1966 included *The Norman Conquest: its setting and impact*, ed. C. T. Chevallier (Eyre and Spottiswoode for the Battle and District Historical Society) and the lectures published by the Historical Association for its Hastings and Bexhill Branch (including F. Barlow on 'Edward the Confessor', H. R. Loyn on 'Harold Godwinsson' and J. Le Patourel on 'Norman Barons'). Among more recent work that of J. Le Patourel has been exceptionally valuable with its proper emphasis on the Norman Conquest as a colonizing movement. Also of great importance has been the contribution of R. Allen Brown both personally and through his creation and active editing of the proceedings of the Battle Historical Conference (Woodbridge, 1979, etc., referred to below under individual articles as *Battle Conference 1978*, etc.). Among older work, there is still much of permanent value in E. A. Freeman, *History of the Norman Conquest* (five vols. and Index, London, 1867–79, and subsequent editions), in F. W. Maitland, *Domesday Book and Beyond* (Cambridge, 1897; reprinted by Fontana Books, with an introduction by E. Miller, London, 1960) and in the work of J. H. Round, W. J. Corbett (in the Cambridge Medieval History) and P. Vinogradoff.

Chapters 1 and 2

(a) *The European background* R. W. Southern, *The Making of the Middle Ages* (London, 1953) and Marc Bloch, *Feudal Society* (two vols., Paris, 1939–40; trs. London, 1961) provide the essential background. Good introductions to various aspects of the age are given by G. Barraclough, *Medieval Germany* (two vols., London, 1938), R. Fawtier, *The Capetian Kings of France* (Paris, 1942; trs. London, 1960), E. Hallam, *Capetian France, 987–1328* (London, 1980) and Sir Steven Runciman, *History of the Crusades*, vol. 1 (Cambridge, 1951). C. H. Haskins, *The Normans in European History* (Boston, 1915) is still valuable as a vigorous treatment of the topic, but J. Le Patourel, *The Norman Empire* (Oxford, 1976) should now be treated as authoritative for its generation. R. H. C. Davies, *The Normans and their Myth* (London, 1976) provides a valuable correction to undue adulation of intrinsic Norman virtue. An appreciation of the sensitive modern approach to social and institutional problems in early medieval France is best gained from the studies of O. Guillot, *Le comté d'Anjou et son entourage au XIe siècle* (Paris, 1972), T. Reuter (ed.), *The Medieval Nobility* (Amsterdam, New York and Oxford, 1978) and E. Hallam, 'The King and the Princes in Eleventh-Century France', *B.I.H.R.* (1980).

(b) *The Norman duchy and the Norman church* D. R. Bates,

Normandy before 1066 (forthcoming), M. de Bouard (ed.), *Histoire de la Normandie* (Toulouse, 1970) and the work of D. C. Douglas and J. Le Patourel provide dependable modern guides. The periodical *Annales de Normandie*, ed. M. de Bouard (Caen, 1951–), is the best means of keeping in touch with Norman studies. Particularly valuable are the contributions of M. de Bouard, Lucien Musset, J. Adigard des Gautries (on place-names and personal names), and of Jean Yver. Frequent references occur in the periodical to historians of an earlier generation, such as L. Delisle and H. Prentout. Much important original material has been edited by Mme Fauroux in her *Recueil des Actes des Ducs de Normandie de 911 à 1066* (Caen, 1961).

The following studies are especially useful: H. Prentout, *Histoire de Guillaume le Conquérant*, vol. I, 'Le Duc de Normandie' (Caen, 1936), D. C. Douglas, 'The Earliest Norman Counts', *E.H.R.* (1946) and 'The Rise of Normandy' (British Academy, 1947), M. de Bouard, 'De la Neustrie Carolingienne a la Normandie féodale', *B.I.H.R.* (1955) and *Guillaume le Conquérant* (Paris, 1958), Jean Yver, 'Les châteaux forts en Normandie', *Bull. de la Société des Antiquaires de Normandie* (Rouen, 1957), J. Boussard, 'Les destinées de la Neustrie du IXe au XIe siècle', *Cahiers de civilisation médiévale, x–xiie siècles* (Poitiers, 1968), J. Yver, 'Les premiers institutions du duché de Normandie', *I Normanni e la loro espansione in Europa nell'alto medioevo* (Spoleto, 1968) and 'Le "Très Ancien Coutumier" de Normandie, miroir de la legislation ducale?', *Revue d'histoire du droit: Tijdschrift voor rechtsgeschiedenis*, vol. xxxix (Groningen, Brussels and the Hague, 1971), J. Le Patourel, 'The Norman Colonization of Britain', *I Normanni e la loro espansione in Europa nell'alto medioevo* (Spoleto, 1969), *Normandy and England, 1066–1144* (Reading, 1971) and 'The Norman Succession, 996–1135', *E.H.R.* (1971), Lucien Musset, 'Pour l'étude comparative de deux fondations politiques des Vikings: le royaume d'York et le duché de Rouen', *Northern History*, vol. x (1975), *Essays in Honour of John Le Patourel* (Leeds, 1975) and 'L'aristocratie normande au XIe siècle', *La noblesse au moyen age, XIe siècles: Essais a la mémoire de Robert Boutrouche,* ed. P. Contamine (Paris, 1976).

On ecclesiastical history special attention is drawn to J. Le Patourel, 'Geoffrey, bishop of Coutances', *E.H.R.* (1944) and to D. C. Douglas, 'The bishops of Normandy, 1035–66', *Cambridge Historical Journal* (1957). There is much valuable material in *Jumièges* (Congrès scientifique du xiiie siècle, Rouen, 1955), including articles by Dom David Knowles, Marjorie Chibnall, C. T. Clay, and D. C. Douglas. Mrs Chibnall (neé Marjorie Morgan) has made many important contributions to Anglo-Norman monastic history, especially *The English Lands of the Abbey of Bec* (Oxford, 1946), and an article on 'Ecclesiastical Patronage and the Growth of Feudal Estates at the Time of the Norman Conquest', *Annales de Normandie* (1958).

(c) *The Normans in England before 1066* J. H. Round, 'The Normans in England under Edward the Confessor', *Feudal England* (London, 1895) still repays careful attention. There is interesting material in J. Ritchie, *The Normans in England before the Norman Conquest* (Exeter, 1948) and in A. Campbell's valuable introduction to his edition of the *Encomium Emmae Reginae* (Camden series, London, 1949). D. C. Douglas has published an important article in *E.H.R.* (1953), 'Edward the Confessor, Duke William of Normandy, and the English Succession'; see also J. S. Beckerman, 'Succession in Normandy, 1087, and in England, 1066: the role of testamentary custom', *Speculum* (1972). The best indication of recent advance on the cultural side comes from G. Zarnecki, 'Romanesque Sculpture in Normandy and England in the Eleventh Century', *Battle Conference 1978*, and R. D. H. Gem, 'The Romanesque Rebuilding of Westminster Abbey', with a reconstruction by W. T. Ball, *Battle Conference 1980.*

Chapters 3 and 4

(a) *The English background* F. M. Stenton, *Anglo-Saxon England* (3rd ed., Oxford 1971) and D. Whitelock, *The Beginnings of English Society* (Pelican Books, 1952) provide the essential background. F. Barlow has written a reliable modern biography of *Edward the Confessor* (London, 1970), following his fine edition of the *Vita Ædwardi* (Nelson's Medieval Texts, London, 1962). He has also presented a thorough and reliable constitutional history of the church in late Anglo-Saxon England in *The English Church, 1000–1066* (London, 1963). Other studies of value include R. R. Darlington, 'Ecclesiastical Reform in the late Old English Period', *History* (1937), H. R. Loyn, 'The King and the Structure of Society in Late Anglo-Saxon England', *History* (1957), D. Bethurum, 'Regnum and Sacerdotium in the Early Eleventh Century', *England before the Conquest*, ed. P. Clemoes and K. Hughes (Cambridge, 1971), N. Brooks, 'Anglo-Saxon Charters: the work of the last twenty years', *Anglo-Saxon England*, vol. 3, ed. P. Clemoes (Cambridge, 1974), H. R. Loyn, 'Church and State in England in the Tenth and Eleventh Centuries', *Tenth-Century Studies*, ed. D. Parsons (Chichester, 1975) and Ann Williams, 'Land and Power in the Eleventh Century: the estates of Harold Godwinsson', *Battle Conference 1980*. There is much of importance for these chapters and also as background to Chapter 6 in Simon Keynes, *The Diplomas of King Æthelred 'the Unready', 978–1016* (Cambridge, 1980).

(b) *The events of 1066* The best introduction remains the edition of *The Bayeux Tapestry*, ed. F. M. Stenton (London, 1957). It should now be read in conjunction with the valuable article by N. P. Brooks (and the late H. E. Walker), 'The Authority and Interpretation of the Bayeux Tapestry', *Battle Conference 1978*. Important studies of the Old English army include the early chapters of M. R. Powicke, *Military Obligations in Medieval England* (Oxford, 1962) and C. W. Hollister, *Anglo-Saxon Military Institutions* (Oxford, 1962). The most reliable account of the battle of Hastings is that of R. Allen Brown, 'The Battle of Hastings', *Battle Conference 1980*. Great interest was aroused by the new edition of the *Carmen de Hastingae Proelio of Guy of Amiens*, by Catherine Morton and Hope Muntz (Oxford,

1972), and a discussion led by R. H. C. Davis, L. J. Engels *et al.* appears in *Battle Conference 1979.*

Chapter 5: Conquest and settlement

Good short introductions to the problems are provided in R. R. Darlington, *The Norman Conquest* (London, 1963), R. H. C. Davis, 'The Norman Conquest', *History* (1966), R. Allen Brown, 'The Norman Conquest', *T.R.H.S.* (1967), J. Le Patourel, *Normandy and England, 1066–1144* (Reading, 1971) and 'The Norman Conquest, 1066, 1106, 1154?', *Battle Conference 1978.* The most important single paper to appear in recent years on the general nature of the conquest and settlement is probably the essay by J. Le Patourel, 'The Norman Colonization of Britain', *I Normanni e la loro espansione in Europa nell'alto medioevo* (Spoleto, 1969). Reliable accounts and interpretations appear in F. M. Stenton, *Anglo-Saxon England*, F. Barlow, *The Feudal Kingdom of England* (London, 1955), G. W. S. Barrow, *Feudal Britain* (London, 1955), C. N. L. Brooke, *From Alfred to Henry III* (London, 1962) and *Saxon and Norman Kings* (London, 1963), F. Barlow, *William I and the Norman Conquest* (London, 1966) and R. Allen Brown, *The Normans and the Norman Conquest* (London, 1969). F. M. Stenton gives what is still within its terms of reference a definitive guide to feudal problems in *The First Century of English Feudalism* (2nd ed., Oxford, 1961). Other useful studies of the feudal question are: C. Stephenson, 'Feudalism and its Antecedents in Anglo-Saxon England', *A.H.R.* (1942–3), C. W. Hollister, 'The Norman Conquest and the Genesis of English Feudalism', *A.H.R.* (1961), J. C. Holt, 'Feudalism Revisited', *Econ.H.R.* (1961) and J. O. Prestwich, 'Anglo-Norman Feudalism', *Past and Present* (1963). Among numerous special studies, mention should be made of H. A. Cronne, 'The Salisbury Oath', *History* (1934), D. C. Douglas, 'The Companions of the Conqueror', *History* (1943) and the introduction to *Domesday Monachorum of Christ Church, Canterbury* (Royal Historical Society, London, 1944), F. M. Stenton, 'English Families and the Norman Conquest', *T.R.H.S.*

(1944), M. Hollings, 'The Survival of the Five-hide Unit in the western Midlands', *E.H.R.* (1948), L. C. Loyd, *The Origin of some Anglo-Norman Families* (Harleian Society, Godalming, 1951), J. G. Edwards, 'The Normans and the Welsh March' (British Academy, London, 1956), B. D. Lyon, the relevant section of *A Constitutional and Legal History of Medieval England* (New York, 1960) and D. R. Cook, 'The Norman Military Revolutions in England', *Battle Conference 1978.* I. J. Sanders, *English Baronies: a study of their origin and descent* (Oxford, 1960) provides a very useful work of reference to the feudal world, and R. H. M. Dolley, *The Norman Conquest and the English Coinage* (London, 1966), a study of fundamental importance on a complicated and important aspect.

Chapter 6: Norman government in state, church and duchy

The chief constructive developments in this field have come in connection with Domesday Book studies. V. H. Galbraith, *The Making of Domesday Book* (Oxford, 1961) and *Domesday Book, its place in Administrative History* (Oxford, 1974) established authoritatively the probable method by which the record was made. R. Welldon Finn also made a valuable contribution, notably in his *Introduction to Domesday Book* (London, 1963; with excellent bibliographical guides). Further advance of the first importance has been made by Sally Harvey, notably in 'Domesday Book and its Predecessors', *E.H.R.* (1971) and 'Domesday Book and Anglo-Norman Governance', *T.R.H.S.* (1975). Other useful studies include Edmund King, 'Domesday Studies', *History* (1973), J. Campbell, 'Observations on English Government from the Tenth to the Twelfth Centuries', *T.R.H.S.* (1975; with valuable comment on continental parallels), and H. R. Loyn, 'Domesday Book', *Battle Conference 1978.* F. E. Harmer, *Anglo-Saxon Writs* (Manchester, 1952), R. C. Van Caenegem, *Royal Writs in England from the Conquest to Glanvill*

(Selden Society, London, 1959), the relevant section of F. J. West, *The Justiciorship in England, 1066–1232* (Cambridge, 1966) and D. R. Bates, 'The Land Pleas of William I's Reign, Penenden Heath Revisited', *B.I.H.R.* (1978) present much valuable material. The introductions to *E.H.D.* ii and to the first two volumes of the *Regesta Regum Anglo-Normannorum*, ed. H. W. C. Davis (Oxford, 1913) and C. Johnson and H. A. Cronne (Oxford, 1956) repay careful study, as does the work of T. A. M. Bishop and Pierre Chaplais in the *Facsimiles of English Royal Writs to A.D. 1100* (Oxford, 1957). S. B. Chrimes, *An Introduction to the Administrative History of Medieval England* (2nd ed., Oxford, 1959) provides a reliable general analysis of the problems.

For the Anglo-Norman Church F. Barlow, *The English Church, 1066–1154* (London, 1979) is now the basic guide. Z. N. Brooke, *The English Church and the Papacy* (Cambridge, 1931) remains valuable, though modified by the work of later scholars. M. Gibson, *Lanfranc of Bec* (Oxford, 1978), has written a good modern biography, and much original material is available in *The Letters of Lanfranc, Archbishop of Canterbury*, ed. H. Clover and M. Gibson (Oxford, 1979). There is an important article on Odo by D. R. Bates, 'The Character and Career of Odo, Bishop of Bayeux', in *Speculum* (1975), and the work of R. A. L. Smith on 'The Place of Gundulf in the Anglo-Norman Church', *E.H.R.* (1944) remains important. C. Morris, 'William I and the Church Courts', *E.H.R.* (1967) advances understanding of the legal side of the work of William and Lanfranc. Dom David Knowles, *The Monastic Order in England* (Cambridge, 1940), the magisterial work on monasticism, sheds much light also on the general structure of the Anglo-Norman church. H. P. R. Finberg, *Tavistock Abbey* (Cambridge, 1951), E. Miller, *The Abbey Bishopric of Ely* (Cambridge, 1952) and E. King, *Peterborough Abbey, 1086–1310: a study in the land market* (Cambridge, 1973) provide valuable regional studies. R. W. Southern's *The Life of St. Anselm* (Oxford, 1963) has replaced all previous general work on Anselm.

Chapter 7: The general effects of the Conquest

The outstanding contribution of the last generation has been that of R. Lennard, *Rural England, 1086–1135* (Oxford, 1959). The older work of F. W. Maitland and P. Vinogradoff remains extremely important. The best regional studies are by F. M. Stenton, *Types of Manorial Structure in the Northern Danelaw* (Oxford, 1910) and by D. C. Douglas, *The Social Structure of Medieval East Anglia* (Oxford, 1927). The work of scholars such as Stenton, J. H. Round, and R. R. Darlington in analysing and translating the Domesday Book accounts of individual counties in the Victoria County History remains of enduring value. H. C. Darby and his helpers have brought their splendid surveys of the *Domesday Geography of England* to a successful close (Cambridge, 1952–79). For urban development, J. Tait, *The Medieval English Borough* (Manchester, 1936) and S. Reynolds, *An Introduction to the History of English Medieval Towns* (Oxford, 1977) give reliable guides. C. N. L. Brooke (assisted by Gillian Keir), *London 800–1216: the shaping of a city* (London, 1975) and Martin Biddle *et al.* (eds.), *Winchester in the Early Middle Ages: an edition of and discussion of the Winton Domesday* (Winchester Studies, vol. i, Oxford, 1976) give the best insight into modern work in progress. G. Zarnecki, *English Romanesque Sculpture, 1066–1140* (London, 1951) remains an indispensable guide.

INDEX

ABINGDON, 116, 119, 132, 133, 164
Abingdon Chronicle, 98
Adam, Domesday commissioner, 146
Adela, countess of Blois, 93
Adelaide, daughter of Robert I of Normandy, 33
Aelfgar, earl of Mercia, 66, 69
Aelfgeard of Worcester, 50
Aelfgifu of Northampton, 62
Aelfheah, archbishop of Canterbury, 156
Aelfmar, 74
Aelfric, abbot of Eynsham, 83, 197
Aelfric, archbishop, 55, 74
Aelfstan, abbot, 74
Aelfwig, abbot of Winchester, 104
Aelfwig, monk, 165
Aethelmaer, bishop of Elmham, 155
Aethelnoth, abbot of Glastonbury, 104
Aethelnoth, archbishop of Canterbury, 74
Aethelric, 74
Aethelwig, abbot of Evesham, 109, 129, 152, 164, 174
Aethelwine, knight (son of Brihtmær), 133
Aimery, viscount of Thouars, 120
Alan the Red, 121
Aldborough, 90
Aldermaston, 69
Aldwin, prior of Winchcombe, 165
Alençon, 42
Alexander II, Pope, 48
Alfred, king of Wessex, 70, 73, 102, 175
Alfred, prince, 52, 63
Alice, daughter of Richard II of Normandy, 25

Alwine, the Child, 162
Anglo-Saxon (language), 137, 144
Anglo-Saxon Chronicle, 55, 57, 79, 88, 91, 114, 137, 140, 144, 148
Anjou, 14, 17, 19, 26–7, 40, 68, 87
Anselm of Aosta, archbishop of Canterbury, 48, 49, 79, 133, 166, 190, 196, 197
Antioch, 30
Aosta, 80
Apulia, 28, 31
Aquitaine, 17, 26
Arques, 39
Arundel, 124, 129
Asbjorn, 106
Ascelin, 188
Athelhelm, abbot of Abingdon, 133
Athelstan, king, 70, 73
Avranches, 45

BALDWIN, abbot of Bury St. Edmunds, 56, 132, 134
Baldwin IV, count of Flanders, 25
Baldwin V, count of Flanders, 43, 44, 51, 88
Baldwin, king of Jerusalem, 196
Baldwin, son of Herluin, 50
Barking, 103
baronage, 14, 42, 115–17, 125–31, 142, 168, 171
  honorial, 127–30
Barton-on-Humber, 197
Bassett (family), 142
Bath, 162
Battle Abbey, 93, 98, 161, 162
Baudri, abbot of Bourgueil, 95
Baudri FitzNicholas, 28
Bayeux, 45, 124, 171
  see of, 39, 45, 132
  Tapestry, 58, 91–6

Bec, 47–9, 157, 161–3
Becket, Thomas, 158
Bede, 165
Bedford, 176
Bellême, 33, 36, 46
Benedict of St. More, 23
Benedict, Pope, 81
Benedictine Order, 48, 49, 83, 161, 162, 165
Beorn Estrithsson, 63, 64
Berengar of Tours, 47
Berkeley (Harding family), 174
Berkhamstead, 99
Berkshire, 78, 82, 98, 116
Bermondsey, 162
Bernard (chaplain), 52
Bernard of Neufmarché (Brecon), 30, 182
Besançon, 80
le Bessin, 20, 37
bishops, consecration of, 81, 155
Blois, 17
blood-feud, 171
Bohemund, 30, 196
Bonneville, 58
bookland, 76
boroughs, 69, 72, 149, 175 etc., 182
de Bouard, Prof. M., 23, 36
Brand, abbot of Peterborough, 104
Brecon, 109, 182
Breteuil, 179, 181
Bretons, 21, 42, 94, 121, 126
Brionne, 38–9, 170
Bristol, 169, 192
Bristol Channel, 61, 63, 69, 90, 93
Brittany, 97, 114, 168
Brooke, Prof. Z. N., 166
Burford, 182
Burgundy, 38, 39
Burton, 82
Bury St. Edmunds, 56, 132–4, 162
  abbot of, 130, 135, 180
Byrhtnoth, earl, 77, 79

CAEN, 37, 40, 48, 195
Caerleon, 125
Cambridge, 105, 176, 178
  -shire, 186
Canterbury, 99, 175, 177
  archbishops, 55, 71, 108
  Christ Church, 74, 83, 131, 160, 161, 185
  St. Augustine's, 156, 160, 185

see of, 64, 82, 130, 133, 137, 152, 155, 156, 166
Canute, king of England, 19, 51–4, 63, 68, 71–4, 77, 83, 87, 196
  laws, 190
Capetians, 16–17, 25–6, 39, 70, 101, 168
Cardiff, 169, 182, 184
Carolingian Empire, 15
Carolingian minuscule, 148
carucage, 149
castles, 36, 38–40, 92, 102, 103, 105–7, 110, 119, 125–6, 138, 170, 177
cavalry, 30, 93–7, 112
celibacy, 46, 82, 159
chancellor, 73, 104, 141, 144
chancery, 40, 144
Chanson de Geste, 25
Charles the Simple, 20, 21
Chertsey, abbey, 80
Cheshire, 68, 75
Chester, 69, 72, 95, 107, 158, 162, 177, 179
Chibnall, Mrs. Marjorie, 162
Chichester, 158
Church, 13–15, 38, 44 etc., 67, 70, 79 etc., 87, 108, 131 etc.
  and Papacy, 165 etc.
  government, 153 etc.
Cinque Ports, 65, 78, 177
de Cioches (family), 119
Cistercian Order, 49, 165
Clare (family), 124, 163
Clarendon, 131
Clavering, 126
Clifford, 125
Clinton (family), 142
Cluny, 48, 161, 162
Cnut, son of Danish king, 110
coinage, 72, 150–1, 171, 184; see also mints
Colchester, 176
Coleswain of Lincoln, 173, 174
communes, 183
Conan, duke of Brittany, 42
constables, 114, 131
Constance, 26
Constantinople, 87, 117
Copsi, earl, 89, 103, 106
Cordova, Caliphate of, 14
Cornwall, 75, 180
coronation
  anointing, 70, 139
  ceremony, 15, 99, 105, 138, 166
  charter, 142, 184

consecration, 71, 155
  oath, 139
Cotentin, 21, 37, 49
Coucy de, 110
councils, ecclesiastical, 154–9, 166, 168
  papal, 43, 80
  royal, 69, 107, 124, 128, 130, 139–42
Courts, 18, 40, 182, 188
  ducal, 58, 143
  ecclesiastical, 82, 159, 169
  papal, 27, 156
  private, 126, 129 (honorial), 165, 171, 186, 194
  public (shire and hundred), 18, 69, 71, 73, 118, 141, 146, 149, 152–3, 157, 171, 190
  royal, 19, 27, 54, 76, 112, 124, 141, 151, 187
  see also *Curia Regis*, Exchequer, Honour
Coutances, 45, 46, 109, 132
Coventry, 82
Cowick (Devon), 163
Cranborne, 162
Crediton, 158
Crowland, 82
Crusades, 14, 29, 196
Curia Regis, 141, 151
Cynesige of York, 81

DANEGELD, 71
Danelaw, 23, 49, 52, 82, 185, 186
Danes, 19, 63, 87, 104, 106–7, 110, 129, 132; see also Scandinavia
Deerhurst (Glos.), 163
demesne, 125, 128, 163
  lord's, 187, 193–4
  royal, 40, 68, 75, 181
Derby, 176
Devon, 125, 126, 127
Dialogue of the Exchequer, 175
Dives, 120
Domesday Book, 72, 75, 76, 99, 104, 117–20, 125, 129, 132, 135, 144–50, 152, 178, 183, 193, 196
Domesday Inquest, 95, 146, 152
  commissioners, 146, 185, 188, 189
  Survey, 99, 140, 153, 189, 193
Dorchester-on-Thames, 79, 80, 156, 158
Douglas, Prof. D. C., 57, 58, 120, 124, 198
Dover, 58, 64, 119, 177

Dreux, count of Nantes, 52
Dublin, 65
Dudo of St. Quentin, 20, 21
dues, 18, 39, 116, 149, 179, 190
Duncan, 108
Dunster, 127
Dunwich, 179
Durham, 106, 146, 156, 165, 179, 197

EADNOTH, 174
Eadric Wild, 106, 107, 174
Eadsige, bishop, 74
Ealdred, archbishop of York, 71, 81, 82, 86, 98, 99, 106, 154, 155
earldom, 67 etc.
  earl's 'third penny', 179, 180
Earl's Barton, 197
East Anglia, 54, 63, 66, 68, 69, 82, 150, 158, 162, 185, 186, 191
Edgar, king of England, 77, 102
Edgar the Aetheling, 57, 99, 103–7
Edith Swannehals, 86
Edith, wife of Edward Confessor, 63, 65, 183
Edith, wife of Harold II, 86
Edith (Matilda), wife of Henry I, 105
Edmund Ironside, king of England, 52, 87
Edward Confessor, king of England, 16, 50–79, 85, 87, 92, 99, 102–4, 120, 132, 138, 142–4, 150–3, 163, 180, 181, 184
Edward Aetheling, son of Edmund Ironside, 56, 70, 99
Edwin, earl of Mercia, 66–8, 86, 89, 90, 96, 103–8
Einhard (*Life of Charlemagne*), 195
Elmham, 81, 104, 144, 155, 158
Ely, 80, 82, 108, 162, 164
  abbot of, 152
Emma, sister of Roger, earl of Hereford, 109
Emma, wife of king Ethelred and of king Canute, 50–3
enfeoffment, 128, 131–4
Ermenfred, bishop of Sitten, 154
Ernost, bishop of Rochester, 48
Ernulf de Hesdin, 188
Essex, 66, 75, 79, 125, 146, 147, 150, 185, 187, 192, 193
Estrith, sister of king Canute, 87
Ethelred, king of England, 49–52, 65, 71, 79, 87

Eton, 163
Eu, 39
  count of, 171
Eustace II, count of Boulogne, 64,
  95, 121, 125, 196
Evesham, 83, 132, 165
Évreux, 39, 45, 132
Ewias Harold, 54, 125
Exchequer, 142, 151, 196
Exeter, 50, 105, 137, 158, 177
  Exeter Domesday Book, 149

FALAISE, 33, 37, 120
fealty, 58, 86, 124, 134, 165, 166, 167
Fécamp, 25, 26, 46, 48, 52
Fens (the), 108, 164
de Ferrers (family), 180
feudal institutions, 14, 102, 108, 187
  etc.
  rights, 40
  service, 39, 44, 76, 111, 128 etc.
  see also fief and Honour
fief, 16–19, 25, 26, 30, 40, 44, 68, 76,
  103, 110–36, 173, 187
  money-fiefs, 114
  papal, 166
  subinfeudation, 114–29
  see also Honour
Finberg, Prof. H. P. R., 134
FitzGilbert (Clare family), 124
FitzsObern (family), 124
Flanders, 17, 20, 27, 43, 44, 51, 61,
  65, 86, 88, 89, 114, 129
Florence, 46
Florence of Worcester, 85, 86, 137,
  164
folk-burdens, 76
Fordwich, 179
Forest, Law of, 150
Foreville, Mlle Raymonde, 58
freemen, 18, 189 etc.
French language, 174
Fulbert, 33
Fulford, 86, 89, 96, 98
fyrd, 76–9, 89, 90, 115

GALBRAITH, Prof. V. H., 147
gavelkind, 185
geld, 71, 76, 103, 147, 149, 152, 173,
  190, 191, 195
  see also Danegeld
Geoffrey, abbot of Westminster, 164
Geoffrey, bishop of Coutances, 46,
  109–10, 121, 141, 151, 152, 196

Geoffrey, count of Anjou, 42
Geoffrey of Mandeville, 125
Geoffrey of Mowbray, see Geoffrey,
  bishop of Coutances
Geoffrey, son of Rotrou, 121
Gerefa, 189
Germany, 12, 14, 16–18, 27, 87, 159
Gilbert, count of Brionne, 35, 163
Gilbert Crispin, abbot of West-
  minster, 161
Giso, bishop of Wells, 80
Glamorgan, 109
Glastonbury, 129, 132
Gloucester, 144, 177, 178
  abbey, 82
  -shire, 64, 79, 127, 174, 179, 183
Godfrey, Protector of the Holy
  Sepulchre, 196
Godgifu, 52, 64
Godred Crovan, 90
Godwin, earl of Wessex, 52, 55–7,
  61–5, 75, 77, 81, 196
  House of, 68, 69, 105
Goldcliff (Mon.), 163
Gospatric, earl, 105
Gregory VII, Pope (Hildebrand),
  29, 80, 154, 166–7
Grimold of Plessis, 37
Gruffyd ap Llywelyn, 66
Gundulf, bishop of Rochester, 48,
  154
Guy, count of Brionne, 37–9, 170
Guy of Amiens, 95
Guy of Ponthieu, 95
Gwynedd, 109
Gyrth, son of Godwin, 63, 66, 94, 98
Gytha, wife of Godwin, 63

HAKON, 57
Hamo Dapifer, count of Eu, 130, 150
Hampshire, 51, 82
Harold I, king of England, 52, 63
Harold II (Godwinson), earl of
  Wessex, king of England, 16,
  42, 56–8, 61–79 passim, 81, 85,
  86, 88, 90 etc., 112, 196
Harold (Hardrada), king of Nor-
  way, 85, 87–90
Harthacnut, 51, 52, 63, 88
Hastings, 33, 52, 77, 86, 91 etc., 116,
  117, 119–21
  castle, 121
Hauteville (family), 28, 30
Hayling Island, 164
Heming's Cartulary, 164

Henry III, Emperor, 43, 80
Henry IV, Emperor, 87, 167
Henry V, Emperor, 50
Henry I, king of England, 70, 105, 109, 114, 138, 139, 142, 151, 157, 163, 166, 169, 182, 184, 193, 195–6
Henry II, king of England, 25, 131, 133, 169
Henry of Beaumont, 173
Henry I, king of France, 26, 27, 37, 42–4
Henry de Ferrers, 125, 141, 146
  family, 180
heredity, 19, 24, 27, 72, 103, 117–18, 192
  hereditary service, 111
  inheritance, 113, 187
  partible inheritance, 185
Hereford, 72, 104, 177, 180, 181
  bishop of, 72
  see of, 82
  -shire, 54, 64, 66, 75, 106, 124, 179
Hereward the Wake, 108, 110, 132, 174
Herfast, bishop of Elmham, 104, 144
heriot, 115, 181
Herleva, mother of William the Conqueror, 33, 34
Herluin, founder of Bec, 48, 165
Herluin, viscount of Conteville, 34
Hertfordshire, 63, 75
hides, 71, 78, 115, 144
  five-hide unit, 116
Hiémois, 33, 39
Hildebrand, see Gregory VII
Hockley (Essex), 188
Hollister, Prof. C. W., 97
Holy Land, 14, 28, 116, 196
Honour, 113, 125, 128, 130, 131, 180
  honorial courts, 129
  see also fief
household, royal, 142–51, 169
  see also Exchequer
House of Lords, 140
Hrolfr, son of Rognvald, 21
Hugh of Avranches (Lupus), earl of Chester, 109, 121, 163, 181
Hugh the Chantor, 156
Hugh of Grandmesnil, 121
Hugh of Montfort-sur-Risle, 95, 121, 130
Humber (R.), 13, 42, 67, 79, 89, 176, 177
Humphrey of Tilleul, 120

Hungary, 52
Huntingdon, 105, 178
  -shire, 188
Hythe, 179

ILBERT de Lacy, 125
Investiture Contest, 14, 18, 167
  decrees, 166
  investiture of bishops, 44
Ireland, 105
Isle of Man, 91
Italy, 14, 16, 28, 29, 80, 87, 117, 159, 196

JARROW, 165
John, king of England, 25
John of Worcester, 137, 164
Judith, niece of William the Conqueror, 107, 110
Judith, wife of Richard II of Normandy, 25
Judith, wife of Tostig, 88
Jumièges, 55, 163, 164
jury, 30, 74, 153, 191

KENT, 66, 74, 89, 99, 104, 151, 152, 185, 186
Kentford, 152
kindred, 51, 159, 171, 191
  succession, 139
kingship, 15–18, 77, 171
  see also monarchy
knighthood, 114, 128
  knight's fee, 115, 116, 119, 128 etc.
Knighton, 130

LAMBERT, count of Lens, 33
land-gable, 181
land-holding, 15, 39, 74 etc., 104, 112, 113, 116–21, 130, 180–1, 187, 190
  ecclesiastical, 131 etc.
  forfeiture, 117, 150
  land-grant, 52
  see also fief, Honour
Lanfranc, archbishop of Canterbury, 43, 46–9, 56, 79, 108, 109, 133, 151, 152, 154–61, 165–7, 196
Latin, 74, 137, 144

law, 27, 50, 75, 179
  canons of church, 157
  estates, 117, 118
  marriage, 33
  Roman, 58
  see also courts, writs
Leges Henrici Primi, 190
Leicester, 176
  -shire, 191
Le Mans, 42
Lennard, R., 188
Leo IX, Pope, 43, 47, 80
Leofric, abbot of Peterborough, 82, 104
Leofric, bishop of Exeter, 174
Leofric, earl of Mercia, 63, 66, 68
Leofwine, son of Godwin, 63, 66, 94, 98
Leominster, 64
levies, 71, 78, 107, 114, 129, 134, 184
Lewes, 134, 162
Liber Eliensis, 82, 86
Lichfield, 82, 155, 156, 158, 162
Lillebonne, Council of, 169
Lincoln, 105, 131, 158, 163, 174, 176, 178
  -shire, 75, 127, 191
Lindsey, 89
Lisieux, 45, 46
Lombards, 28, 30
London, 50, 71, 97–9, 103, 163, 174–6, 178, 180, 182, 183
  council (1075), 157, 158
Lorraine, 13, 54, 55, 158

Magnum Concilium, 140
Magnus, king of Norway, 88
Maine, 20, 40, 42, 44
Maitland, F. W., 135, 147, 153, 183, 190
Malcolm Canmore, king of Scotland, 105
Maldon, battle of, 77, 79
Manor, 13, 68–9, 135, 150, 185 etc.
Manzikert, Battle of, 14
Marches (The) of Wales, 66, 75, 106, 107, 109, 124, 125, 179, 182
Margaret of Scotland, 57, 70
Marmoutier, 161
marriage, 33, 34, 46 (clergy), 50, 113, 159 (laws)
marshals, 114, 129, 143

Matilda, daughter of Henry I of England, 50
Matilda, wife of Aelfgeard, 50
Matilda, wife of William the Conqueror, 43, 45, 47, 70, 105
Mauger, archbishop of Rouen, 45, 46
Maurilius, archbishop of Rouen, 46
Mayenne, 42
Melrose, 165
Mercia, 66, 68, 106, 107, 110, 117, 125, 164
Merleswein (sheriff), 105, 127
Middlesex, 75

military organization, 39, 69, 77, 102, 111 etc.
  see also fyrd
mints, 28, 72, 171, 176, 177, 182, 184
monarchy, 13–19, 25–7, 67, 70 etc., 77, 197
monasteries, 46, 48, 49, 160–5
monetagium, 184
Montgomery, 125
Morcar, earl of Northumbria, 67, 86, 89, 90, 96, 103–5, 107, 108
Mortain, 39
Mortemer, 42, 170
Moslems, 28, 30
murdrum, 151

NEWCASTLE-ON-TYNE, 110
Nicea, 25, 35
Nicholas II, Pope, 28, 80
Norfolk, 75, 147, 152
Normandy, duchy of, 17, 20 etc., 27 etc.
  consolidation of, 38 etc.
  government of after 1066, 168 etc.
Norman-French, 137
Northampton, 119, 176
  -shire, 67, 119, 149
Northumbria, 67–9, 79, 86, 88, 106, 107, 110, 117, 165, 185
Norwegians, 87
  see also Scandinavia
Norwich, 158, 162, 176, 179, 183
Nottingham, 105, 176
  -shire, 125

ODENSE (Denmark), 165
Odo of Bayeux, 34, 39, 46, 91, 95, 104, 109, 121, 141, 152, 167, 196
Ogbourne (Wilts), 163

Olaf Haroldsson (St. Olaf), 77
Olaf, Prince, 90
Ordericus Vitalis, 34, 50, 127, 195
Orkney Islands, 89, 90
Osbern, lord of Ewias Harold, 54
Osbern, seneschal, 35
Osmund, bishop of Salisbury, 144
Oswald, bishop of Worcester, 77
Otto the Great, 143
Ouse, R. (Yorks), 89, 176, 177
Oxford, 182, 183

PALESTINE, 30
pallium, 45, 55–7, 80
Papacy, 14, 80, 87, 154 etc., 165 etc.
   Papal decrees, 166
   Reformed, 55, 56, 79, 155
Paris, 16, 19, 26
Paul, abbot of St. Albans, 161
Pavia, 28, 47, 80
Pays d'Auge, 21, 23
le Pays de Caux, 21
Peace of God, 112, 113
Pembrokeshire, 108
penalties, 18, 78, 181
penance, 37, 40, 155, 162
Peter of Valognes, 130, 141, 150
Peterborough, 82, 83, 104, 108, 132, 137
Peter's Pence, 80, 165, 167
Pevensey, 91, 93
Philip I (of France), 44, 87, 168
Philip Augustus, 25
Pinkenys (barony), 119
pleas, judicial, 147, 152, 170
   of the sword, 149
   reserved, 113
   royal, 181
   spiritual, 157
Plumberow (Essex), 188
Pons, 121
Pontefract, 125
Powys, 109

RALF PAYNEL, 127
Ralf the Staller, 54
Ralf, son of Ralf the Staller, 109, 110
Ralf the Timid, 54
Ralf of Tosny, 121
Ralph de Gacé, 35, 36
Ramsbury, 82
Ramsey, 132
Ranulf, brother of Ilger, 188

Ranulf Flambard, 109
Ranulf Peverel, 125
Rayleigh, 125, 126, 130, 146, 150
Rectitudines Singularum Personarum, 189
reeve, 69, 150, 188, 189
Regenbald, 104, 144
Reinfrid, 165
Remigius, bishop of Dorchester, (Lincoln), 146, 154
Renaud I, count of Burgundy, 25
Rheims, 43
   Papal Reforming Council (1049), 45, 80
Rhuddlan, 181, 184
Rhys ap Tewdwr, 108, 109
Riccall, 89
Richard I, duke of Normandy, 24, 25, 39, 49, 51
Richard II, duke of Normandy, 24, 25, 33, 39, 49, 51, 53
Richard, III, duke of Normandy, 25, 33
Richard FitzGilbert, 121, 125, 141
Richmond, 110, 125, 126
rights, blood, 51, 87
   civil, 103, 189, 190, 192
   dominical, 188
   honorial, 113
   jurisdiction, 181
   land, 180, 187
   metropolitan, 157
   royal, 27, 76, 104, 149, 180, 182
   succession, 88, 187
   village, 185, 186
Ripon, 165
Robert (of Jumièges), archbishop of Canterbury, 55–8, 64, 80, 81
Robert, archbishop of Rouen, 35
Robert, bishop of Hereford, 144, 146, 151
Robert de Comines, 106
Robert Curthose, 168–70, 195, 196
Robert Fitzhamon, 30, 182
Robert FitzWimarc, 54, 126
Robert of Gloucester, 182
Robert Guiscard, 14, 28
Robert the Magnificent, 25, 26, 33–5, 53
Robert of Mortain, 24, 39, 118, 120, 121, 126, 180
Robert d'Oilly, 141
Robert of Rhuddlan, 109, 181
Rochester, 162, 185
   bishop of, 48
Rockingham, 119

Roger of Beaumont, 121
Roger Bigot, 121, 130, 141, 150
Roger Blunt, 130
Roger de Busli, 125
Roger Fitzwilliam, 179
Roger, brother of Robert Guiscard, 29
Roger, earl of Hereford, 109
Roger of Montgomery, 121, 124, 129, 141
Roger of Salisbury, 109, 151
Roger of Tosny, 35
Rognvald, earl of Möre, 21
Rollo, 19–21, 23, 24
Rome, 27, 29, 57, 80
    Council, 47
Romney, 72
Roncesvalles, 120
Rouen, 21, 37, 45, 46, 48, 50, 83, 88, 104, 128, 161, 176
    council of, 45
    count of, 20
    mint, 171
le Roumois, 21
Rudolph, 52
Rutland, 75

ST. ALBANS, 132, 197
St. Andrews, 165
St. Augustine's, see Canterbury
St. Clair-sur-Epte, 20
St. Cuthbert, 165
St. David's, 184
St. Denis (of Paris), 163
St. Évroul, 29, 164
St. Gervais, 194
St. Neots (Hunts), 163
St. Oswald, 138
sake and soke, 134, 135, 152
Salisbury, Oath of (1086), 129, 130
    see of, 158, 163
Sandwich, 89, 179
Saxony, 19
scaccarium, 151
Scandinavia, 13, 21, 52, 71, 72, 78, 83, 87–9, 117, 165, 178, 192, 193
Scot and lot, 181
Scotland, 89, 105, 107, 108, 156, 165, 194
    Scottish court, 117
scutage, 133
Seasalter, 179
Sées, 45, 164
Seine, R., 37
seisin, 74
Selby, 162

Selsey, 153, 155, 158
Serlo, abbot of Gloucester, 161
service, military etc., 44, 76–8, 111 etc., 128 etc., 187
    see also fyrd and military organization
Sherborne, 83, 162
    see of, 158
sheriff, 40, 69, 107, 126, 129, 150, 151, 157, 180, 188
ship-building, 92
ship-soke, 78
Shrewsbury, 162, 179
Shropshire, 75, 124, 129
Sicily, 14, 28–30, 116, 196
Siward, earl of Northumbria, 63, 66, 104
slaves 190, 192, 193
sokemen, 191
Somerset, 127, 180, 192
Southampton, 177
Spain, 28
Spearhafoc, 80
Stafford, 107
    -shire, 106
Stamford, 176, 178
Stamford Bridge, Battle of, 85, 86, 89, 90, 97, 98
Stenton (F.M.), Sir Frank, 72, 200, 201
Stephen, king of England, 169, 196
Stigand, archbishop of Canterbury, 55, 71, 79, 81–3, 104, 154, 165
Stoke-by-Clare (Suffolk), 163
Suen of Essex, lord of Rayleigh, 125, 130, 146, 150, 188
Suffolk, 75, 124, 147, 152
Sussex, 75, 89, 93
suzerainty, 26
Sweyn (Estrithson), king of Denmark, 87, 106, 107
Sweyn, son of Godwin, 63, 64
synod, diocesan, 82
    ecclesiastical, 45, 158
    Lenten, 167
    provincial, 159
    public, 45

TADCASTER, 90
Taillefer, 120
Taini Regis, 118
Tancred de Hauteville, 29
Tancred, nephew of Bohemund, 30, 196

Tavistock, 134
taxation, 116, 190
  monetagium, 184
  national, 71
  royal (collectors), 113
tenants-in-chief, 115, 118–20, 124, 127, 130, 140, 146, 183, 188
  in Normandy, 131
Terra Regis, 150
Tewkesbury, 162, 183
thegn, 78, 98, 112, 113, 115, 117, 127, 130, 143
Theobald, archbishop of Canterbury, 49
Theodore of Tarsus, archbishop of Canterbury, 156
Thetford, 158, 176
Thomas, archbishop of York, 155
Thorkill of Arden, 173, 174
Thorney, 82
Thurstan, abbot of Glastonbury, 161
Tickhill, 125
Tinchebrai, Battle of, 195
Toledo, 14, 28
Toret, 45
Tostig, 16, 63–8, 85, 86, 88–91, 196
Totnes, 126
Tournai, 162
towns, Anglo-Saxon, 175 etc.
trade, 13, 50, 176, 178, 180
Treasury, 148, 150, 151
  see also Exchequer
Truce of God, 37, 112, 113
Turgot, 165
Turold, abbot of Peterborough, 132
Turold, tutor to Duke William, 35
Tutbury, 125, 180
Tynemouth, 165

ULF, earl, 87

VAL-ÈS-DUNES, 35, 37, 43, 170
Varangian Guard, 87, 117
Varaville, Battle of, 35, 170
Venosa, 29
Vercelli, 47, 80
vernacular, 74, 83
Vexin, 101
Victor II, Pope, 80
Vita Ædwardi, 67, 88

WACE, 45
Walcher, bishop of Durham, 110
Wales, 106, 108, 194
  see also Marches
Walter Giffard, 95, 146
Waltham Holy Cross, 81, 83
Waltheof, 104, 106, 107, 110
Warden, 119
Warwick, 105, 173
  -shire, 50, 78, 173
Watling Street, 176, 186
Wearmouth, 165
Wells, 162
wergeld, 112, 190, 192
Wessex, 19, 68, 76, 117
  earldom, 75, 110
Westminster, 33, 83, 164
  Abbey, 59, 71, 85, 99, 105
Wherwell, 65
Whitby, 165
William I, king of England, duke William II of Normandy
  birth, 33
  reception of arms, 36
  early political skill, 37
  consolidation of duchy, 38 etc.
  marriage to Matilda of Flanders, 43
  the Norman Church, 48 etc.
  oath of loyalty sworn by Harold, 58–9, 91
  claim against Harold, 86 etc.
  landing at Pevensey, 91 etc.
  coronation at Westminster, 71, 99
  directions to troops, 102
  return to Normandy, 103
  coronation of Matilda, 105
  rebellion of 1069, Harrying of the North, 106 etc.
  treatment of Waltheof, 110
  Oath of Salisbury, 129
  problems of Normandy, 168 etc.
  death, 194 etc.
  see also Table of Contents passim.
William, bishop of London, 55, 80, 103
William of Bona Anima, archbishop of Rouen, 48
William de Cahanges, 119
William of Dijon, 48
William FitzOsbern, 104, 121, 141, 179
William of Jumièges, 45
William Longsword, 24, 25

William Malet, 106, 141
William of Malmesbury, 29, 52, 83, 96, 137, 175
William, monk, son of Richard II of Normandy, 25
William of Montgomery, 36
William of Percy, 121
William of Poitiers, 17, 36, 45, 51, 58, 86, 91, 92, 96, 98, 102, 127, 174
William II (Rufus), king of England, 109, 133, 138, 139, 141, 148, 161, 168, 178
    succession, 195
William Talvas, 33
William of Warenne, 121, 162
William Werlenc, 39
Wiltshire, 75, 180
Winchcombe, 82, 165
Winchelsea, 52
Winchester, 50, 51, 81, 82, 104, 124, 131, 146, 161, 163, 177, 178
    Council (1070), 154, 156, 157
    New Minster, 104
    Old Minster, 83
    Treasury, 148, 150, 151

Windsor, 119, 133, 164
witenagemot (witan), 55, 73, 76, 128, 139, 140
Worcester, 50, 76, 78, 80, 82, 83, 115, 116, 131, 137, 162, 164, 177
    -shire, 78, 146, 152, 179
writ, 73, 74, 103, 104, 131, 148, 157, 180
    of right, 152, 153
Wulfnoth, 57
Wulfric, abbot of New Minster, Winchester, 158
Wulfstan, archbishop of York, 82, 83, 112
Wulfstan, bishop of Worcester, 80, 86, 109, 160, 164, 174

YORK, 80, 89–91, 93, 105–7, 175–8
    archbishop(ric), 71, 107, 108, 155, 156
    mint, 72
    -shire, 75, 89, 90, 125, 127